The Campus History Series

Overbrook School for the Blind

On the cover: Please see page 63. (Courtesy of Overbrook School for the Blind archives.)

The Campus History Series

OVERBROOK SCHOOL FOR THE BLIND

EDITH WILLOUGHBY
FOR OVERBROOK SCHOOL FOR THE BLIND

ARCADIA PUBLISHING

ISBN 978-0-7385-4916-3

Published by Arcadia Publishing
Charleston, South Carolina

Printed in the United States of America

Library of Congress Catalog Card Number: 2006906167

For all general information contact Arcadia Publishing at:
Telephone 843-853-2070
Fax 843-853-0044
E-mail sales@arcadiapublishing.com
For customer service and orders:
Toll-Free 1-888-313-2665

Visit us on the Internet at www.arcadiapublishing.com

CONTENTS

ACKNOWLEDGMENTS

I want to express my appreciation to the people who assisted me in the preparation of this history. Most of all I want to thank Kathe Archibald, development coordinator of Overbrook School for the Blind, and Dr. Bernadette M. Kappen, director of Overbrook School for the Blind, for their help in writing the captions and organizing the photographs.

A thank-you is extended to Overbrook board member Carolyn Friedman, who cheerfully researched key figures noted in the book. I am also grateful to Maryann Flack for her secretarial support throughout the project.

I am thankful to the talented staff at Overbrook who contributed their photography to the book, including the following: Dennis Brookshire, publications coordinator; Denise Mihalik, computer training specialist; and John Thomas and Tim Macauley, mobility instructors. Images are courtesy of Overbrook's archives, including those by Walter M. Faust, Francis Cauffman Foley Hoffmann, Architects Ltd./copyright Edmund B. Gilchrist Jr. Photography, and copyright Positive Exposure/Rick Guidotti, unless otherwise noted.

Many thanks to the individuals who provided their feedback on the book: Rebecca Ilniski, Jennifer Criscuolo, Carolyn Friedman, and David Archibald.

INTRODUCTION

In the early 19th century, there was little opportunity for children who were blind to be involved in educational programs. Methods for teaching the blind were being used in Europe but had not yet reached the United States.

A dynamic and creative atmosphere existed in Philadelphia that permitted the school to get started. It was during this time that John Vaughan and Roberts Vaux worked together to bring Julius Friedlander to America. These leaders, along with other early members of the board of managers, were active in the political development of the city of Philadelphia. Friedlander, the founder of Overbrook, had been trained to work with the blind in Germany and brought with him to Philadelphia the methods of instruction that he had used there. From 1832 until his death in 1838, Friedlander developed services for students in his own home, constructed the first school building at Twentieth and Race Streets, boosted enrollment to 33 students, and witnessed the production of the first embossed book in the country, the Gospel of Mark, and the publication of the first magazine for the blind, *Lux in Tenebris*.

Several remarkable leaders followed Friedlander. One who came in 1849 and stayed until 1890 was William Chapin. Chapin is credited with starting the kindergarten in 1884, and during his time at Overbrook, the first embossed dictionary for the blind was published. Within the first three years of his employment, he had developed comprehensive schemes for education, advocated for employment opportunities, and established a residence for blind individuals who were working. Gifted administrator Edward Allen, who guided the building of the current campus on Malvern Avenue in Philadelphia, succeeded Chapin. The new campus was selected so that students would have a state-of-the-art school, clean air, and a place for physical activity. A Spanish Renaissance–style building with two interior cloisters offered the students a beautiful environment. Over the years, the buildings have been renovated to meet the needs of the students. Ramps, elevators, and modernized classrooms and dormitories provide the students of today with the same opportunities for activity and independence.

Overbrook School for the Blind continues to fulfill the ideas of its early leaders. The students are provided with strong academic programs, daily living skills, vocational training, and social and recreational opportunities. When the circumstances in the world change, Overbrook adjusts its curriculum. For instance, in the early 1990s, as technology was becoming a part of everyday life, the school developed a strategic plan to put appropriate technology into the hands of every student. This plan, Overbrook 2001, integrated technology into the curriculum and provided the students with the literacy of the 21st century.

Overbrook reaches out beyond the campus to provide services to families throughout the year. During the annual Summer Workshop, families of infants and toddlers receive information and training in specialized techniques that will enhance their child's growth and development.

Staff members also provide early intervention services to families in their homes. The program teaches family members how to work with their child. In addition to the home visits, preschool-age children receive services in their day care or school programs.

In the 1980s, Overbrook developed a program for students from around the world. Students came to the school for one year to study English, develop their computer skills, and learn how to travel independently and to become future leaders in their own countries. Over a period of 15 years, approximately 400 students and adults participated in the program.

Working internationally has thus become a part of Overbrook. Through the years, students from many different countries have attended school on the campus, including Genevieve Caulfield, who founded the school for the blind in Thailand as well as other services for the blind in that country. In the early 1990s, the philanthropy of the Soros Foundation and the Nippon Foundation allowed Overbrook to share its expertise and services with programs for people who are blind or visually impaired in more than 17 different countries.

The focus of Overbrook has always been on the students. Over the years, the board of managers and the dedicated staff have made Overbrook an outstanding educational leader. In fact, educators from around the United States and from various foreign countries visit the campus every year to learn new techniques to share with their students. Into the future, Overbrook School for the Blind will continue to follow the path of its early leaders through the current mission to develop and deliver education enhancing the options available for persons with visual impairment and other challenges, so they have the greatest opportunity to experience active and fulfilled lives.

One

A Great Idea

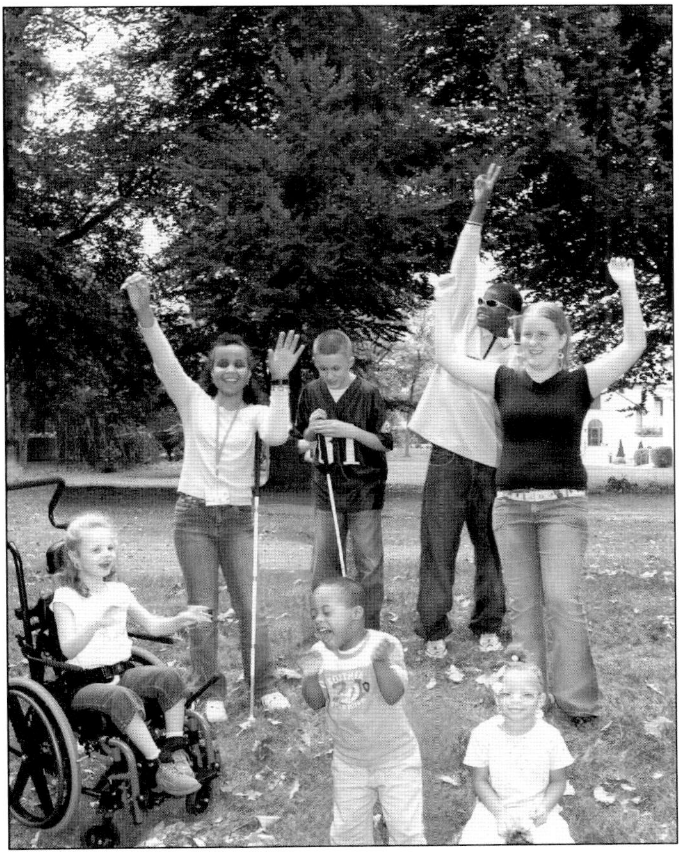

A Dream Comes True. Although there were as many as 8,000 people who were blind in the United States in 1830, most were hidden from view. Many Americans were skeptical of educating the blind, as they were thought unable to function in society. However, a young German named Julius Friedlander thought differently and came to Philadelphia with the hope of starting a school for the blind. With the help of influential leaders from Philadelphia, he made his dream a reality in 1832 with the founding of the Pennsylvania Institution for the Instruction of the Blind, now known as Overbrook School for the Blind.

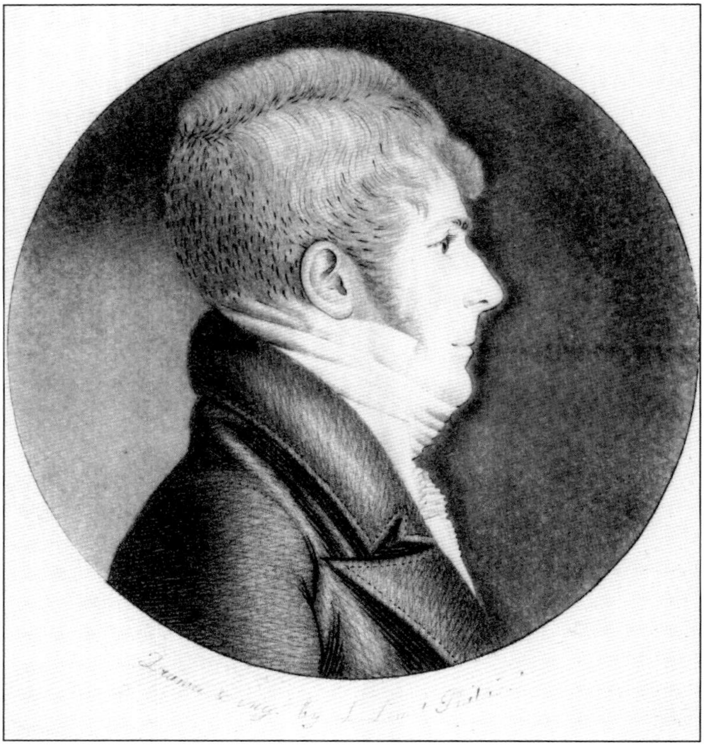

J. Francis Fisher, Board Member and President (1807–1873). The founding of Overbrook School for the Blind grew out of a report made by J. Francis Fisher. Fisher had been asked by Roberts Vaux to investigate the education of the blind in France. He studied the French methods of training and instruction. When he returned to Philadelphia, he worked to establish the Pennsylvania Institution for the Instruction of the Blind. Fisher was affiliated with the school for 40 years, serving as a member and then as president of the board of managers.

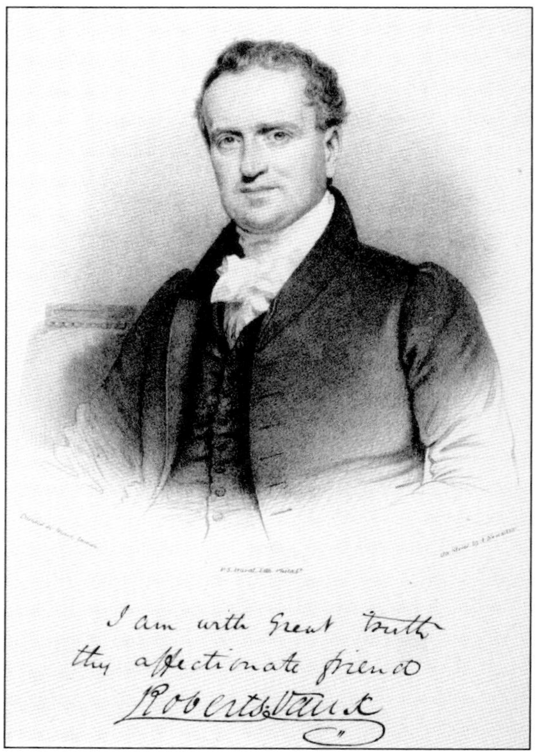

Roberts Vaux, Board Member (1786–1836). Admitted to the Pennsylvania bar in 1808, Roberts Vaux had become a judge in the Court of Common Pleas in Philadelphia by 1835. He was a fervent proponent of prison reform, a founder and 14-year president of the board of public schools, and a founder of the School for the Deaf. He refused several public posts that were offered by Pres. Andrew Jackson, one of which was the mission to St. Petersburg. As early as 1829, Vaux was talking to others about starting a school for the blind. He served on the organizing board of the Pennsylvania Institution as vice president, faithfully carrying out his vision. (Courtesy of the Library Company of Philadelphia.)

SCHOOL SEAL. This official seal of Overbrook School for the Blind shows the embossed profile of John Milton with the slogan Hail Holy Light under the school's name and the year the school was incorporated, 1834.

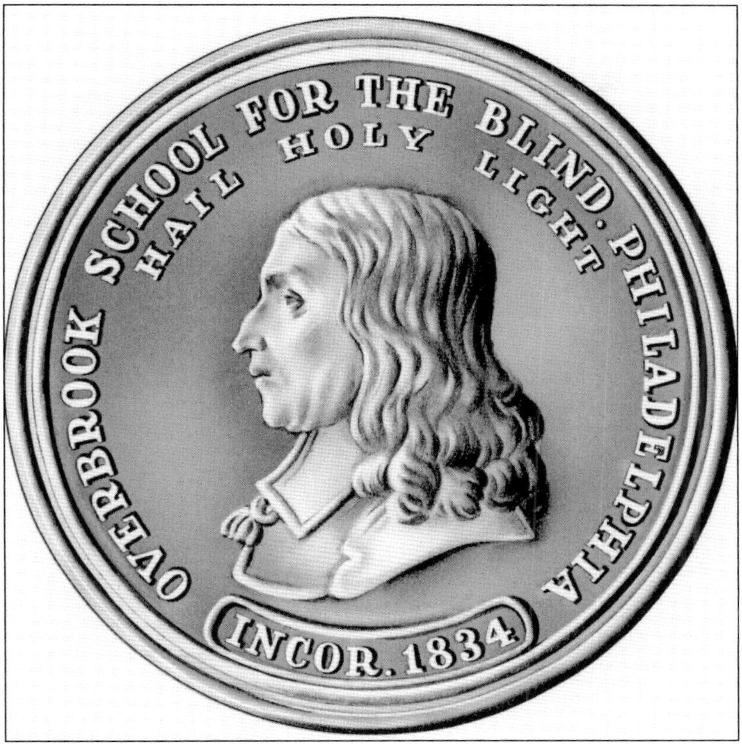

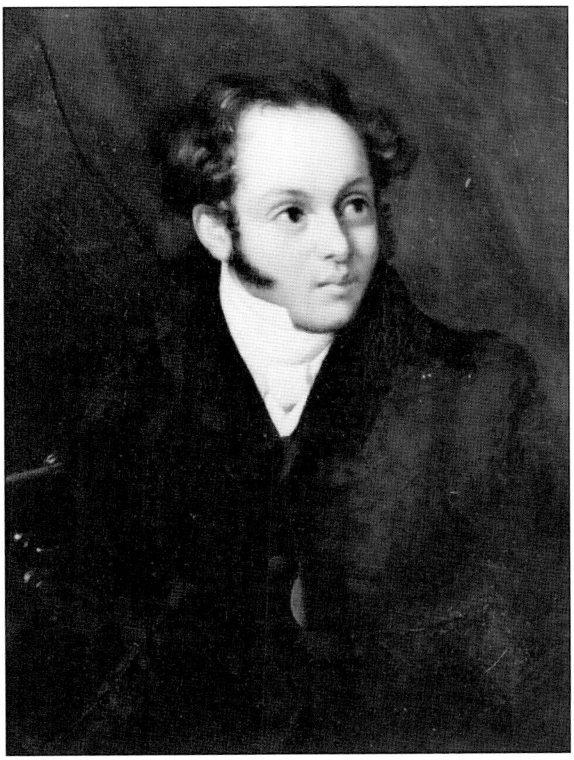

OVERBROOK'S FOUNDER AS A YOUNG MAN, 1826. This portrait of Julius Friedlander was painted in Paris when he was 23 years old.

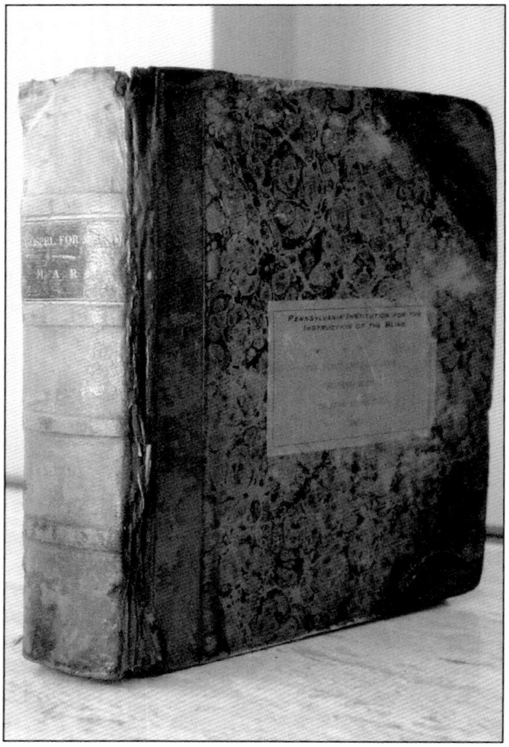

The First Embossed Book. The New Testament's book of Mark was the first embossed book for the blind in North America. It was published and printed by the Pennsylvania Institution for the Instruction of the Blind in 1833.

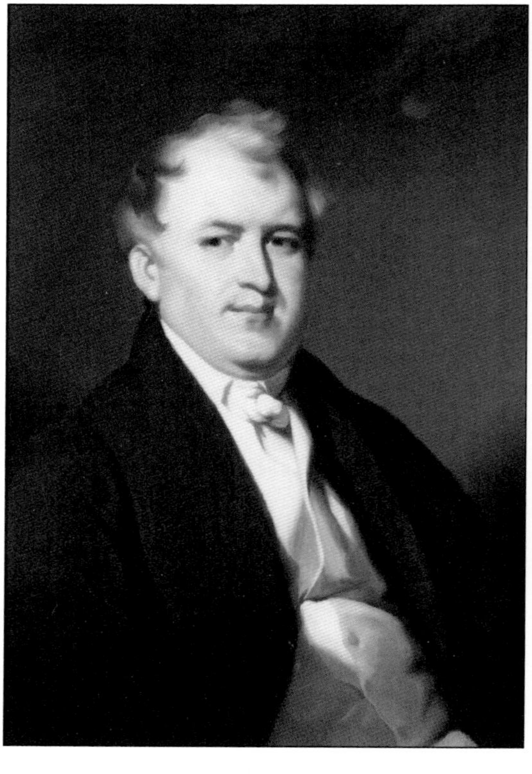

Nathan Dunn, Board Member (1782–1844). Nathan Dunn served in many capacities on the board of managers—board member, member of the Finance Committee, vice president, and president. He financed the production of the book of Mark. (Courtesy of Collections of Philadelphia Museum of Art.)

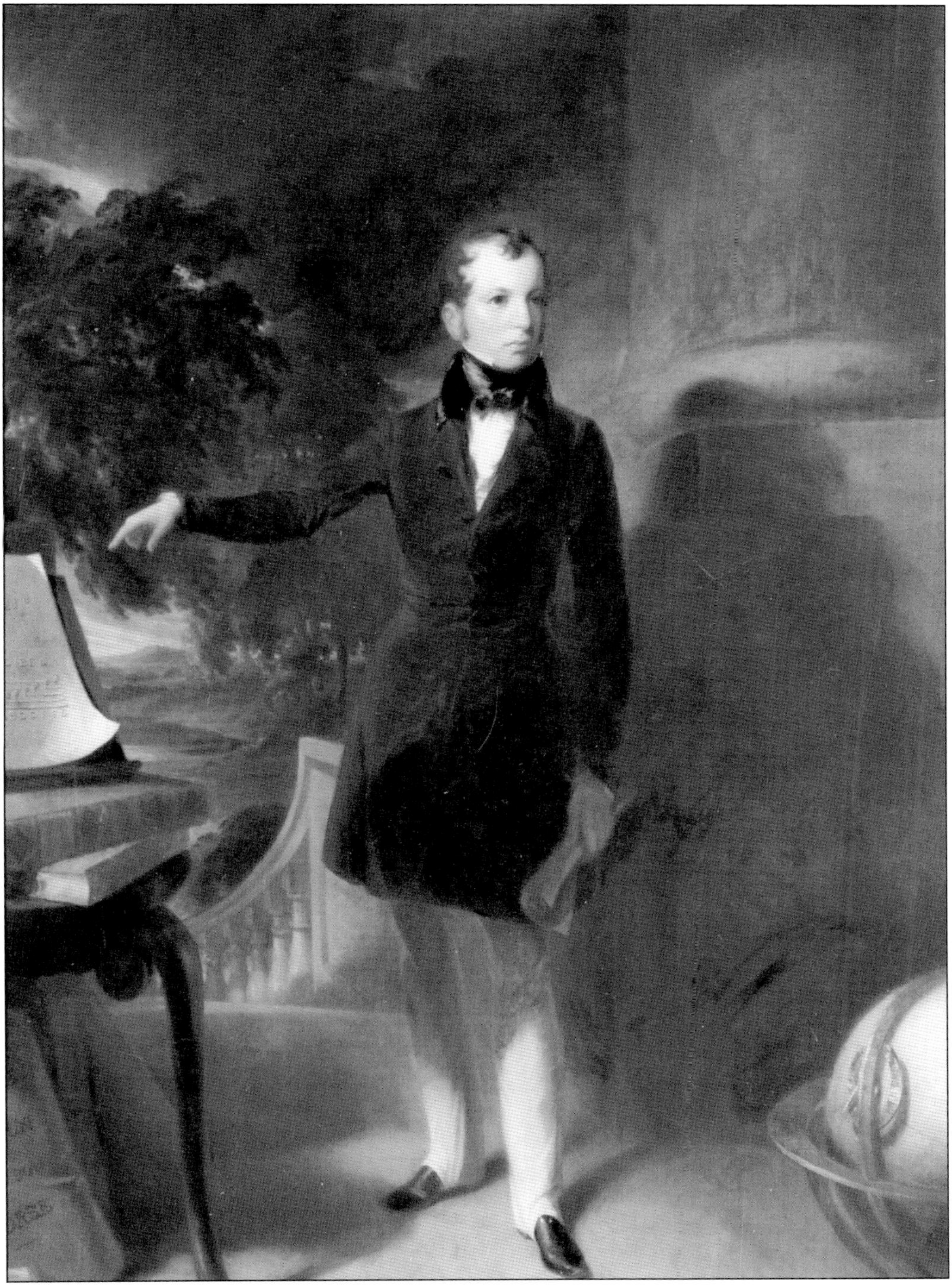

PORTRAIT OF JULIUS FRIEDLANDER, 1841. This oil painting, created by John Neagle on canvas, is owned by the school. Neagle worked diligently to include objects most representative of Friedlander's advances on behalf of people who are blind or visually impaired. A copy of the student magazine *Lux in Tenebris* appears in the left foreground, and the book of Mark is on the table.

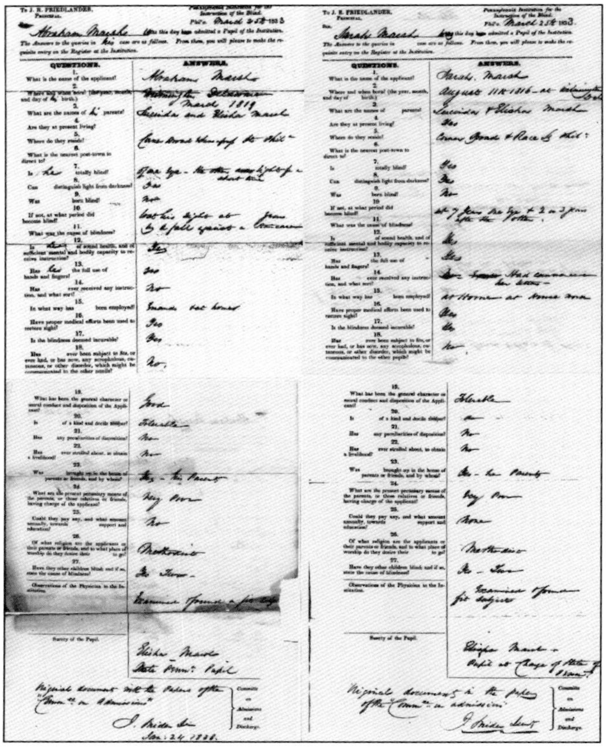

First Student Applications. These are the applications for admission of Abraham and Sarah Marsh in 1838. Taught in their home, the siblings were Julius Friedlander's first students.

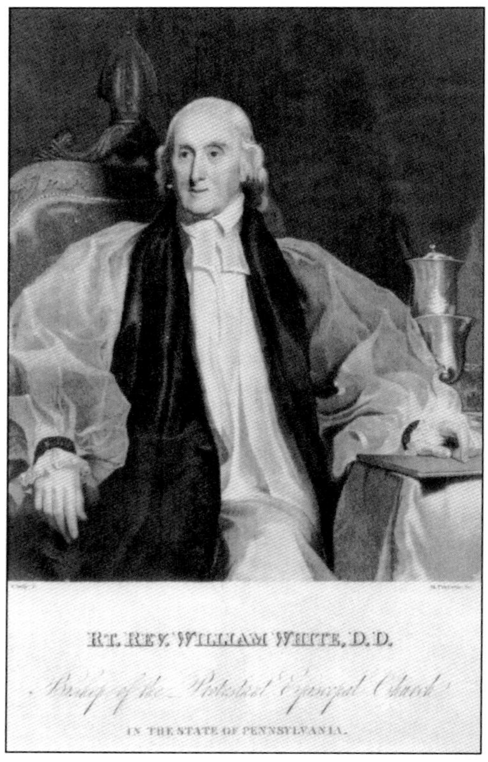

William D. White, D.D., First Board President. Born in Philadelphia in 1748, William D. White was priest of Christ Church and St. Peter's from 1779 to 1836 and chaplain to Congress from 1788 to 1801. He was a friend and pastor of George Washington and was chosen bishop of Pennsylvania, the first Anglican bishop in the country. He died at the age of 88. His home on Walnut Street in Philadelphia is in the Independence National Historical Park. (Courtesy of White-Williams Scholars.)

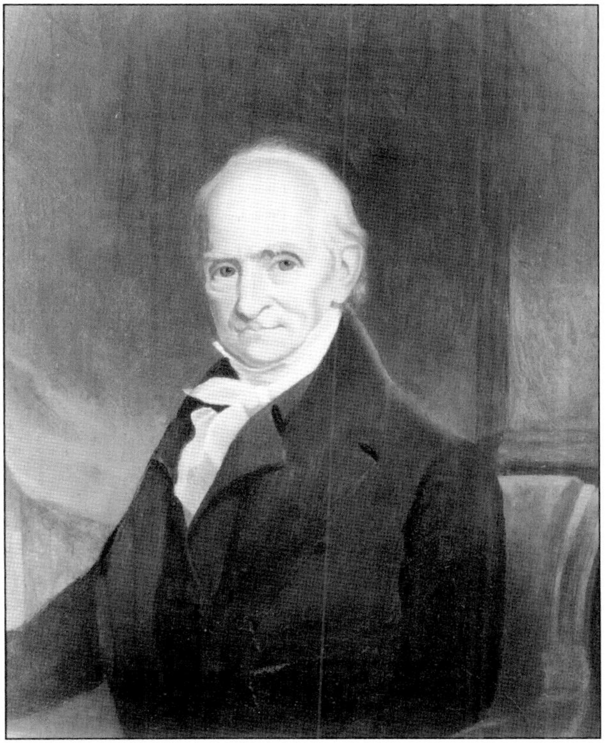

John Vaughan, Second Board President. Born in England, John Vaughan served as the librarian and secretary of the American Philosophical Society for over 40 years, curator of the Academy of Natural Sciences, and a director of the Pennsylvania Academy of Fine Arts. He worked on various committees and, after the death of Bishop White in 1836, became the school's second president until his death in 1847.

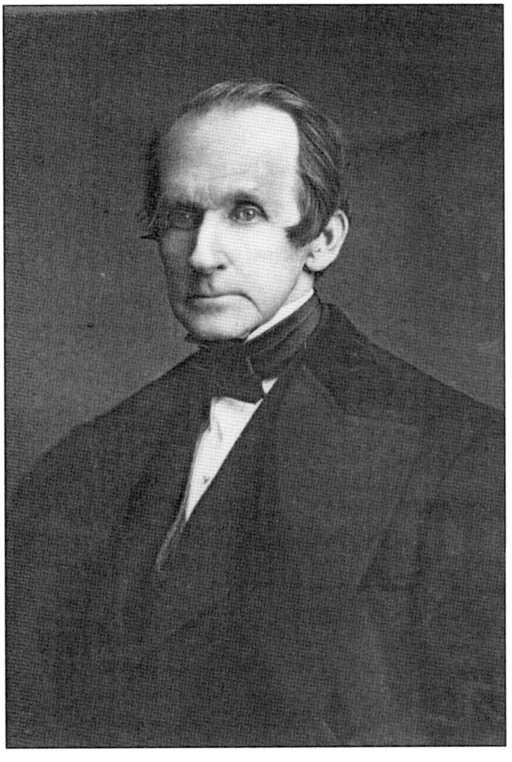

William Chapin (1802–1888). Born in Philadelphia, William Chapin learned the art of engraving at age 15 and eventually moved to New York City. He accepted the position of commissioner of public schools in New York, where he met the principal of the New York Institute for the Blind. In 1839, Chapin accepted an appointment as principal of the newly founded Ohio School for the Blind. He spent the next several years learning better methods of teaching people who are blind. In 1849, Chapin became principal at Overbrook. He took immediate steps to open a store on Walnut Street to sell goods manufactured by students. Chapin was responsible for publishing the first dictionary for the blind with board manager Dr. Robley Dunglison.

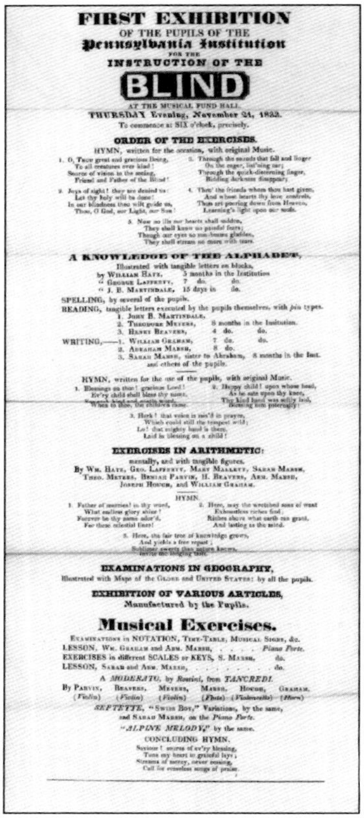

FIRST EXHIBITION

OF THE PUPILS OF THE

Pennsylvania Institution

FOR THE

INSTRUCTION OF THE

BLIND

AT THE MUSICAL FUND HALL,

THURSDAY Evening, November 24, 1833.

To commence at SIX o'clock, precisely.

ORDER OF THE EXERCISES.

HYMN, written for the occasion, with original Music.

1. O, Thou great and gracious Being,
To all creatures ever kind!
Source of vision to the seeing,
Friend and Father of the Blind!

2. Joys of sight! they are denied us:
Let thy holy will be done!
In our blindness thou wilt guide us,
Thou, O God, our Light, our Sun!

3. Through the sounds that fall and linger
On the eager, list'ning ear;
Through the quick-discerning finger,
Bidding darkness disappear;

4. Thro' the friends whom thou hast given,
And whose hearts thy love controls,
Thou art pouring down from Heaven,
Learning's light upon our souls.

5. Now no ills our hearts shall sadden,
They shall know no painful fears;
Though our eyes no sun-beams gladden,
They shall stream no more with tears.

A KNOWLEDGE OF THE ALPHABET,

Illustrated with tangible letters on blocks,
by William Hays, 5 months in the Institution
" George Lafferty, 7 do. do.
" J. B. Martindale, 15 days in do.

SPELLING, by several of the pupils.

READING, tangible letters executed by the pupils themselves, with *pin* types.
1. John B. Martindale,
2. Theodore Meyers, 8 months in the Institution.
3. Henry Beavers, 4 do. do.

WRITING,—1. William Graham, 7 do. do.
2. Abraham Marsh, 8 do.
3. Sarah Marsh, sister to Abraham, 8 months in the Inst.
and others of the pupils.

HYMN, written for the use of the pupils, with original Music.

1. Blessings on thee! gracious Lord!
Ev'ry child shall bless thy name,
When to thee, the children came.

2. Happy child! upon whose head,
As he sate upon thy knee,
The kind hand was softly laid,
Blessing him paternally!

3. Hark! that voice is rais'd in prayer,
Which could still the tempest wild;
Lo! that mighty hand is there,
Laid in blessing on a child!

EXERCISES IN ARITHMETIC:

mentally, and with tangible figures.
By Wm. Hays, Geo. Lafferty, Mary Mallett, Sarah Marsh, Theo. Meyers, Beniah Parvin, H. Beavers, Abm. Marsh, Joseph Hough, and William Graham.

HYMN.

1. Father of mercies! in thy word,
What endless glory shine!
Forever be thy name ador'd,
For these celestial lines!

2. Here, may the wretched sons of want
Exhaustless riches find;
Riches above what earth can grant,
And lasting as the mind.

3. Here, the fair tree of knowledge grows,
And yields a free repast;
Sublimer sweets than nature knows,
Invite the longing taste.

EXAMINATIONS IN GEOGRAPHY,

Illustrated with Maps of the Globe and United States: by all the pupils.

EXHIBITION OF VARIOUS ARTICLES,

Manufactured by the Pupils.

Musical Exercises.

Examinations in NOTATION, Time-Table, Musical Signs, &c.
LESSON, Wm. Graham and Abm. Marsh, ... *Piano Forte.*
EXERCISES in different SCALES or KEYS, S. Marsh, do.
LESSON, Sarah and Abm. Marsh, ... do.

A *MODERATO*, by *Rossini*, from *TANCREDI.*
By Parvin, (*Violin*) Beavers, (*Violin*) Meyers, (*Violin*) Marsh, (*Flute*) Hough, (*Violoncello*) Graham. (*Horn*)

SEPTETTE, "Swiss Boy," Variations, by the same, and Sarah Marsh, on the *Piano Forte.*

"*ALPINE MELODY,*" by the same.

CONCLUDING HYMN.

Saviour! source of ev'ry blessing,
Tune my heart to grateful lays;
Streams of mercy, never ceasing,
Call for ceaseless songs of praise.

FIRST STUDENT EXHIBITION, 1833. These presentations were initiated to show the public that children who were blind could learn to read and write and lead productive lives. As noted on this program from November 24, 1833, the exhibitions showcased student spelling, reading, and performing of musical exercises.

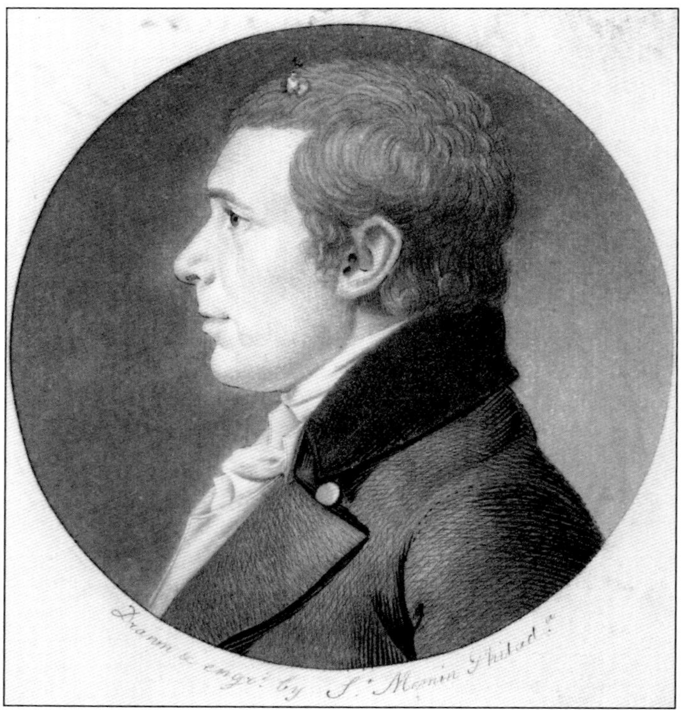

PETER STEPHEN DUPONCEAU, BOARD MEMBER (1760–1844). Peter Stephen Duponceau was born in France and traveled to America as the secretary and aide-de-camp to Baron Friedrich von Steuben. In 1778, he was made a captain in the Continental army, fighting alongside von Steuben and George Washington at Valley Forge. A member of the founding board of managers, Duponceau served as vice president for three years.

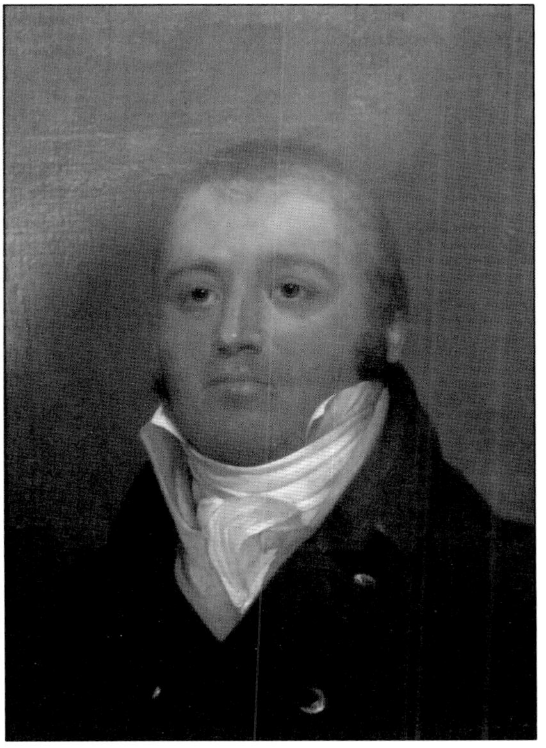

WILLIAM YOUNG BIRCH, BOARD MEMBER AND BENEFACTOR (1765–1837). Born in Scotland, William Young Birch came to America as a sea merchant in 1793. A wealthy bookseller and stationer in Philadelphia, he served as a member of the board of managers from the school's founding until his death. He left almost his entire estate, worth $200,000, to the school; it was used for the first building at the northwest corner of Schuylkill Third and Sassafras, now known as Twentieth and Race Streets. This portrait of Birch was painted by Joseph Wood in the 1830s.

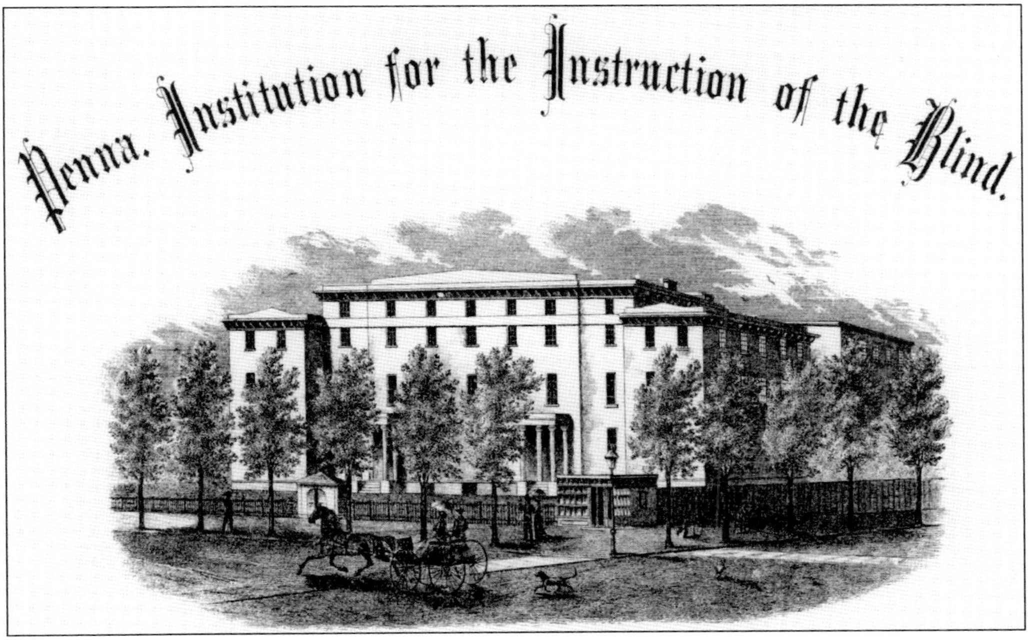

FIRST BUILDING, 1840. This lithograph of the Pennsylvania Institution for the Instruction of the Blind was created by J. T. Bowen. The cornerstone was laid on September 10, 1835, and the building was dedicated in October 1836. The total cost was $38,383.64, made possible by the bequest of his entire fortune by board member William Young Birch.

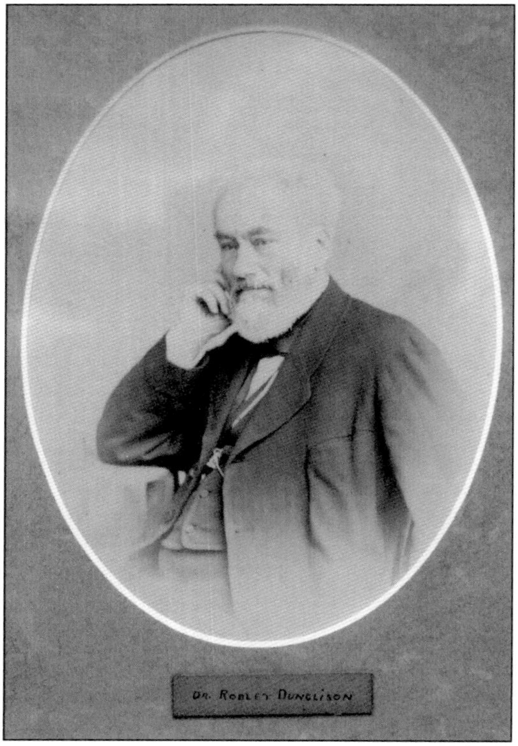

DR. ROBLEY DUNGLISON (1798–1869). A practicing physician by the age of 20, Dr. Robley Dunglison was hired in 1824 by Thomas Jefferson to be professor of anatomy and medicine at the University of Virginia. He was the attending physician to Jefferson at his death in 1826. In 1836, Dr. Dunglison accepted a position at Jefferson Medical College in Philadelphia and was elected to the board of managers of the Pennsylvania Institution for the Instruction of the Blind. He supervised the production of the first embossed dictionary for the blind in 1862. A copy can be seen at the Library Company of Philadelphia.

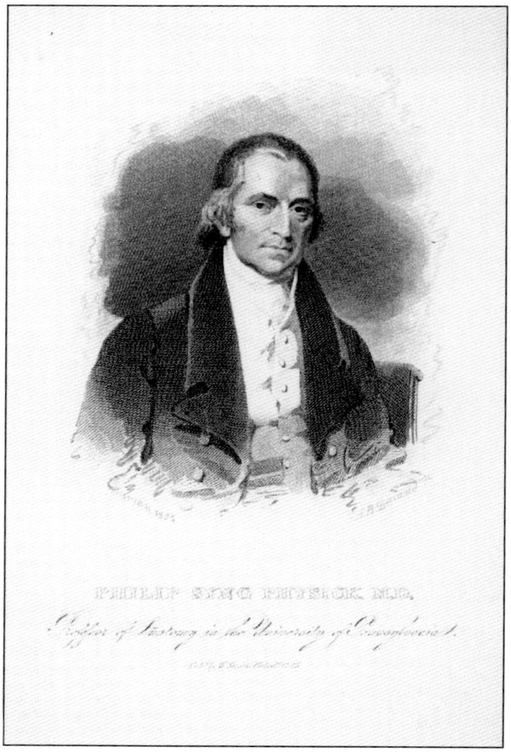

DR. PHILLIP SYNG PHYSICK, BOARD MEMBER AND SCHOOL PHYSICIAN (1768–1837). Known as the "Father of American Surgery," Dr. Phillip Syng Physick sat on the founding board of managers and also served as the consulting physician. Dr. Physick played an active role in treating victims of the yellow fever epidemic in 1793. He became a professor of both surgery and anatomy at the University of Pennsylvania. His many accomplishments include inventing the tonsil guillotine and needle forceps and being the first to use animal ligatures in surgery. (Courtesy of the Library Company of Philadelphia.)

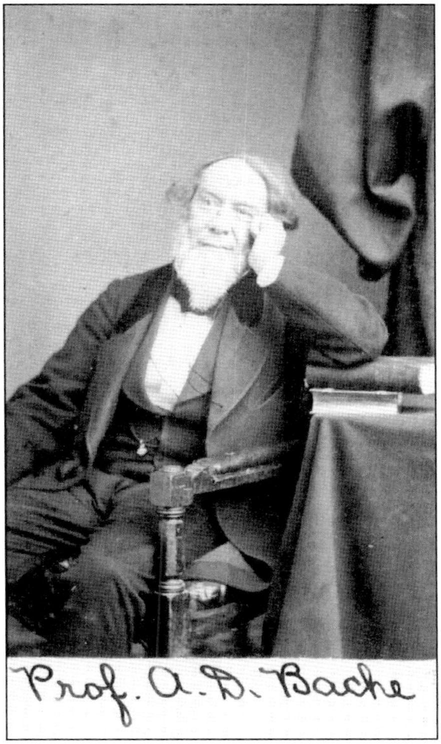

Alexander Dallas Bache, Board Member (1806–1867). A member of the founding board of managers, Alexander Dallas Bache also served on the Committee of Instruction. He was born in Philadelphia, the nephew of former vice president George M. Dallas and great-grandson of Benjamin Franklin. After graduating from the U.S. Military Academy, he served as the chair of natural philosophy and chemistry at the University of Pennsylvania. Bache was the first president of Girard College, a school established for poor orphan boys. (Courtesy of the Library Company of Philadelphia.)

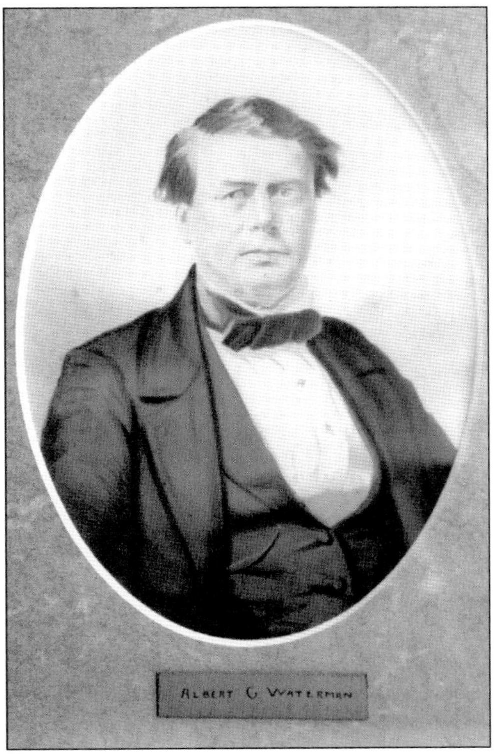

Albert G. Waterman. Son of a surgeon in the Continental army, Albert G. Waterman was born in Virginia and came to Philadelphia in 1832. He brought with him his nephew Jewett Henry Gray to be enrolled in the Pennsylvania Institution for the Instruction of the Blind. Becoming a member of the board of managers in 1838, Waterman served on the select council of Philadelphia and the common council but declined to run for mayor. He was an active participant in the preservation of the State House of the Colony of Pennsylvania, now called Independence Hall.

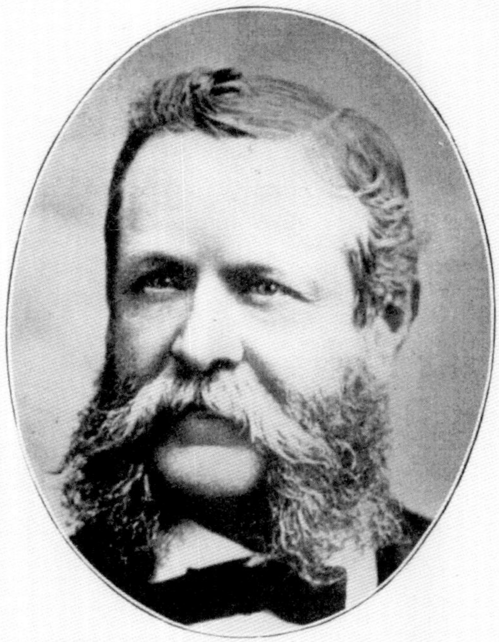

BENJAMIN WOODS RICHARDS
Treas., Gen. Supt. & Trus. Laurel Hill Cemetery
Dir. Girard Trust Co. Capt. & A.-D.-C. U.S.A. (1862)

Benjamin Richards, Third Board President. Benjamin Richards was born in New Jersey and educated at Princeton. He served as a Pennsylvania state senator, a member of the House of Representatives, and a twice-elected mayor of Philadelphia. A member of the founding board of managers, he became the third president of the Pennsylvania Institution for the Instruction of the Blind in 1844 and remained in office until 1850. Richards was also a director of Girard College, a member of the American Philosophical Society, and a trustee of the University of Pennsylvania. (Courtesy of the Library Company of Philadelphia.)

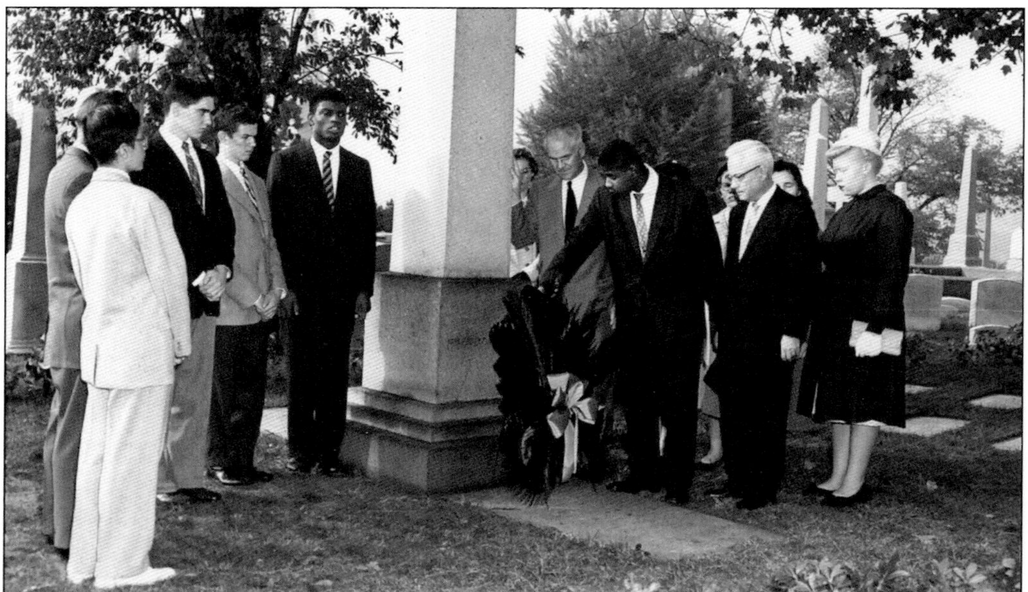

Laurel Hill Cemetery. The board of managers purchased this oval-shaped plot surrounded by small bushes in December 1837 to bury the recently deceased benefactor William Young Birch. Subsequently, Julius Friedlander and other teachers and students were buried in the plot, located on Ridge Avenue in Philadelphia. The space has one large monument in the center with eight single markers in front of it.

Two

The Building and Neighborhood

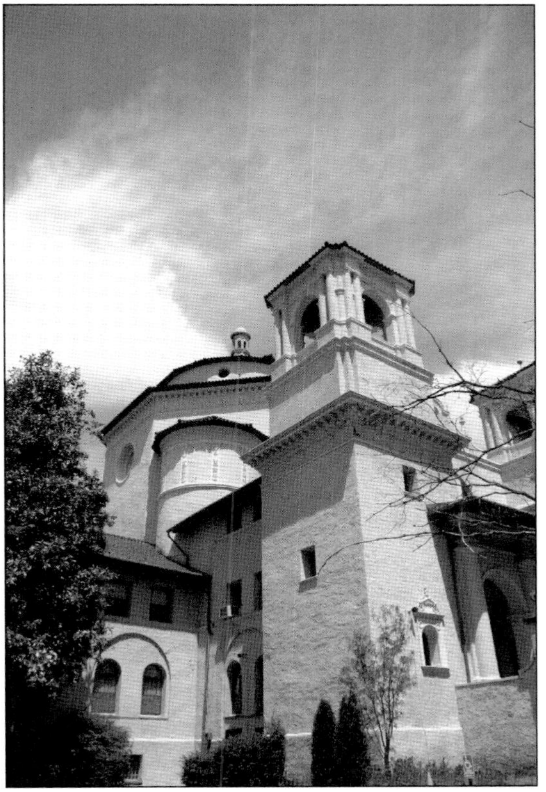

New Location. In 1895, the board of managers decided to look for a new site for the school. The location at Twentieth and Race Streets no longer fulfilled the needs of the students, as philosophies about educating the blind were changing and the building was aging. On July 26, 1896, the 26.3-acre Elizabeth Pleasonton property in the Overbrook section of Philadelphia was purchased for $5,000 an acre (approximately $133,000 total). The site offered proximity to the Overbrook station of the Pennsylvania Railroad and accessibility to streetcar lines. The former farm was surrounded by green open space, perfect for promoting health. The new building, located on Malvern Avenue, was completed in 1899.

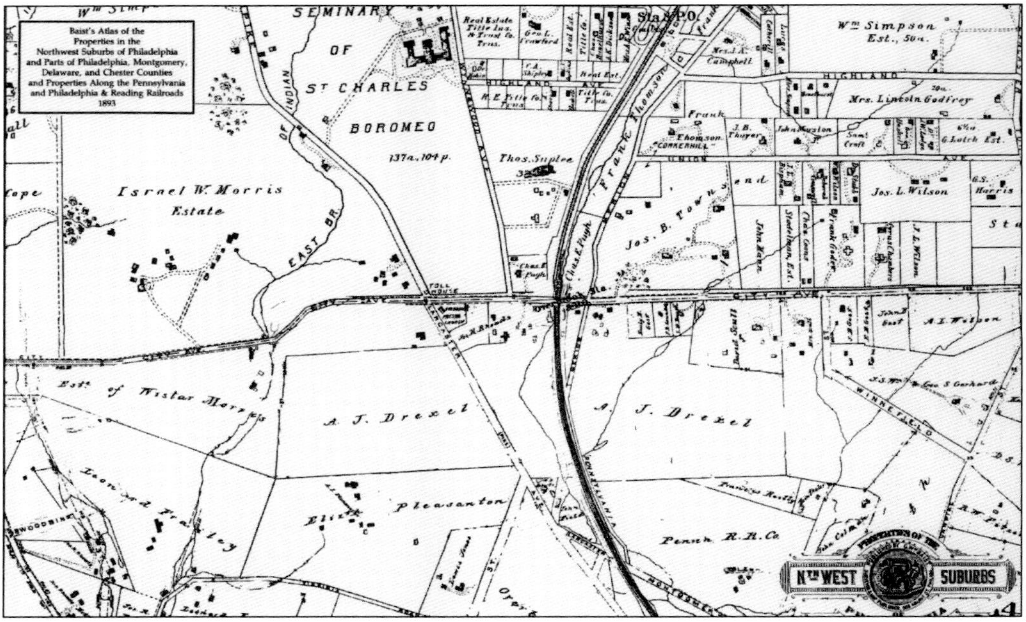

An 1893 Atlas. This map, from an atlas published by G. W. Baist in 1893, depicts the northwest suburbs of Philadelphia. Lancaster Pike was the major east–west highway near the main line of the Pennsylvania Turnpike. The area was thought to be an ideal site for the new school.

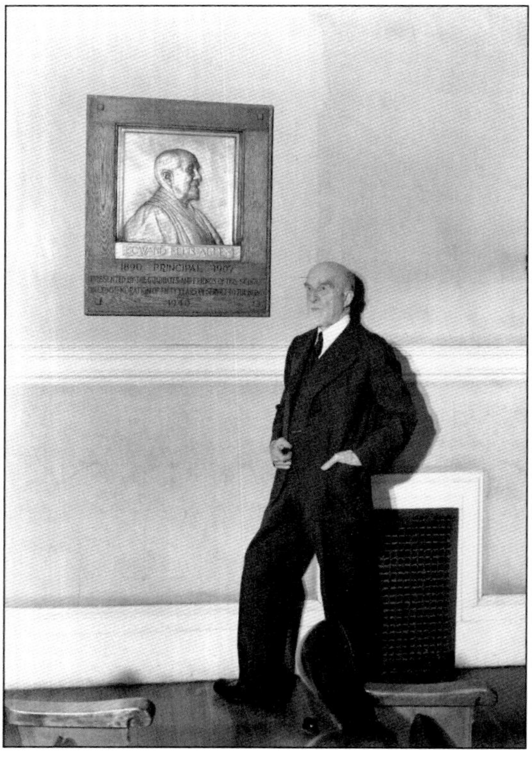

Edward Ellis Allen. Edward Ellis Allen became principal of the Pennsylvania Institution for the Instruction of the Blind in 1890. He came to the school after graduating cum laude from Harvard and teaching for three years in the Royal Normal College for the Blind in London. He also worked for two years at the Perkins School for the Blind as a principal teacher. Allen was perhaps the only superintendent who knew all four braille codes struggling for supremacy in American schools for the blind: Boston Line Letter, New York Point, American Braille, and English Braille. Accordingly, he began to produce books in American Braille in the school's printing office. He had the privilege of erecting a new building in Overbrook, which became a model for other schools for the blind. In 1930, the University of Pennsylvania recognized him with an honorary doctor of science degree.

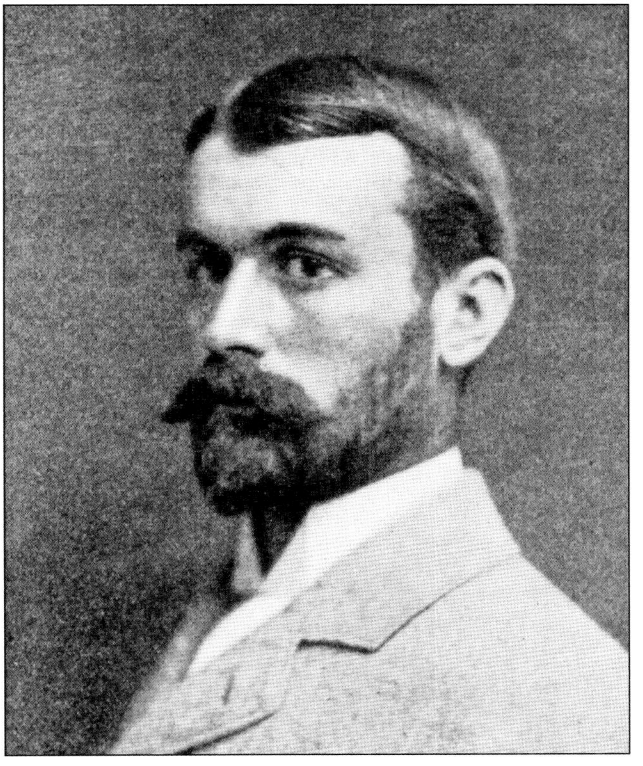

WALTER COPE (1860–1902). Walter Cope served as the architect of Overbrook School for the Blind and, along with John Stewardson, formed the firm of Cope and Stewardson. His other works include buildings at the University of Pennsylvania, Bryn Mawr College, and Princeton University.

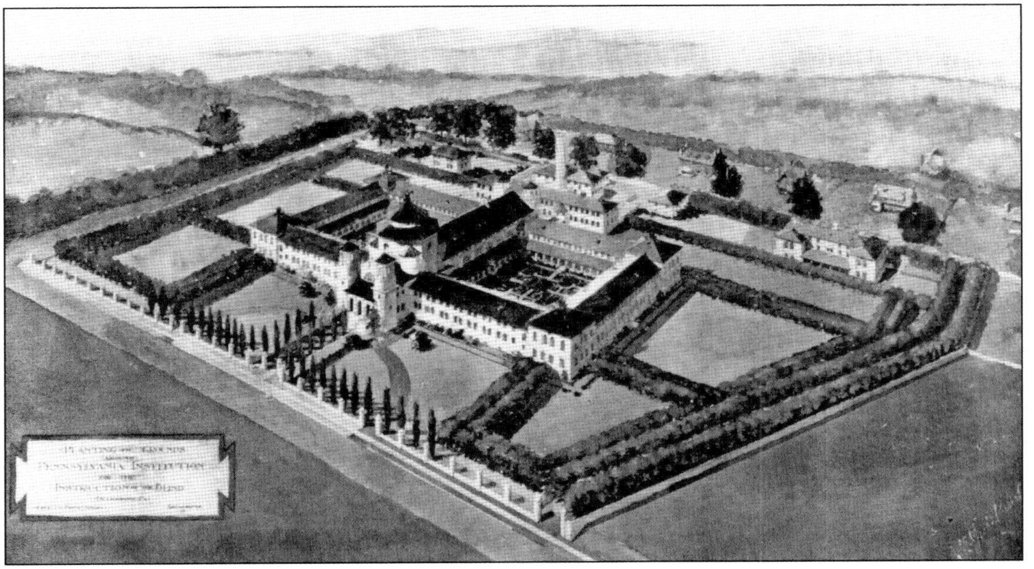

BIRD'S-EYE VIEW. This view of the campus was sketched before the buildings were constructed. The expansive property covers 11 acres and includes playgrounds and buildings. The adjoining 10-acre field is for sports.

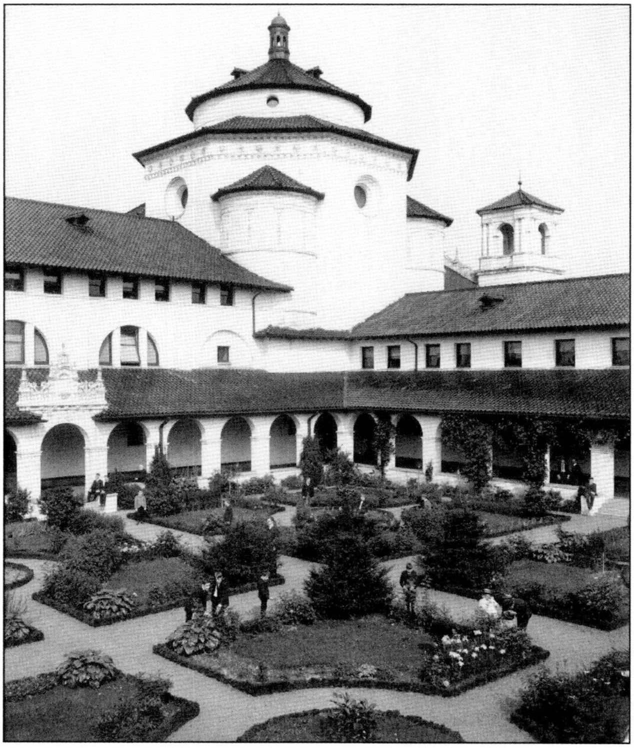

Inside the Boys' Cloister. The rotunda is seen from across the boys' cloister gardens, which are lush with plants and flowers. The roofs are terra-cotta with stucco arches.

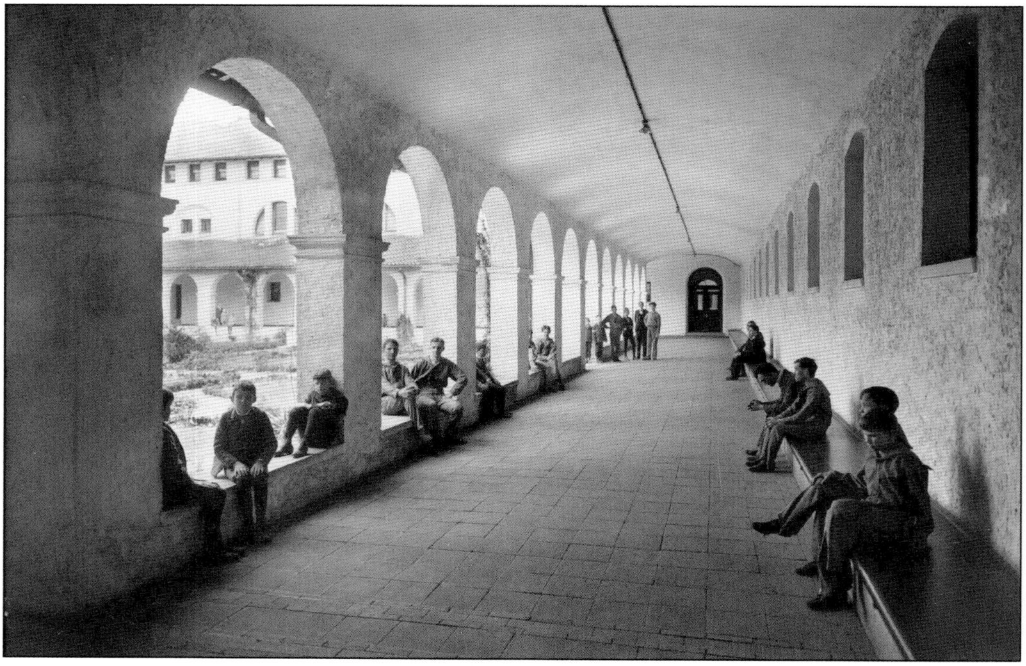

Relaxing in the Boys' Cloister, 1903. A group of boys rests in the boys' cloister, sitting on the long wooden bench. The cloisters were used for outside activity year-round. Some of the boys in the photograph are dressed in the jumpsuits worn for gym class.

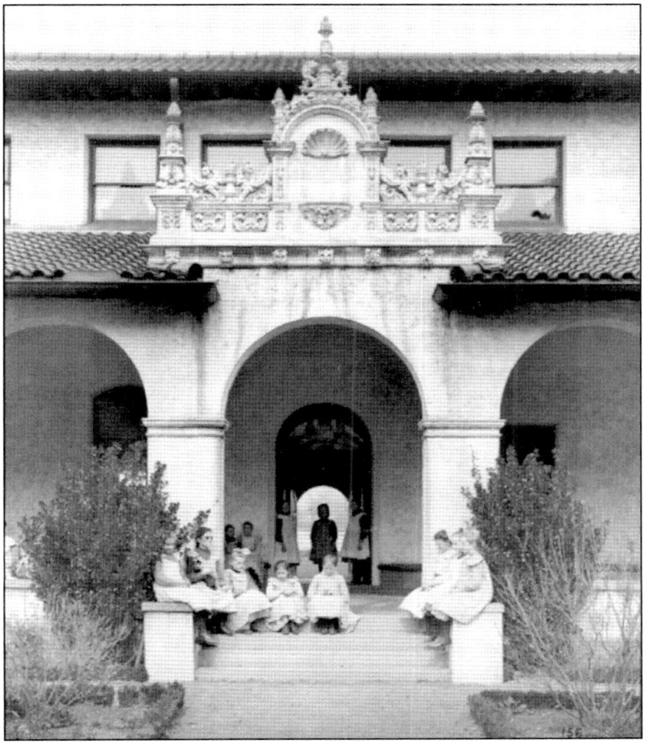

Chatting with Friends. Girls gather in the cloister under the building's elaborate limestone decorations. The openness of the cloister, the beauty of the arch, and the variety of the plantings were important features in the design of the structure.

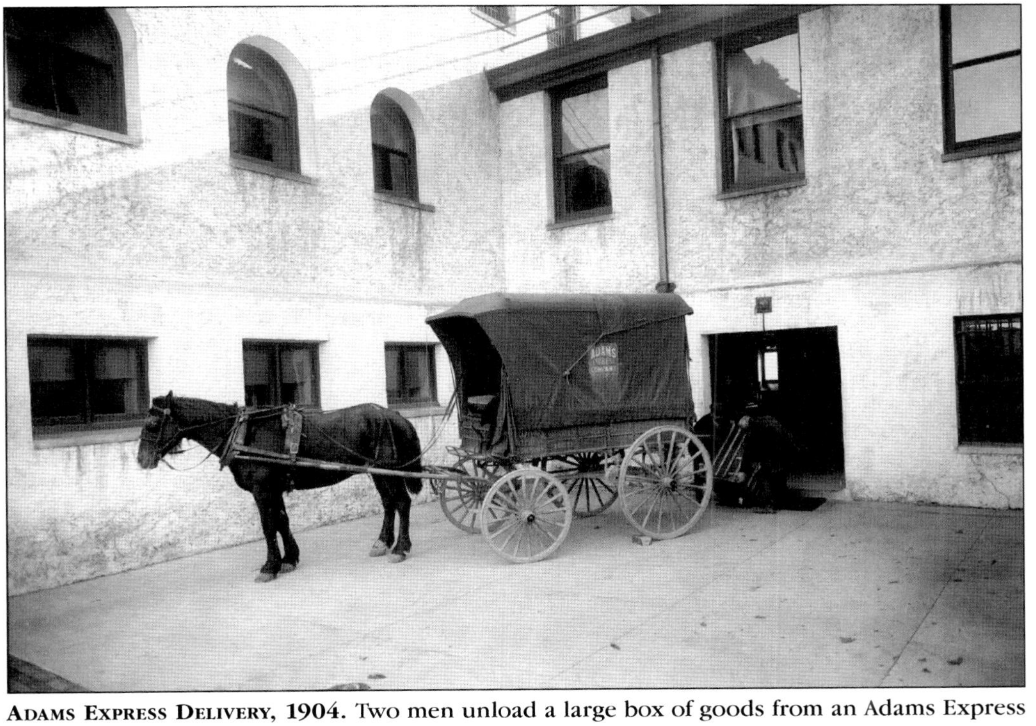

Adams Express Delivery, 1904. Two men unload a large box of goods from an Adams Express horse-drawn delivery carriage.

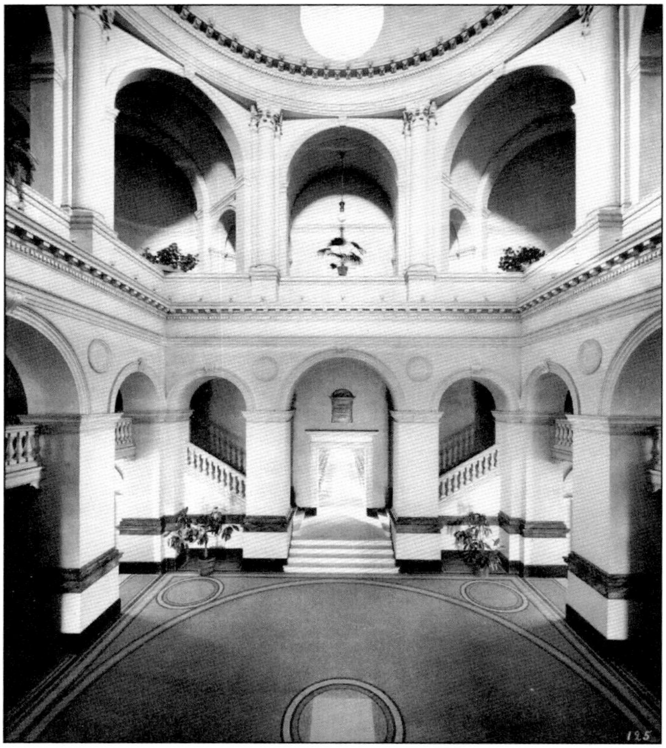

Unforgettable Entrance, 1904. The rotunda, with its domed ceiling and arched opening on the second floor, has always been a gathering place for students and staff. The terrazzo floor and marble steps help create many beautiful sounds. For years, students have enjoyed hearing echoes and even singing in this beautiful entrance.

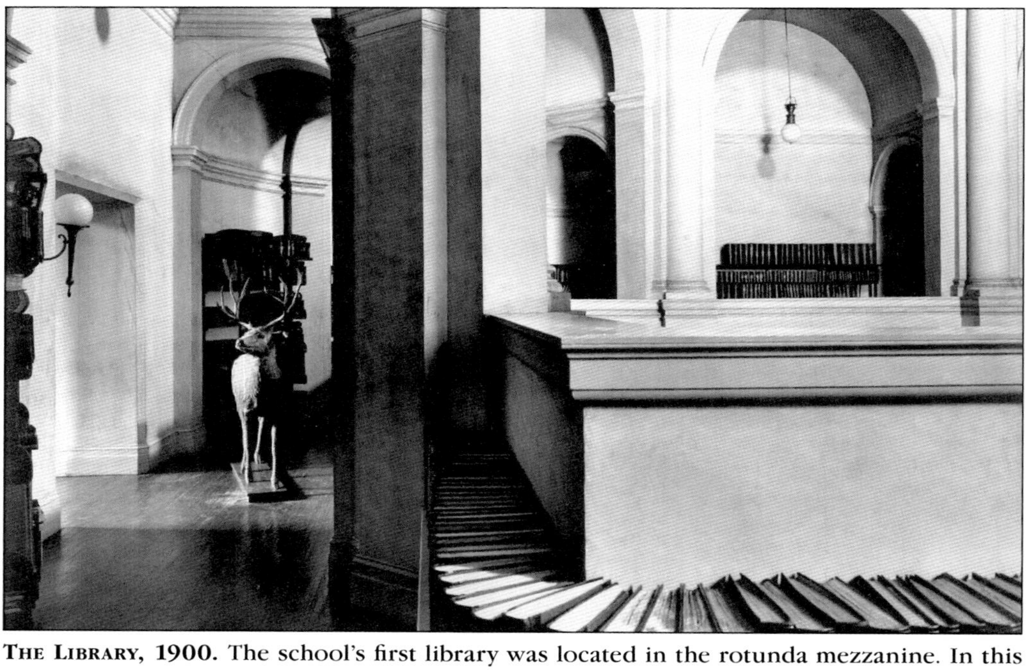

The Library, 1900. The school's first library was located in the rotunda mezzanine. In this photograph, books appear in the foreground and a stuffed deer stands in the back, indicating the entrance. Reading braille and developing strong literacy skills were important goals from the early beginnings of the school.

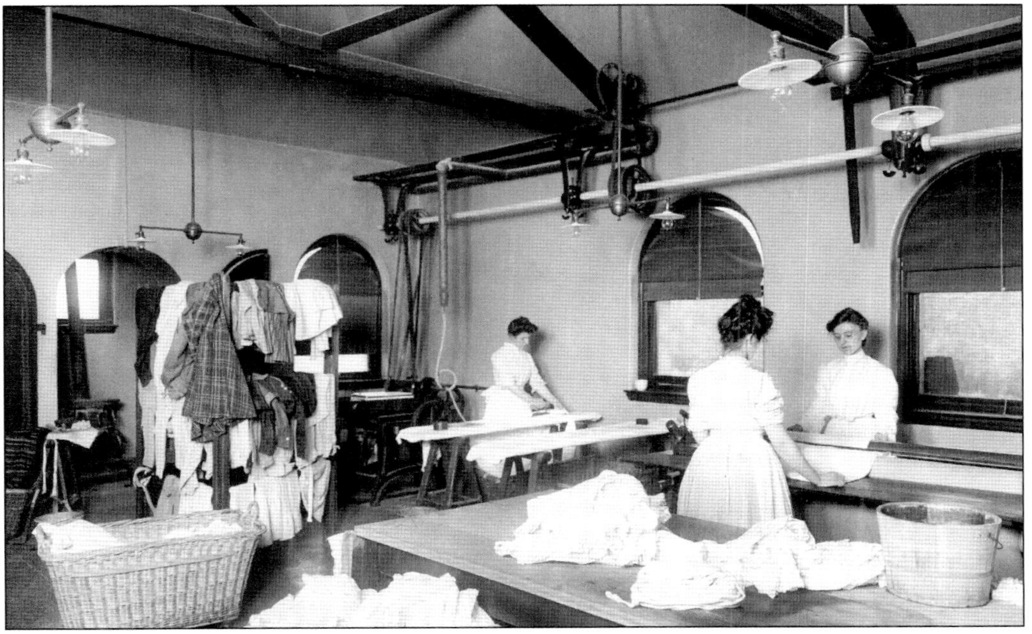

The Laundry Room. Clothing piled on tables and in wicker laundry baskets awaits ironing by three laundresses, who are using a flatiron and a mangle, which is a machine that presses fabric with heated rollers.

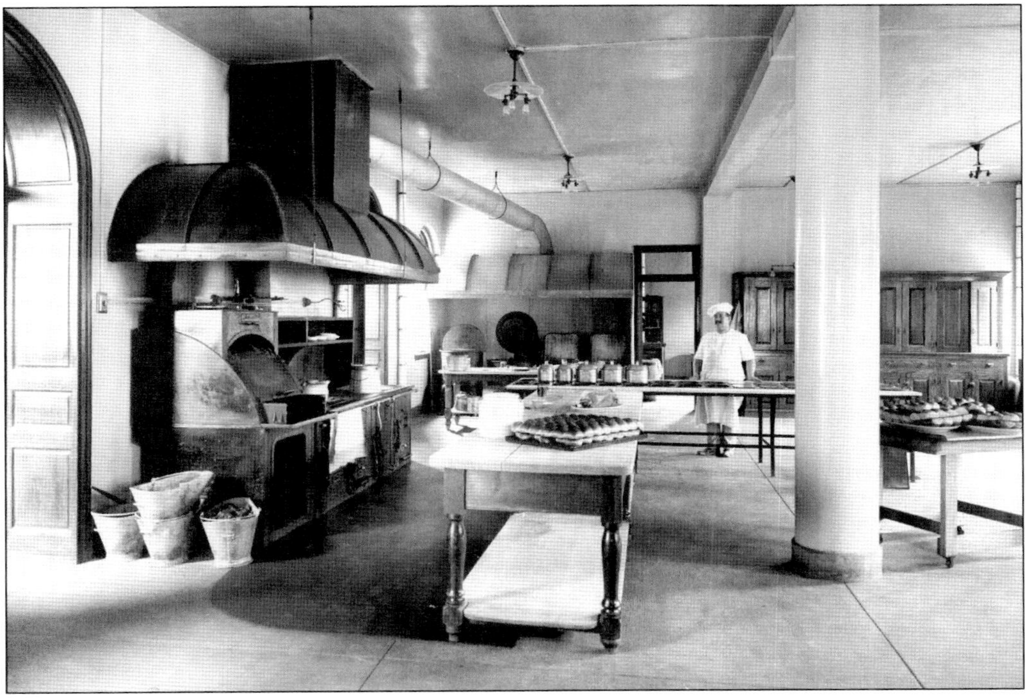

The Kitchen, 1904. One of the features of the school's new building was a centrally located kitchen with the latest equipment. Here baker William Bristle stands in the rear of the kitchen; fresh-baked rolls occupy the foreground.

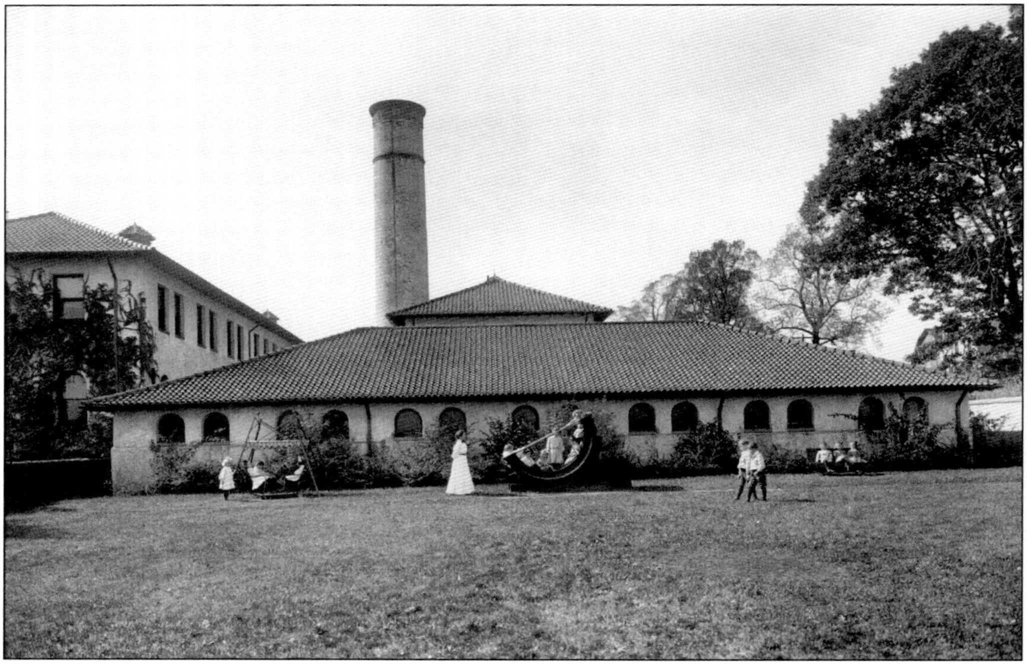

Children Playing, 1909. Children play on a rocking boat and swing in front of the pool building. Constructed in 1906, the building is composed of a terra-cotta tiled roof, stucco walls, and arched windows.

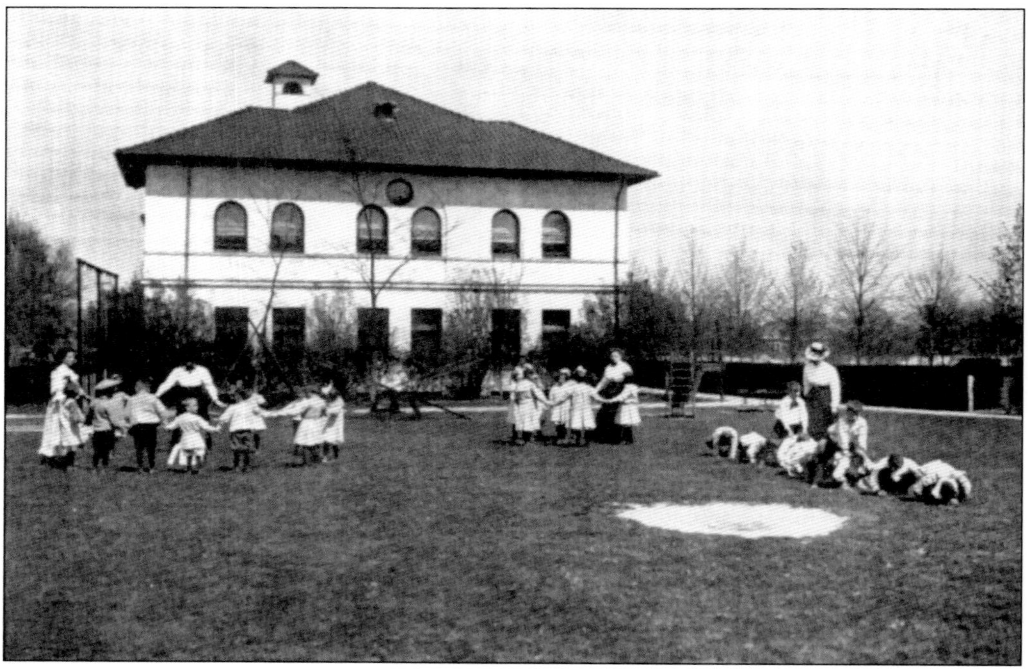

Games on the Green, 1901. Teachers and students play leapfrog and ring games in the field in front of the kindergarten building. From an early age, children were encouraged to be active and enjoy the typical games of the period.

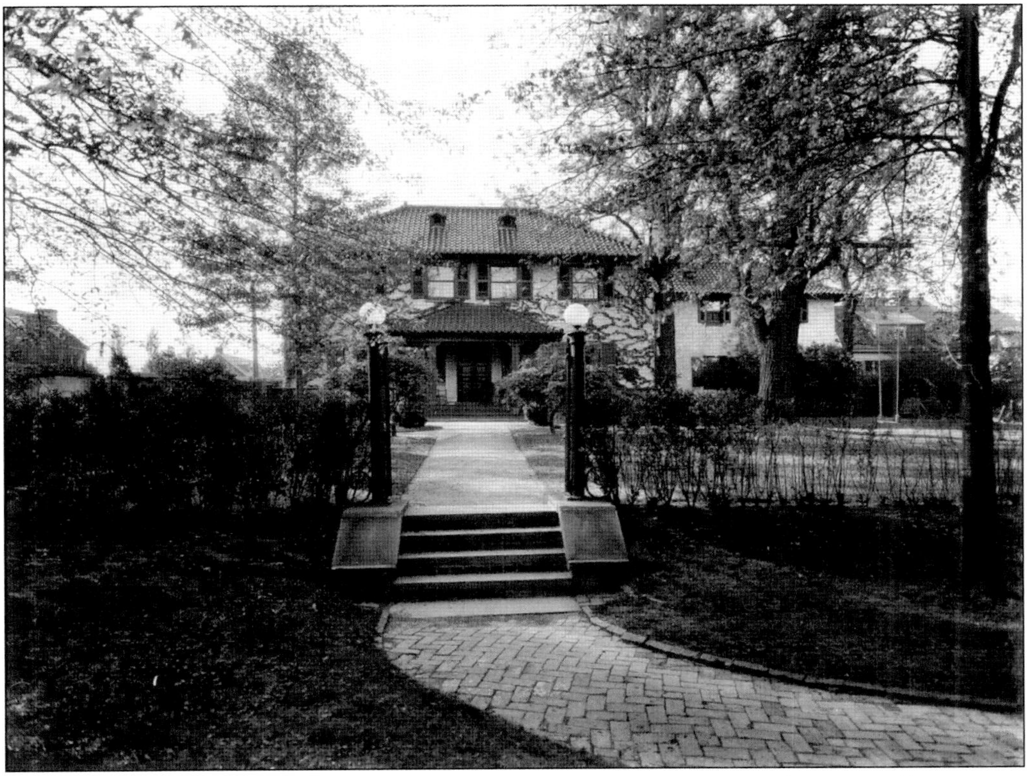

White Hall. A cobblestone path leads to steps approaching the entrance to the principal's residence on the campus. Built in 1899, it was called White Hall in honor of Bishop William D. White.

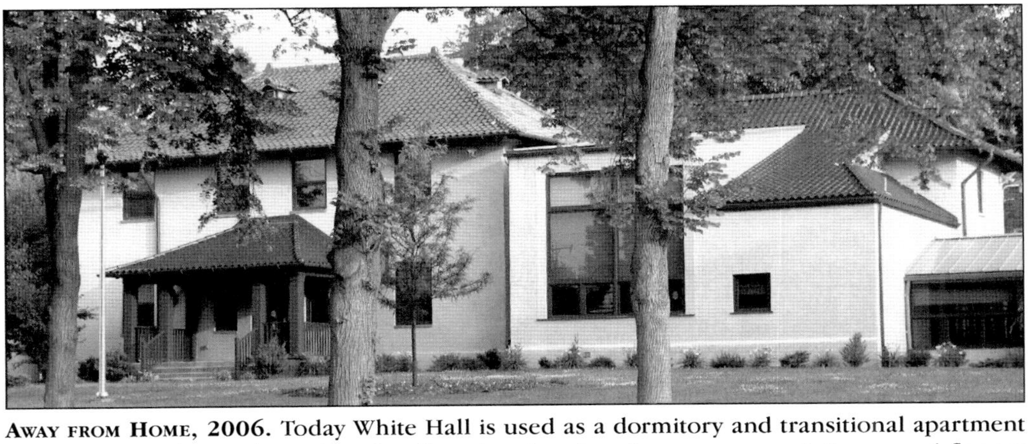

Away from Home, 2006. Today White Hall is used as a dormitory and transitional apartment program for older students. The first floor has five dormitory rooms, and the second floor is divided into two apartments where students have the opportunity to live independently but receive assistance when needed.

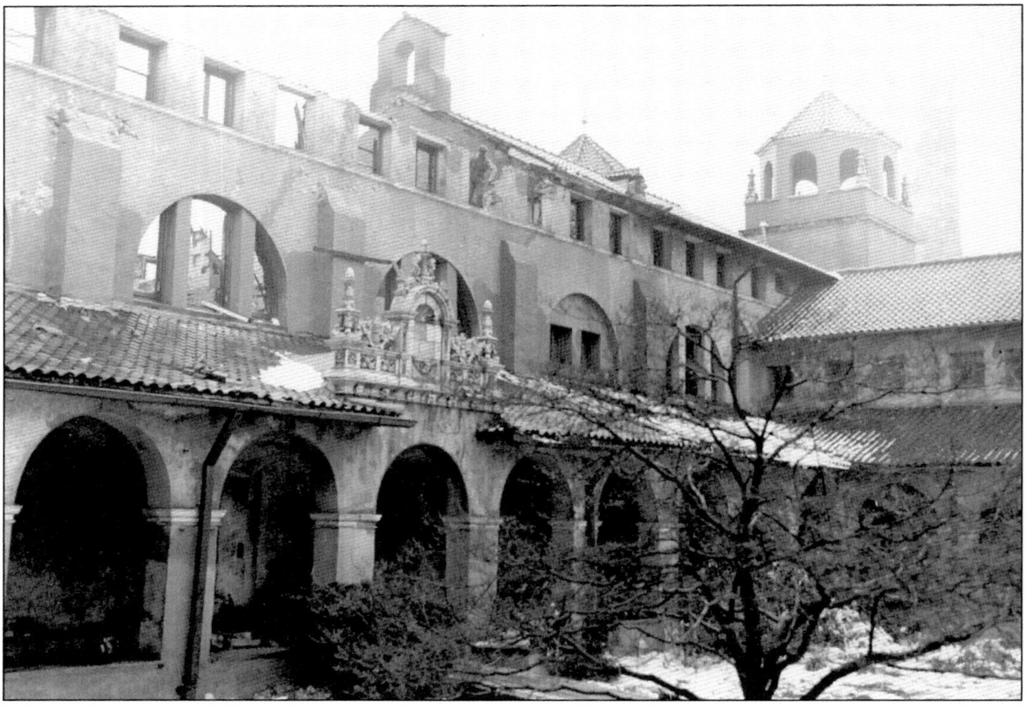

The Fire of 1960. This photograph shows what is left of the exterior of the original auditorium and gymnasium at Overbrook School for the Blind after a fire destroyed it in March 1960. None of the students were injured, but two firemen did lose their lives as a result of the blaze.

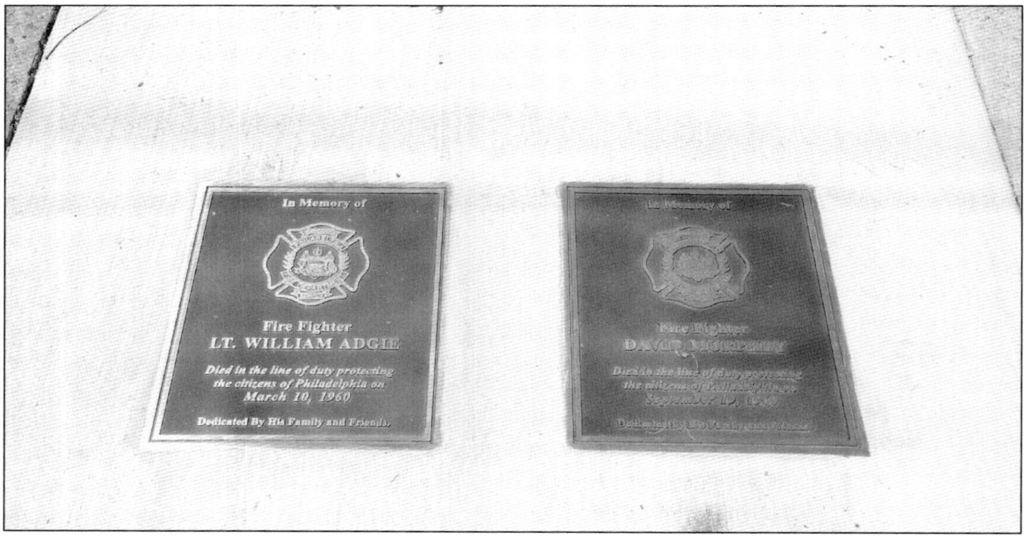

Remembering Fallen Heroes, 2006. On August 11, 2006, two bronze plaques were placed in the sidewalk in front of Overbrook commemorating Lt. William Adgie and David Murphey, who died helping save Overbrook's 338 students and staff members during the fire of 1960. Adgie died at the scene when a roof fell on him and his team, and Murphey died months later from his injuries. Family, friends, community leaders, and Overbrook staff members attended the dedication ceremony to pay their respects to the two fallen firemen.

NEWSPAPER CLIPPING, 1960. On March 10, 1960, Theresa Hayes, a 17-year-old student, was working the switchboard when the fire alarm sounded. She called the fire department and refused to leave her post. Eventually, a fireman led her out of the building. Her story of courage was featured in the *Philadelphia Inquirer*.

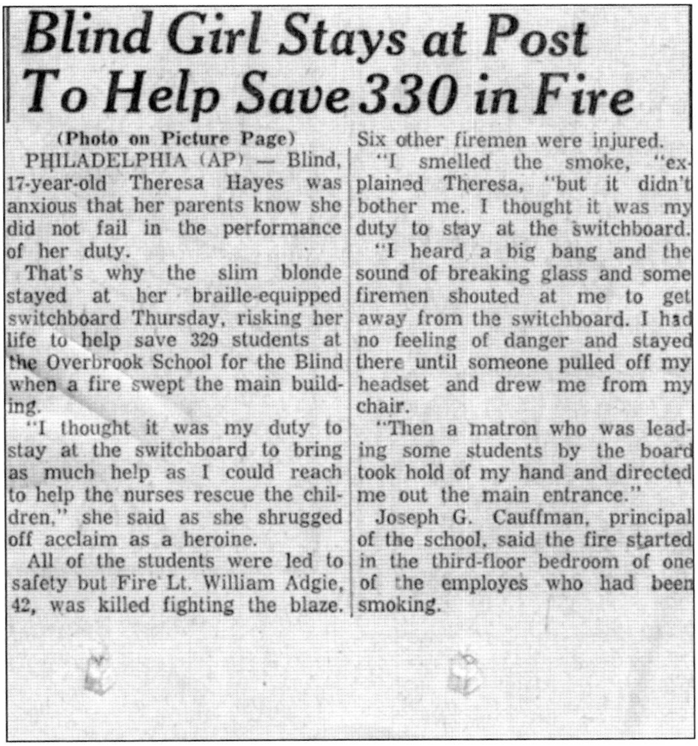

Blind Girl Stays at Post To Help Save 330 in Fire

(Photo on Picture Page)

PHILADELPHIA (AP) — Blind, 17-year-old Theresa Hayes was anxious that her parents know she did not fail in the performance of her duty.

That's why the slim blonde stayed at her braille-equipped switchboard Thursday, risking her life to help save 329 students at the Overbrook School for the Blind when a fire swept the main building.

"I thought it was my duty to stay at the switchboard to bring as much help as I could reach to help the nurses rescue the children," she said as she shrugged off acclaim as a heroine.

All of the students were led to safety but Fire Lt. William Adgie, 42, was killed fighting the blaze. Six other firemen were injured.

"I smelled the smoke," explained Theresa, "but it didn't bother me. I thought it was my duty to stay at the switchboard.

"I heard a big bang and the sound of breaking glass and some firemen shouted at me to get away from the switchboard. I had no feeling of danger and stayed there until someone pulled off my headset and drew me from my chair.

"Then a matron who was leading some students by the board took hold of my hand and directed me out the main entrance."

Joseph G. Cauffman, principal of the school, said the fire started in the third-floor bedroom of one of the employes who had been smoking.

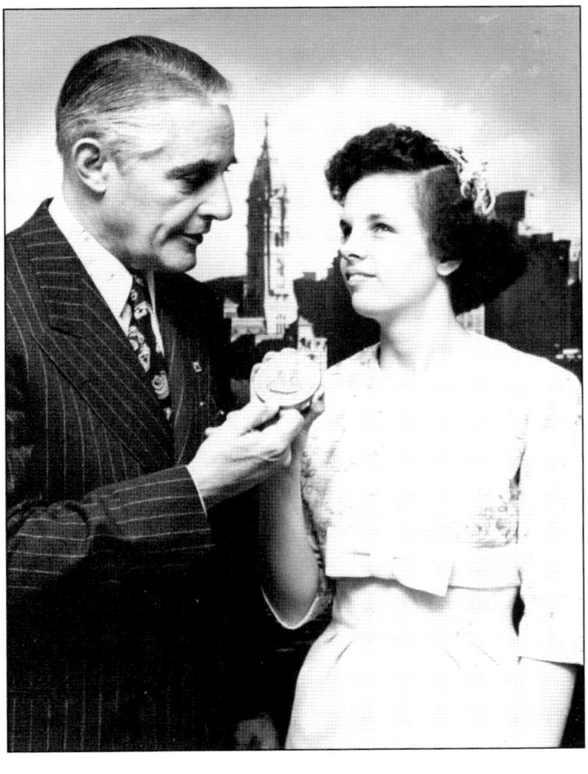

MEDAL PRESENTATION, 1960. Philadelphia mayor Richardson Dilworth presents Theresa Hayes with an award for her courage during the fire of 1960.

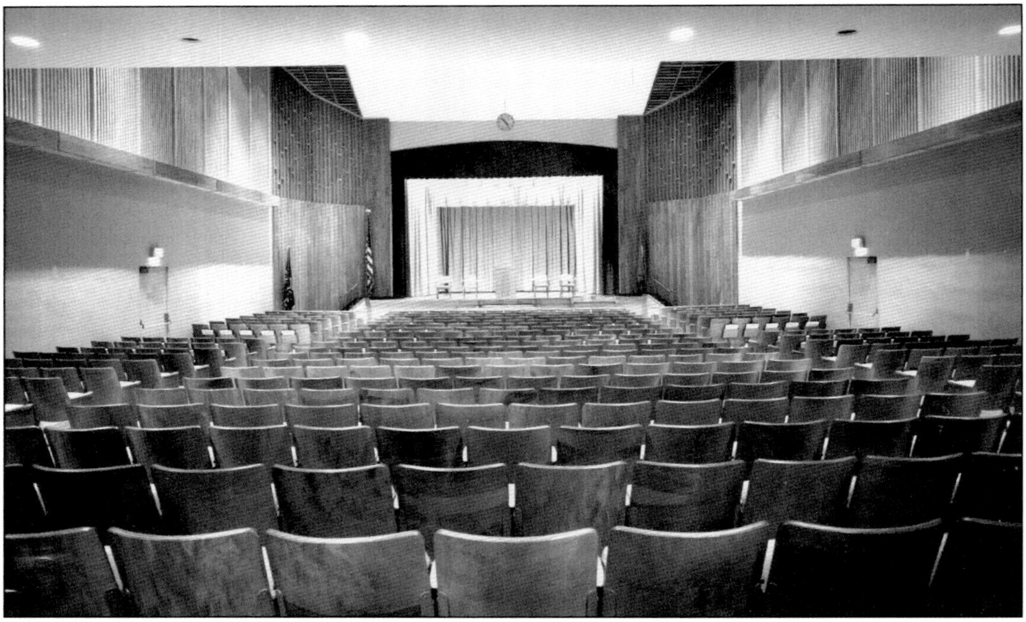

New Auditorium, 1964. The auditorium built after the fire of 1960 offered students a modern facility to perform plays, celebrate the holidays with special performances, share their musical talents, and participate in assemblies. This photograph shows the auditorium, with its rows of wooden chairs for audience members and a stage framed by curtains.

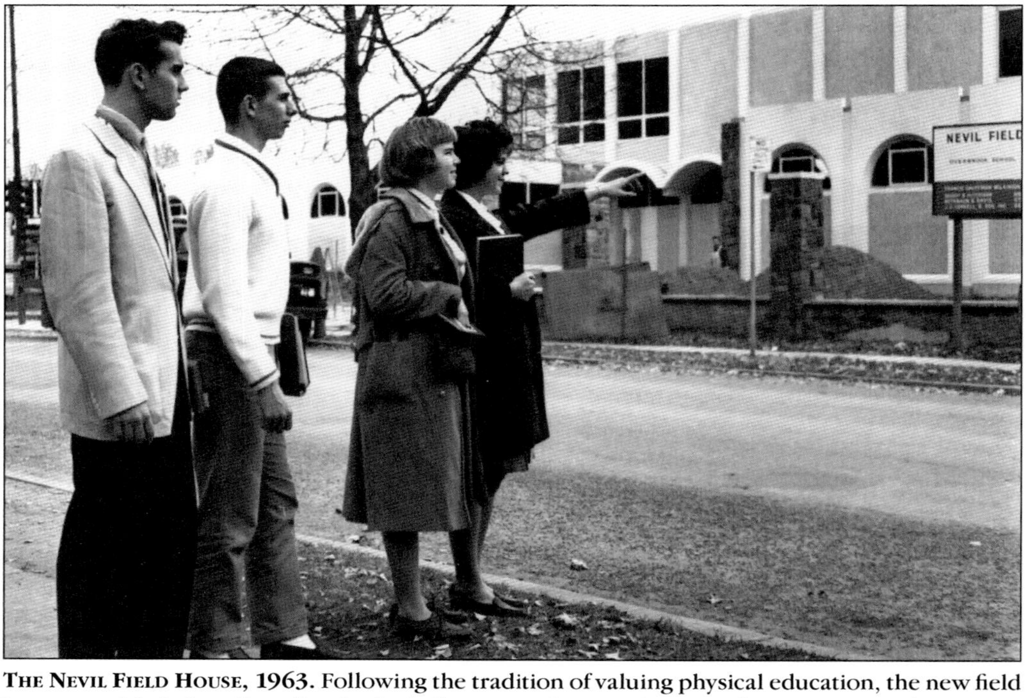

The Nevil Field House, 1963. Following the tradition of valuing physical education, the new field house provided a bowling alley, basketball court, indoor track, rooms for Scouting, and two large locker rooms. Here four students look at the new facility from across the street.

GROUNDBREAKING FOR NEVIL CENTER, 1971. Richard C. Lorbert, vice president of Girard Bank, holds a shovel with two students from the Deafblind Program at the groundbreaking for the Nevil Center.

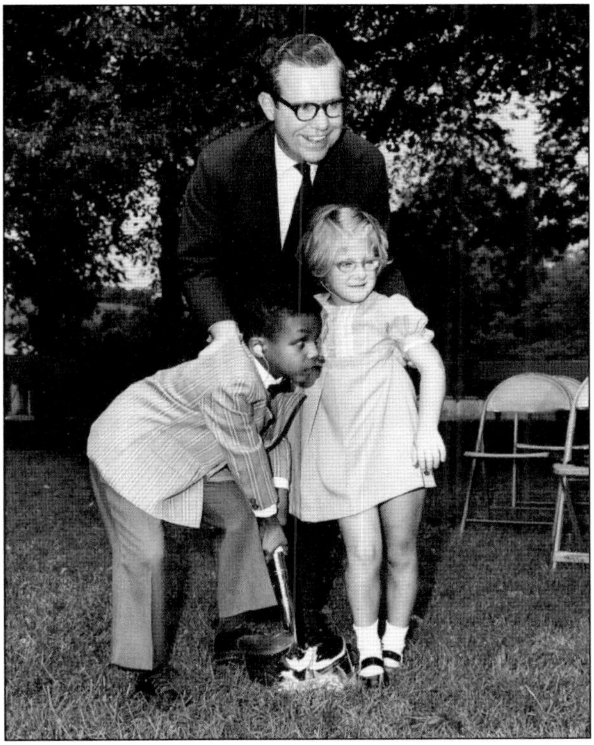

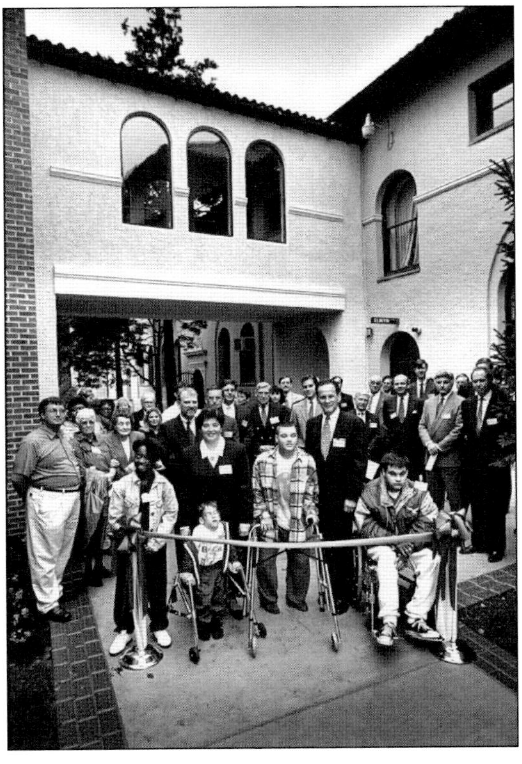

DEDICATION OF NEVIL BRIDGE AND ELEVATOR, 1994. Students, staff, and board members attend the ribbon-cutting ceremony for a new bridge and elevator to make the campus even more accessible.

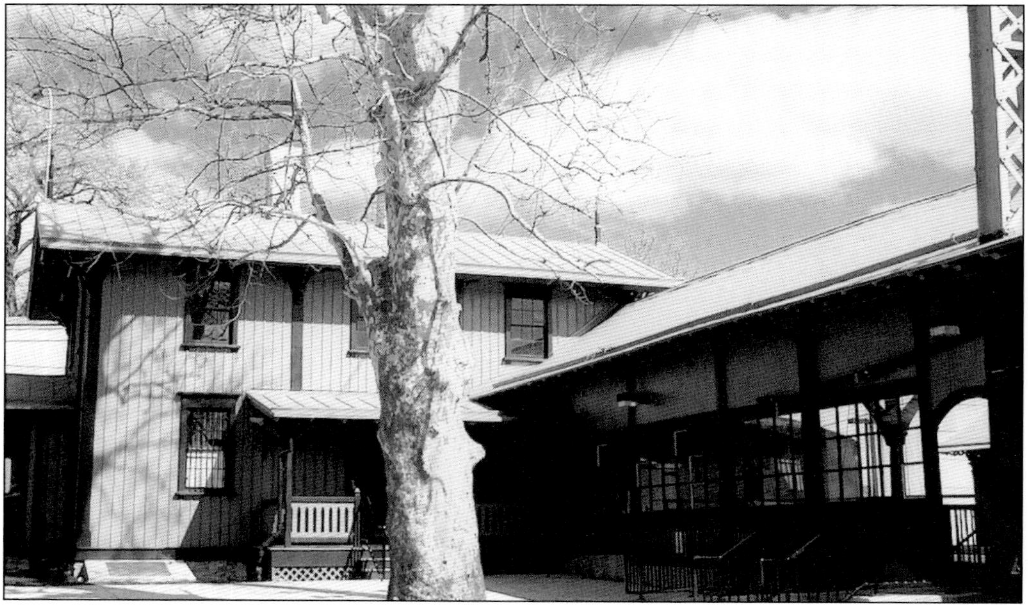

Overbrook Train Station, 2006. This railroad station, of cottage design with wood-carved brackets, was built in 1858. The depot is located half a mile from the school, which was an important factor in selecting the school's site in the Overbrook Farms area. Originally a flag station, the stop dates from 1840 on the Columbia Railroad system. The present station house was built in 1858 and served the local farmers and estate owners whose land straddled both sides of the city boundary.

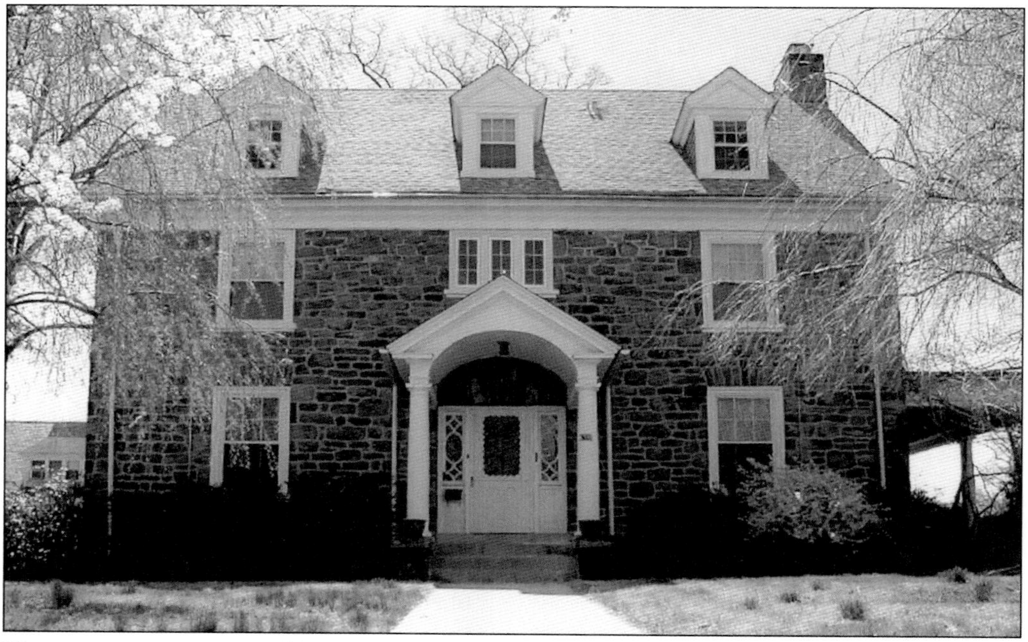

Woodbine House. Owned by Overbrook School for the Blind, this structure showcases the Pennsylvania granite found in many homes in the Overbrook Farms community. The Woodbine House is used as accommodations for guests of the school and as a meeting area for staff.

Three

Lessons and Learning

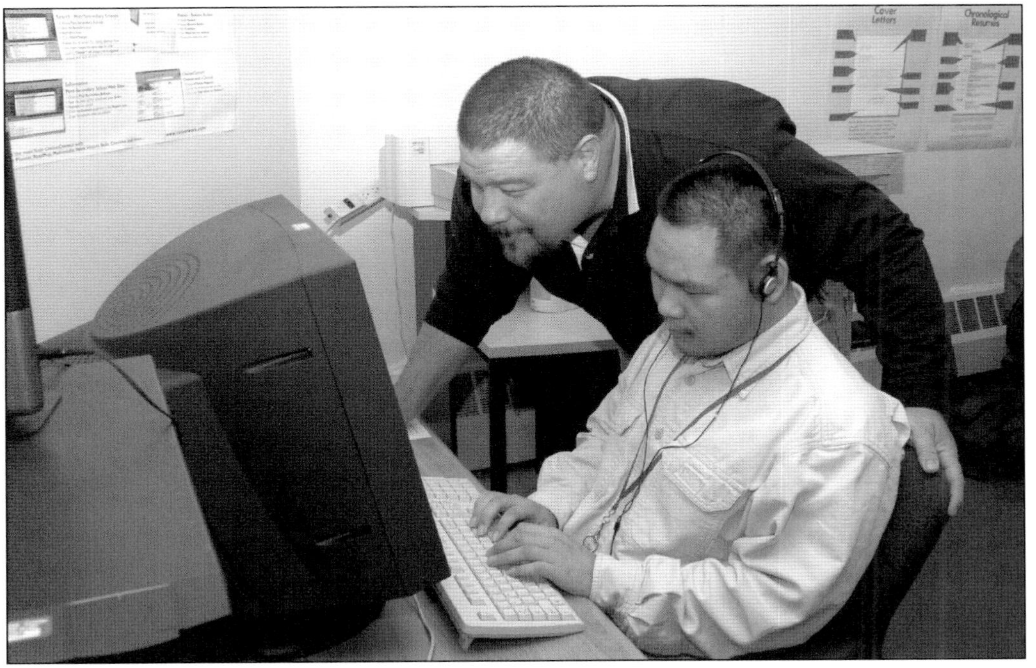

Curriculum Plans. Overbrook's philosophy has always been to involve students in a strong educational program. The curriculum has followed the State of Pennsylvania's plan for all students in the academic areas of learning. As the student population changed to include multihandicapped students, Overbrook adjusted its curriculum. In the early 1990s, a long-range plan was developed to provide appropriate technology to all students, every day, regardless of age or disability. Technology was viewed as a link to the literacy of the 21st century and an important component for communication, daily class work, and employment.

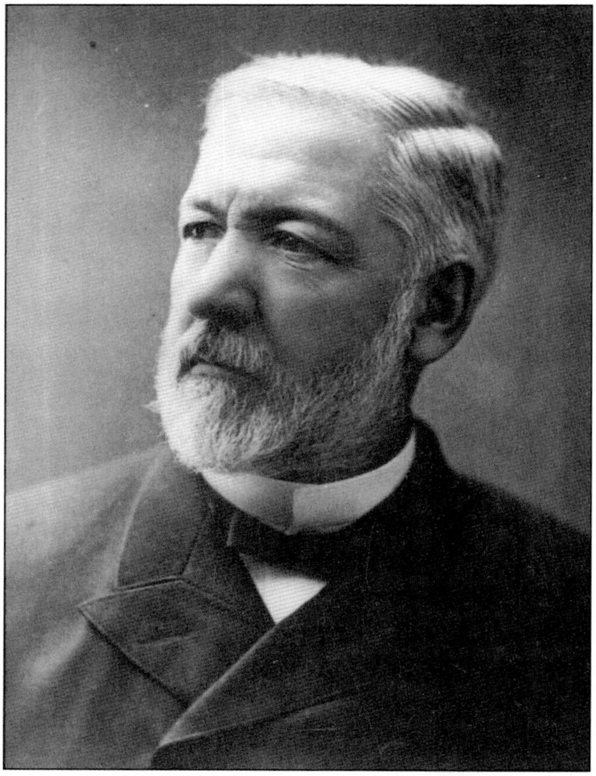

Overbrook Teacher and Presidential Candidate. James Blaine graduated from Washington College in 1847 and taught at the Western Military Institute and the Pennsylvania Institution for the Instruction of the Blind from 1852 to 1854. His wife, Harriet, also worked at the Pennsylvania Institution as an assistant teacher for girls. In 1854, the Blaines moved to Maine, where James edited the *Portland Advertiser* and the *Kennebec Journal*. He was a delegate to the first Republican convention in 1860. After holding many political offices, he was nominated for president by the party in 1884 and became the "Plumed Knight of the Grand Old Party." His opponent—and the victor—was Stephen Grover Cleveland. Interestingly, Cleveland was working at the New York Institute for the Blind at the same time that Blaine was teaching at the Pennsylvania Institution. (Courtesy of Collections of Maine Historical Society.)

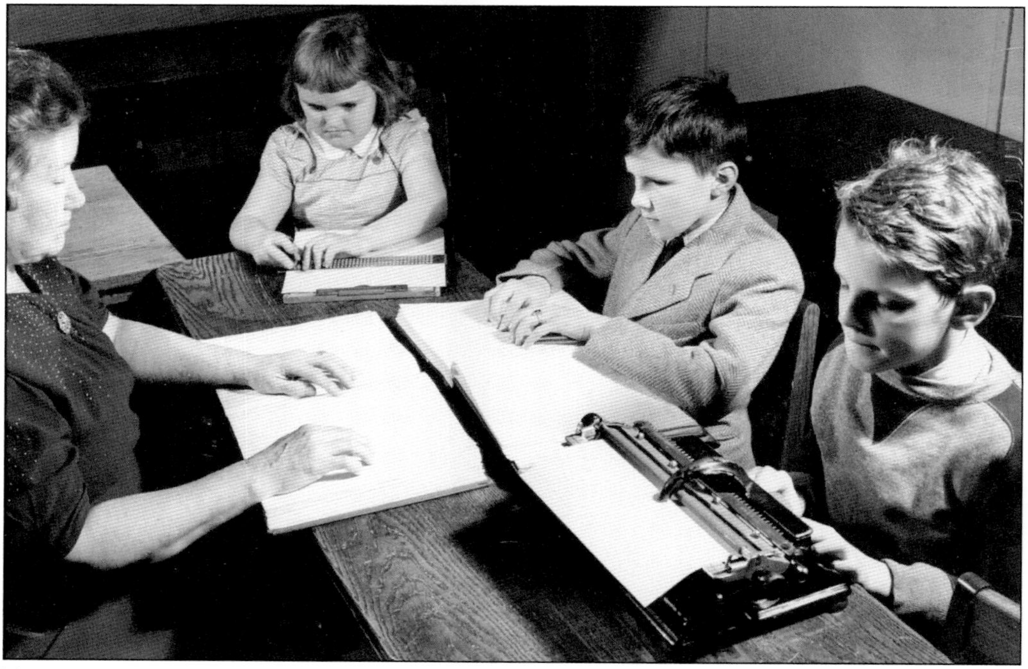

Tools for the Blind, 1923. Anne Ward, a 1900 graduate of Overbrook, works with three students—one using a brailler, one employing a slate and stylus, and one reading braille.

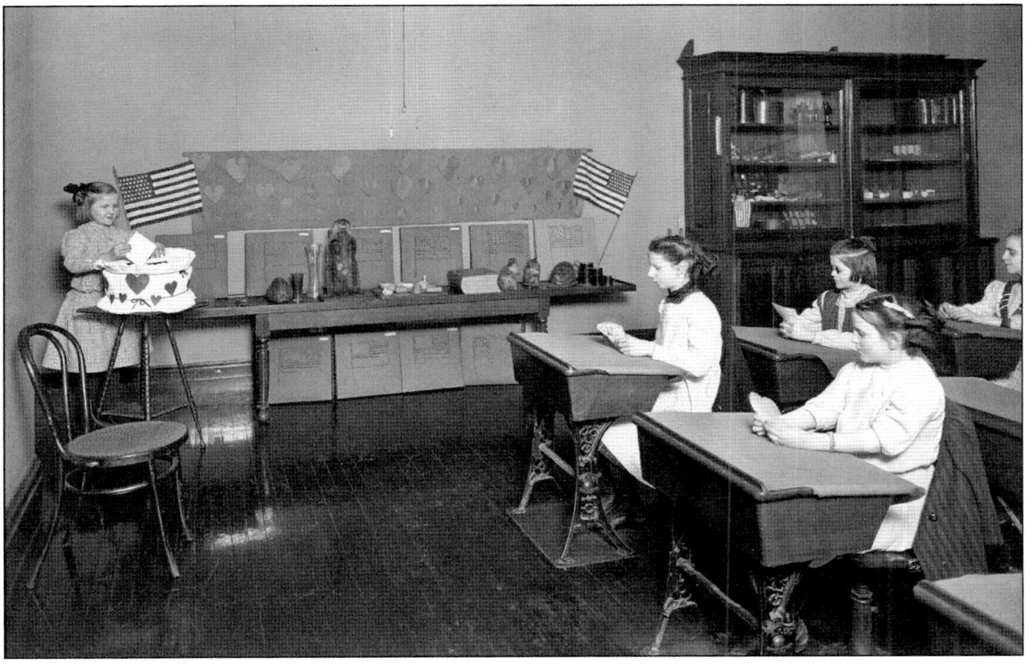

Valentine's Day. Holidays and special celebrations throughout the year have been a big part of Overbrook's history from the beginning. In this photograph, female students read their Valentine's Day cards in the classroom.

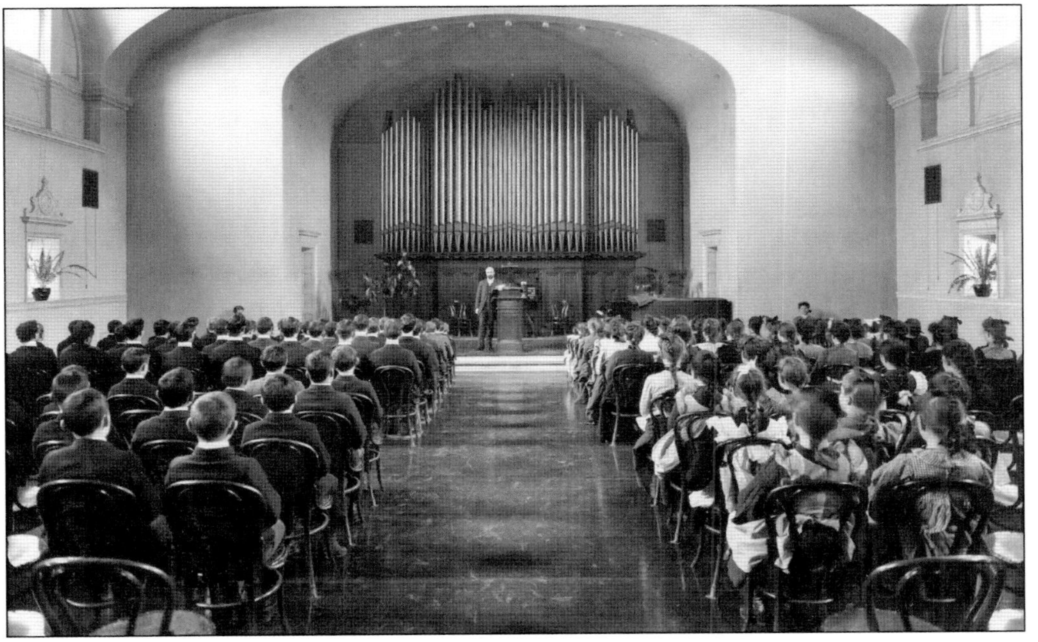

Daily Chapel, 1904. The genders were carefully separated by the design of the building. Chapel, however, was one of the few activities where boys and girls were brought together in the same room. Boys were seated on the left, while girls were on the right, facing the lectern and the large organ, which was also used for teaching.

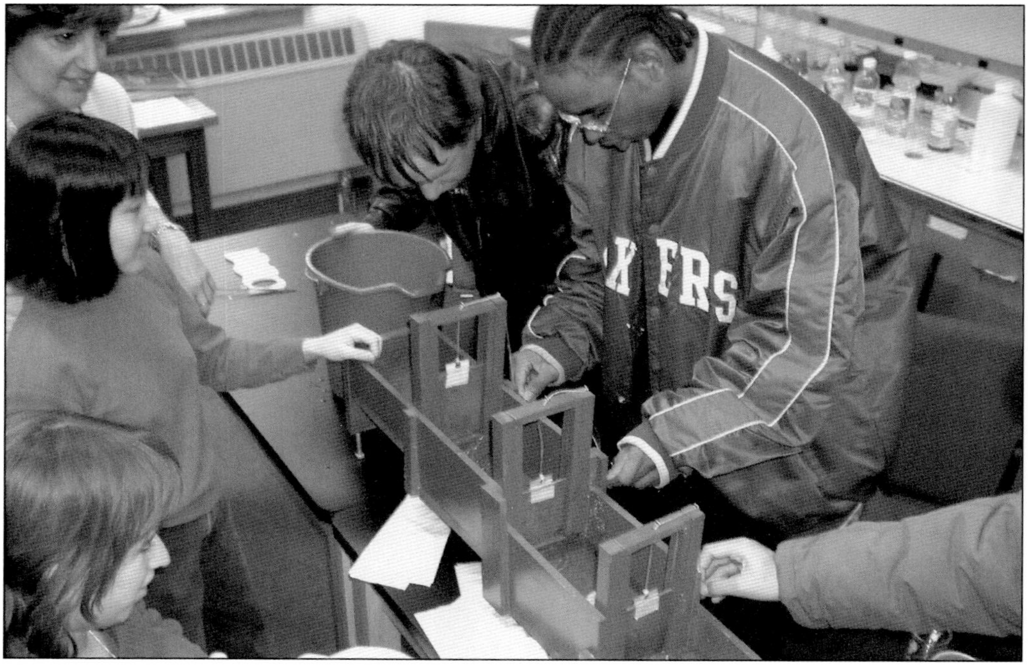

Learning about Canal Locks. In the late 1960s, more coeducational activities started to take place. Today boys and girls join together in classes, sports, and recreational pursuits. Here high school–age boys and girls use a model to understand a canal lock system.

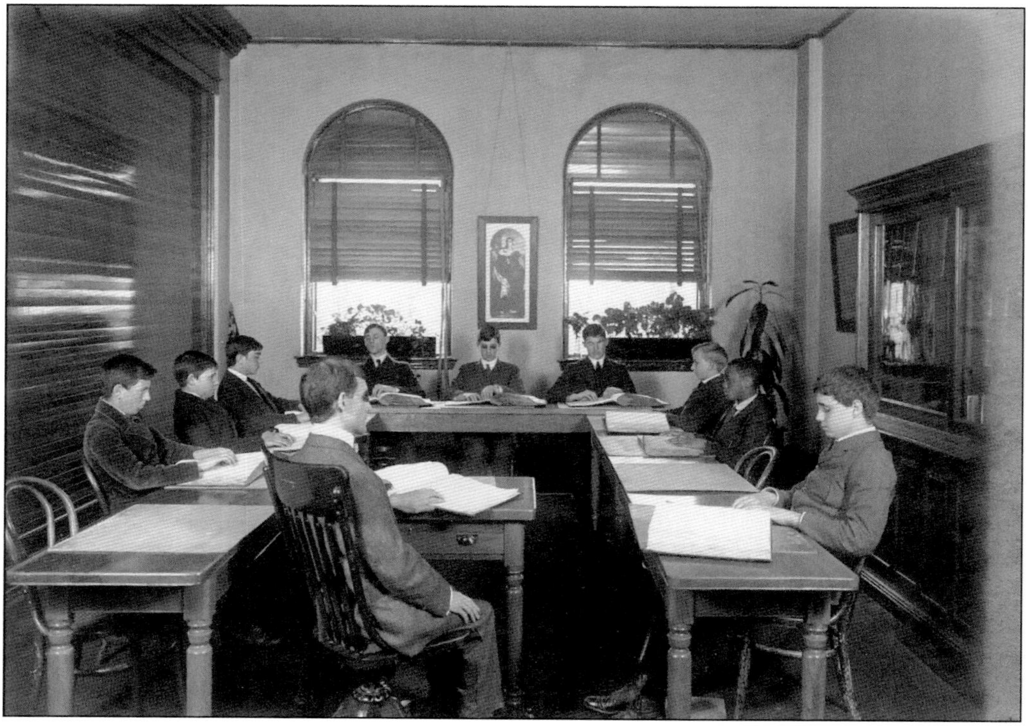

Boys' Classroom, 1910. Boys sit around a U-shaped desk reading braille.

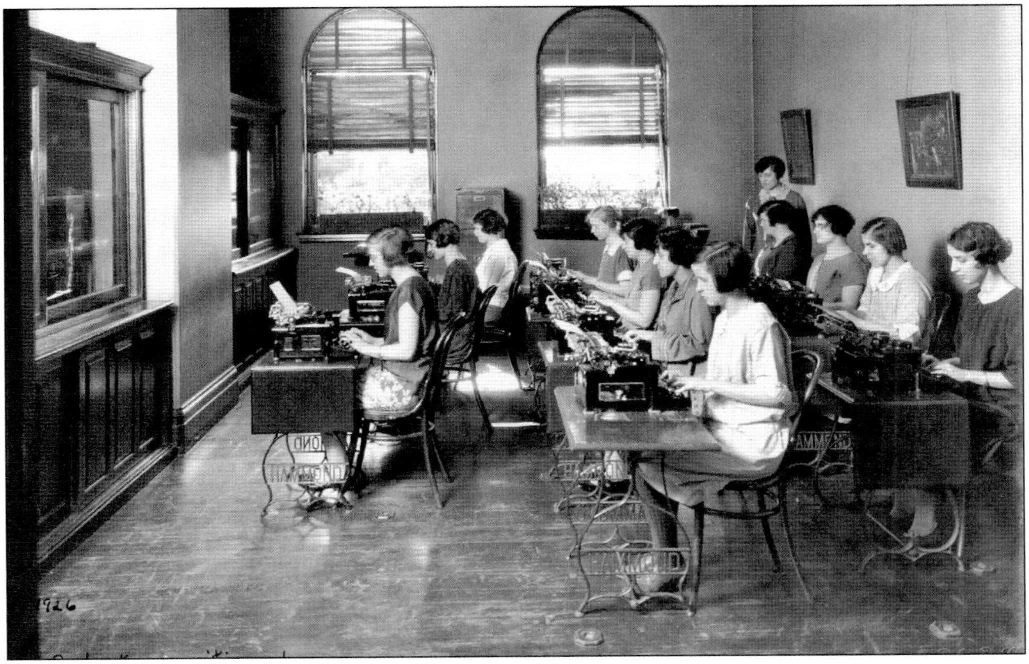

Girls' Typewriting Class, 1926. The early founders of the school recognized the importance of skills for future employment. Built into the curriculum were opportunities for the students to develop practical skills. In this photograph, girls sit at desks and practice typing.

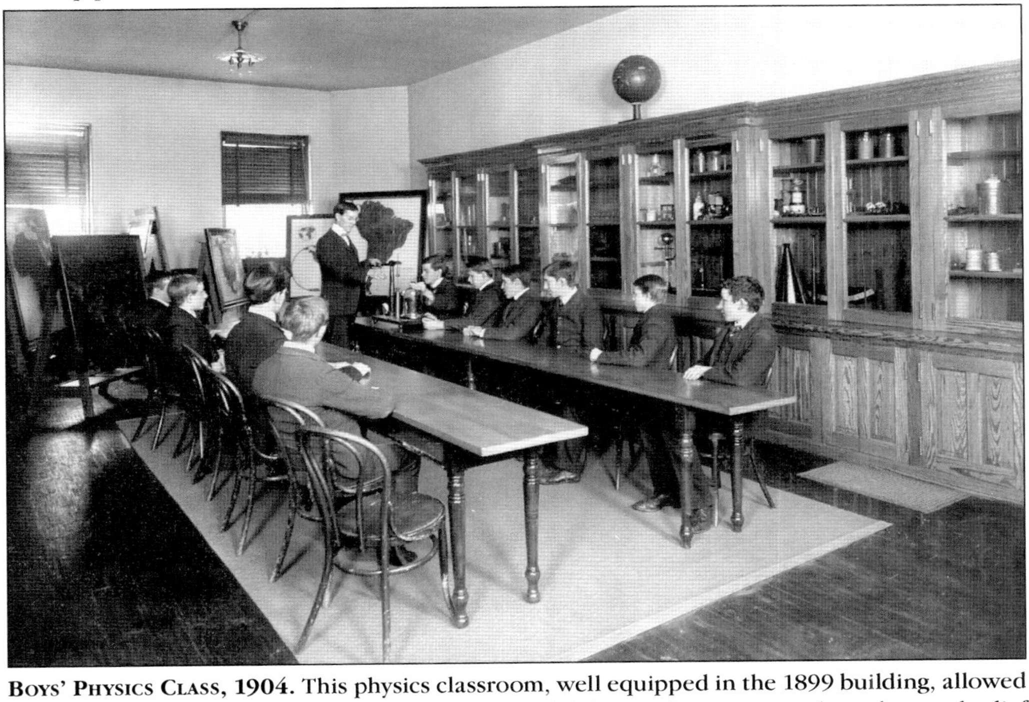

Boys' Physics Class, 1904. This physics classroom, well equipped in the 1899 building, allowed for hands-on learning. Here the teacher uses a model that students can touch, and several relief maps hang around the room.

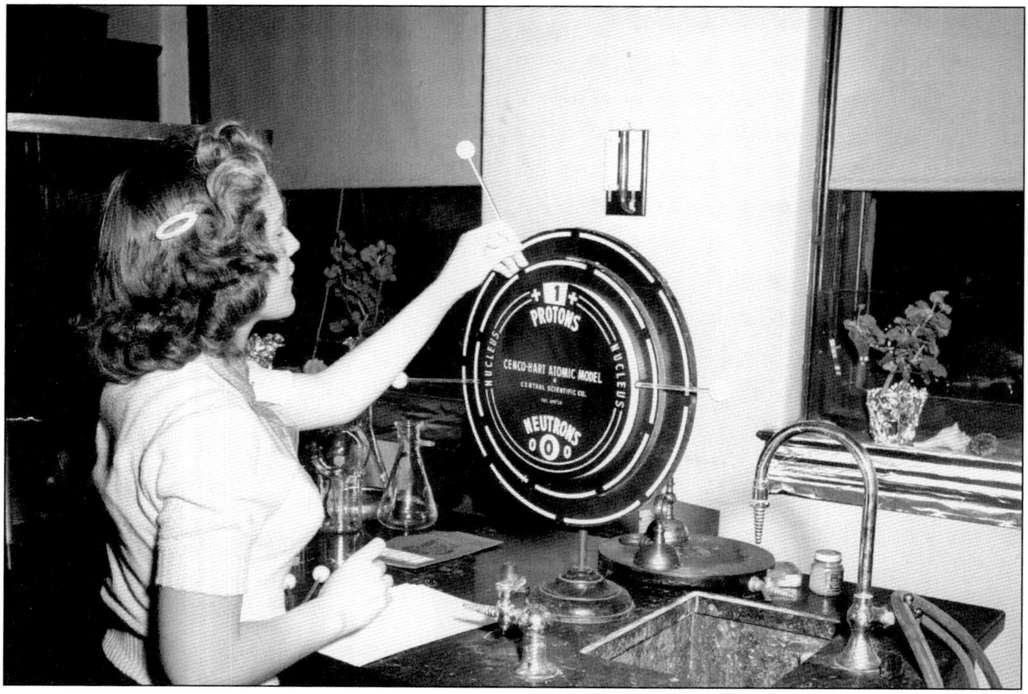

Atomic Model, 1955. A teenage girl uses an atomic model to learn about protons, neutrons, and atoms.

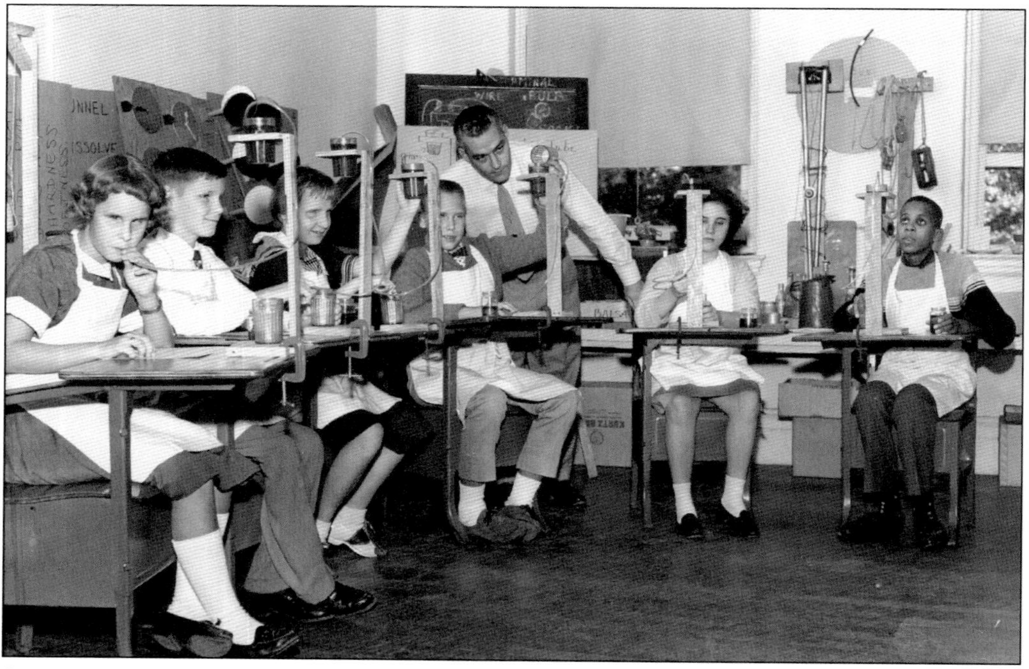

Science Experiment, 1961. Dr. Gilbert Ulrich instructs six students on how to use a siphon with a wooden frame, which holds one cup of liquid at desk level and elevates another cup. Plastic tubing connects the two.

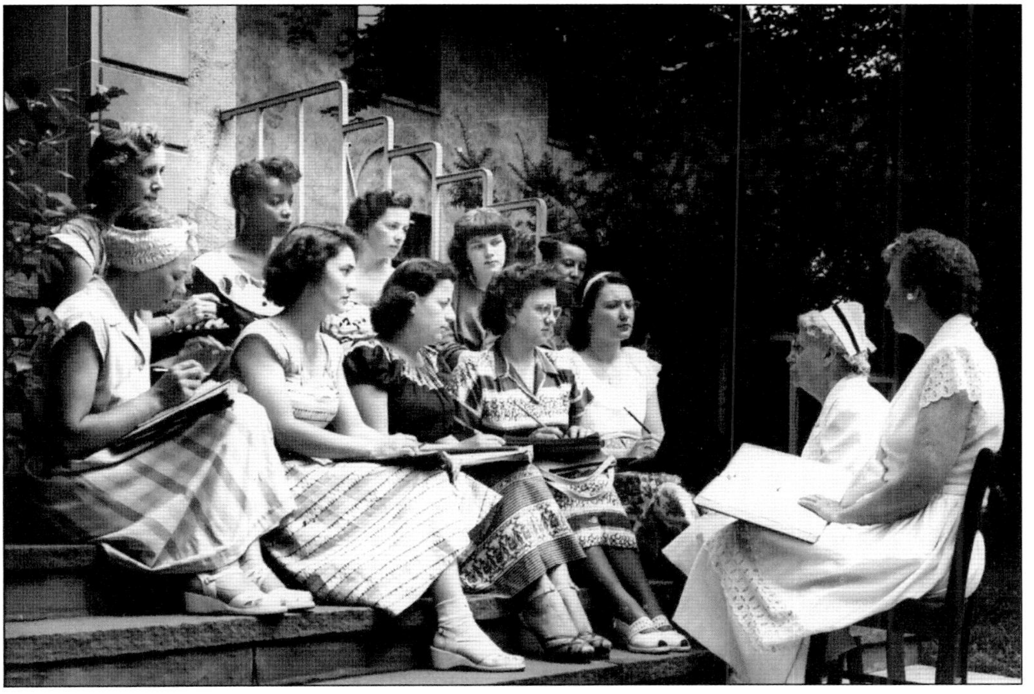

Moms in School. Mothers of infants and toddlers attend classes to learn skills to help their children. Overbrook had the first program of this type to support families.

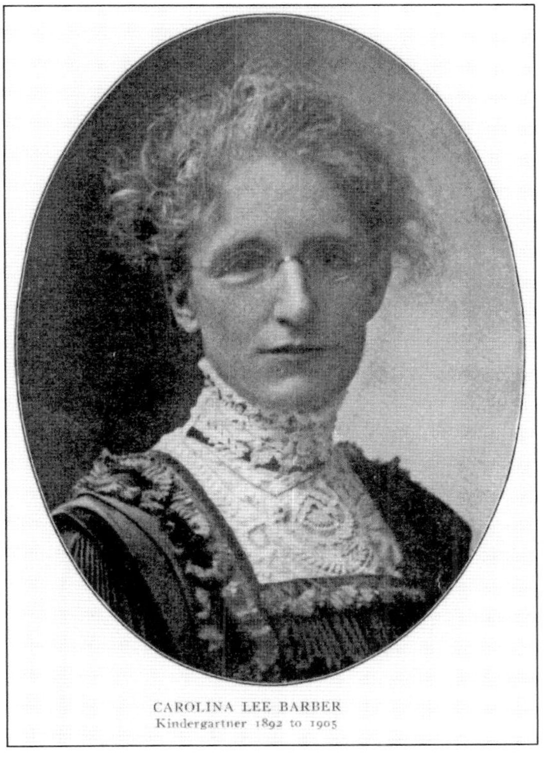

Carolina Lee Barber. In 1884, the first Pennsylvania kindergarten for blind children was opened. Carolina Lee Barber was hired as the kindergarten teacher in 1892 and remained for 13 years.

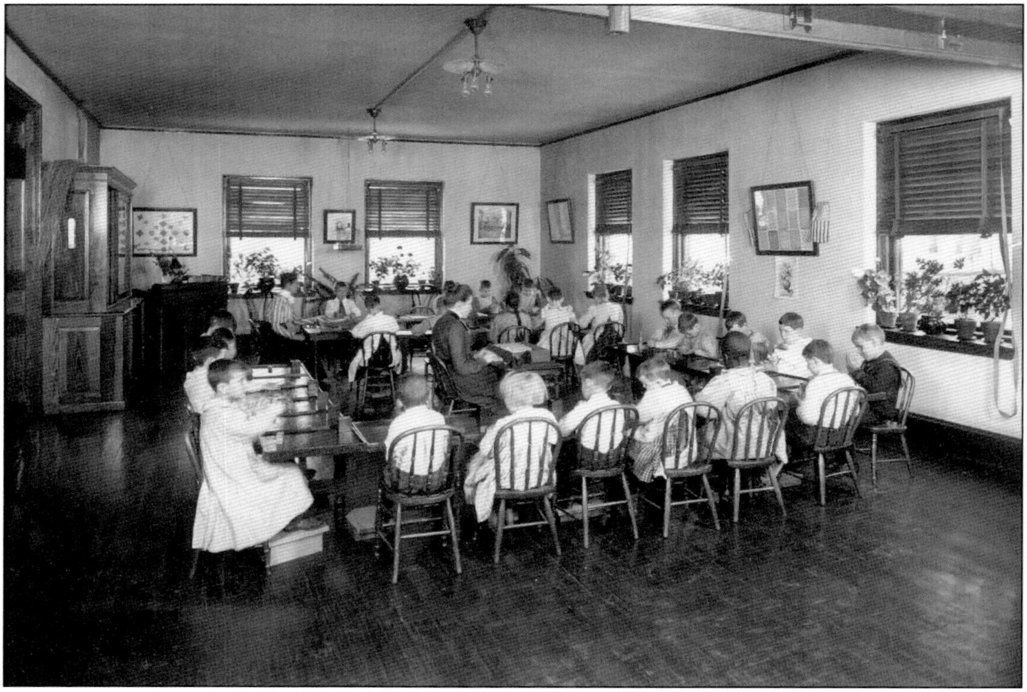

Coeducational Kindergarten, 1910. This was the first class of integrated kindergarten. In the photograph, girls and boys play with wooden blocks on their desks.

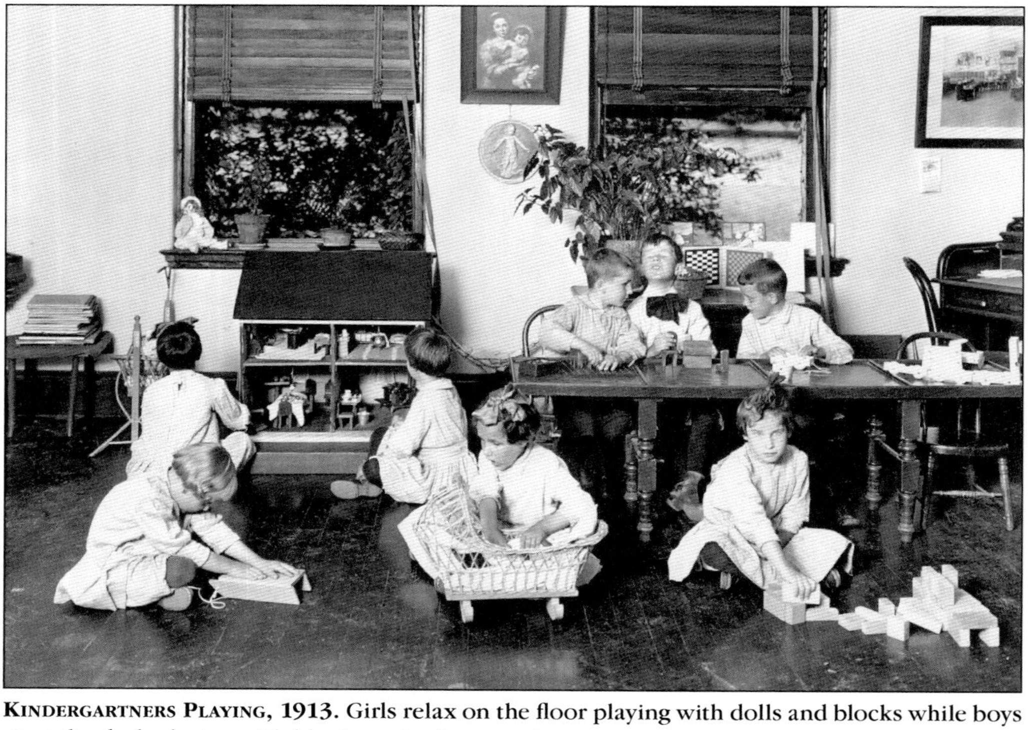

Kindergartners Playing, 1913. Girls relax on the floor playing with dolls and blocks while boys sit at the desk playing with blocks and other wooden toys.

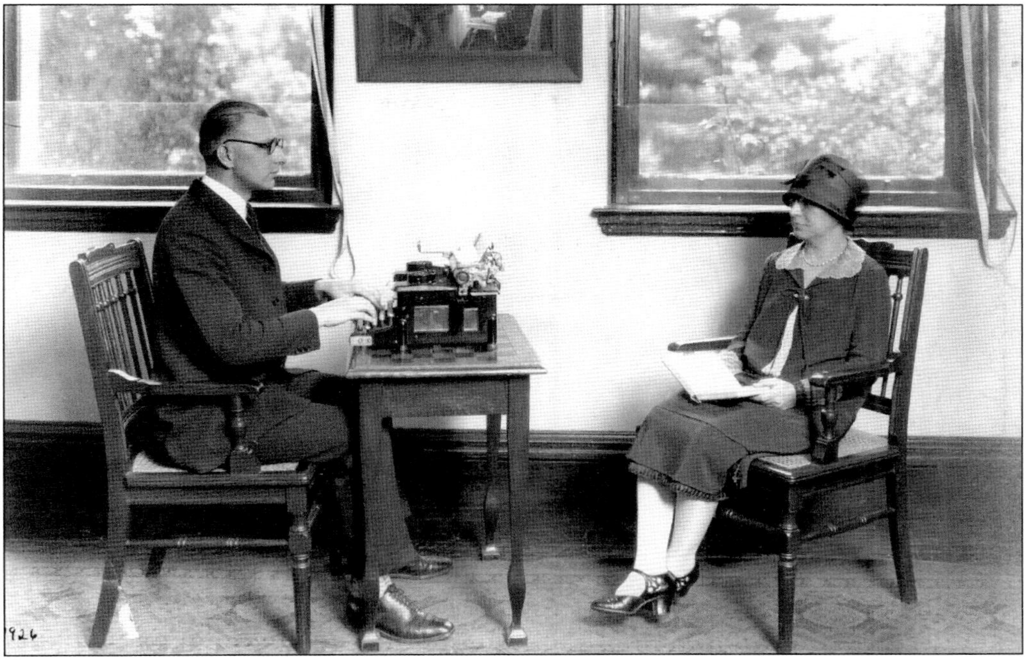

A Volunteer Reader, 1926. Students at Overbrook were fortunate to have volunteers to assist with reading textbooks and current material that was unavailable in braille. Many Philadelphians learned about Overbrook by becoming volunteer readers. Here a volunteer helps an older student with his schoolwork.

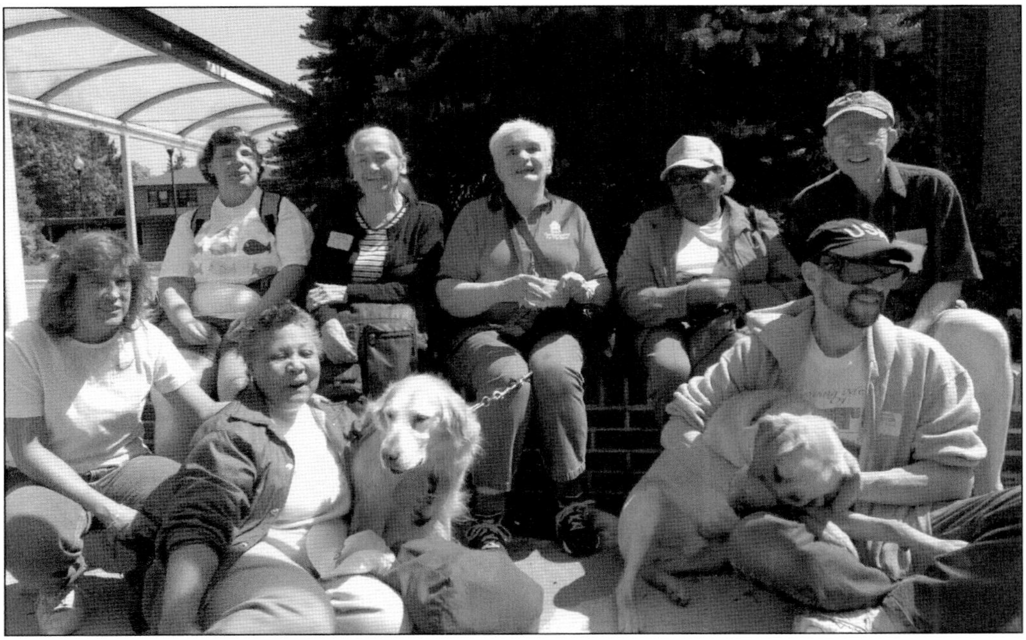

Volunteer Gardeners. Visually impaired role models come and share their skills with students in many different ways. These gardeners who are blind or visually impaired often lend a hand on Overbrook's campus by planting bulbs and flowers.

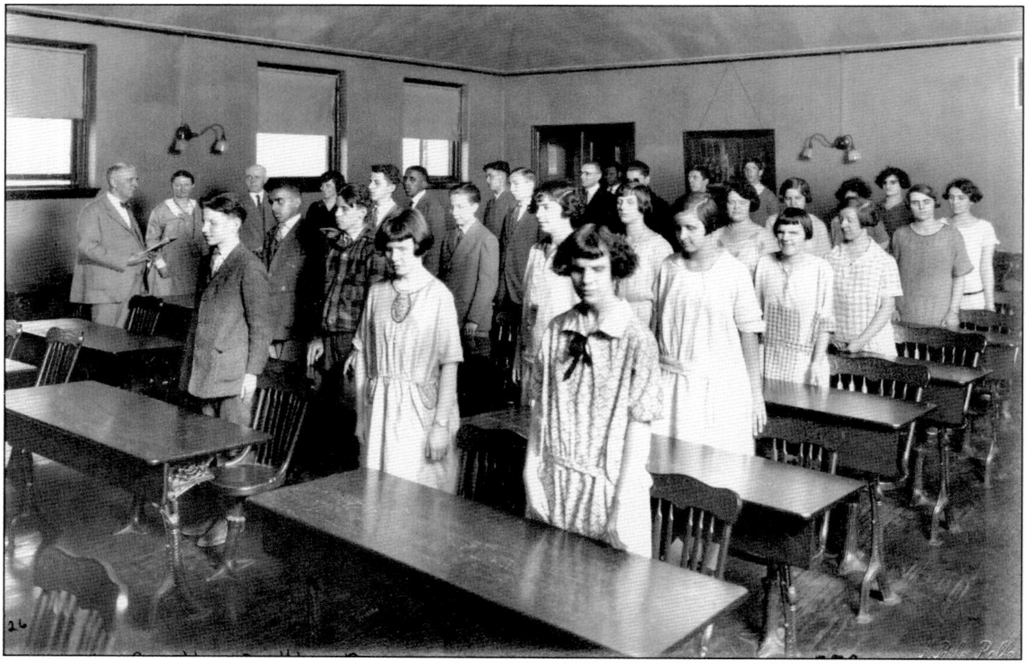

FUN WITH WORDS, 1926. Boys and girls stand in a classroom with three teachers off to the side. The students are practicing for the spelling bee, which was a popular way to learn and have fun at the same time.

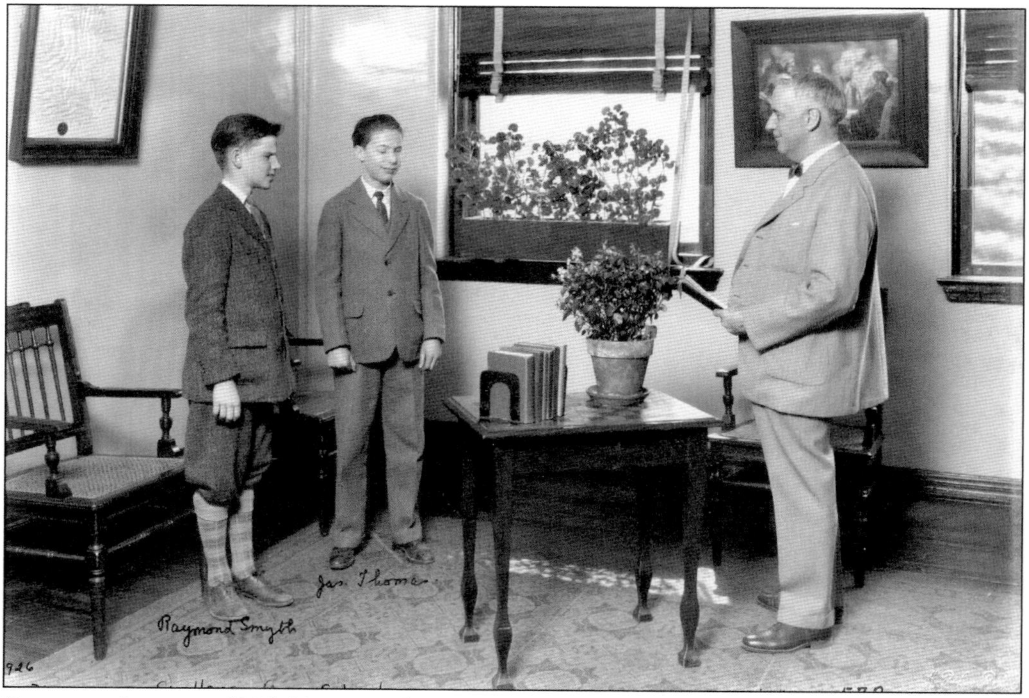

CHAMPION SPELLERS, 1926. Two award-winning spellers from the boys' school stand in front of Dr. Olin H. Burritt, the institution's ninth principal.

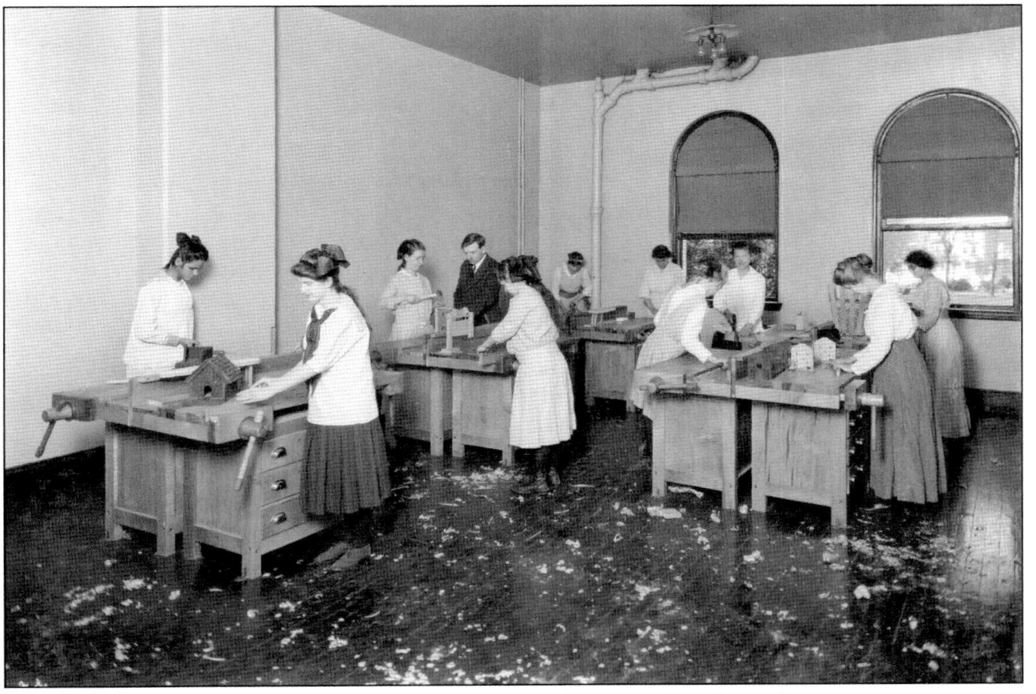

WOODWORKING PROJECTS. Girls create birdhouses in their woodworking class.

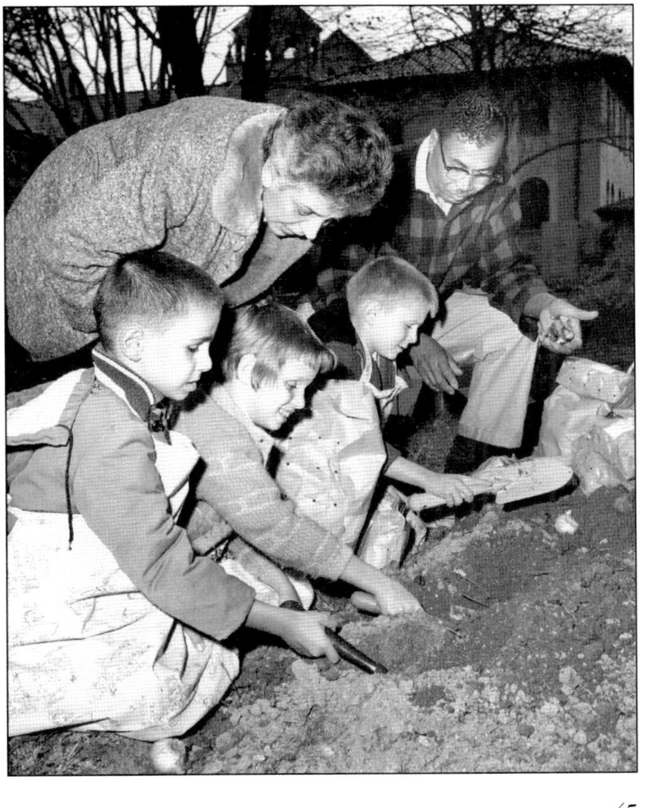

GARDENING, 1963. Two young boys and a girl plant tulip bulbs with the help of Elizabeth Sigafoos, supervisor of the primary school, and one of the gardeners.

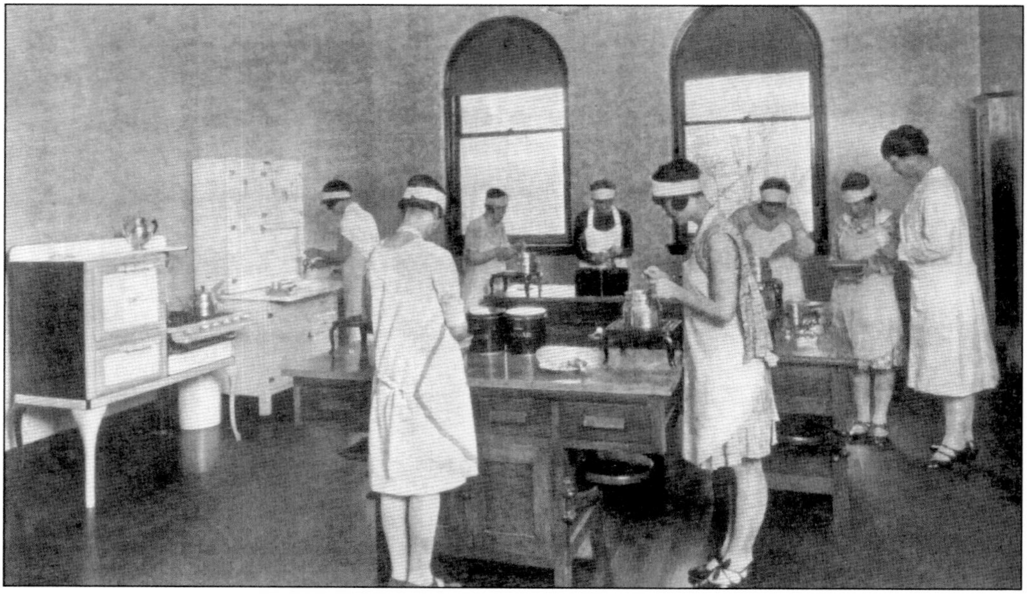

Domestic Science, 1930. Food preparation and cooking have remained an important part of the program. These female students, wearing aprons and headbands, learn how to cook using all the latest kitchen aids of the time.

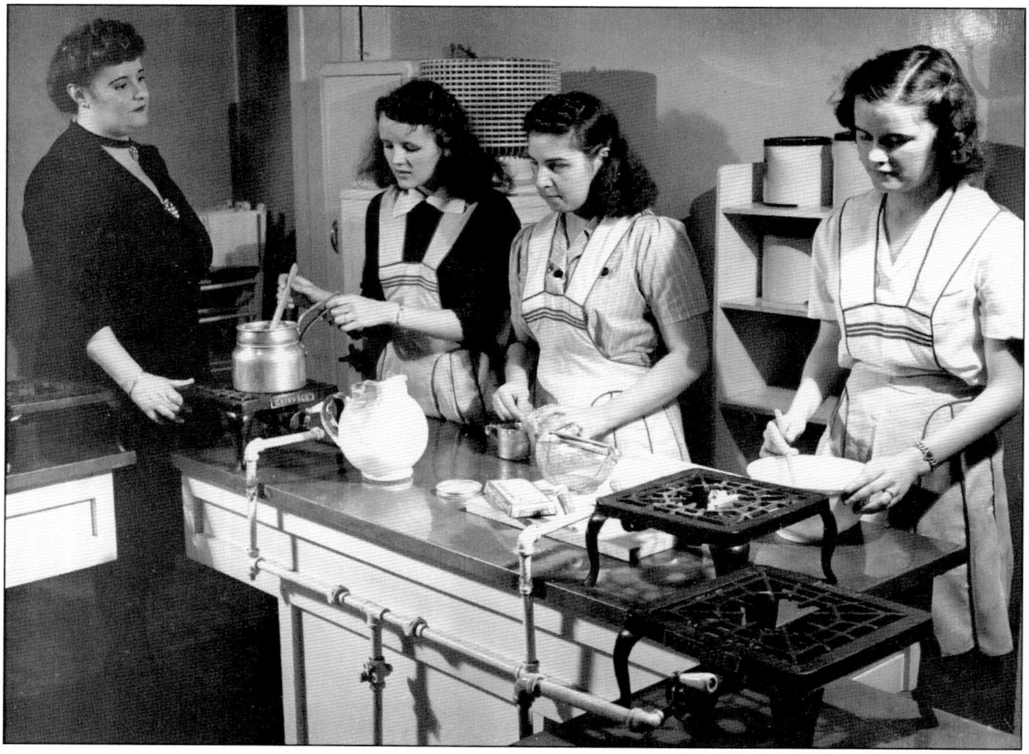

Learning to Cook, 1949. Three teenage girls discover how to use a gas burner and measuring cups in their home economics class.

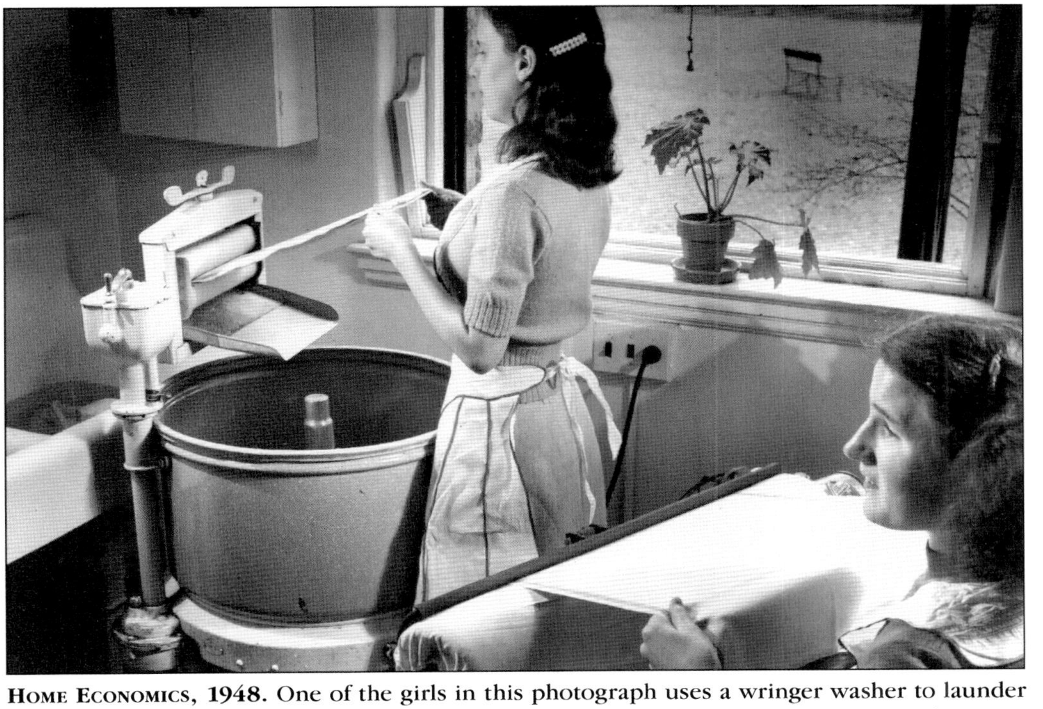

Home Economics, 1948. One of the girls in this photograph uses a wringer washer to launder sheets and pillowcases while the other uses a mangle to iron the linens. Today students are involved in similar activities but have the benefit of modern washers and dryers.

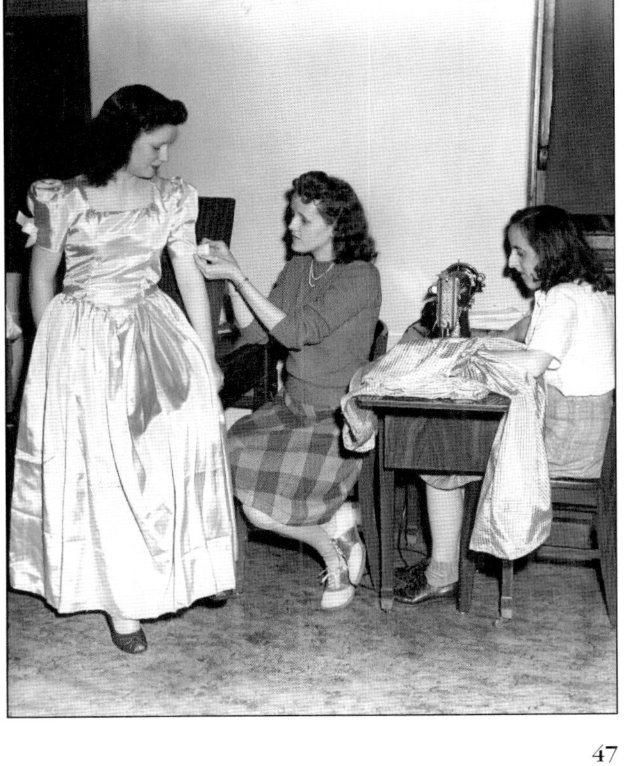

Prom Dress Fitting, 1947. In a home economics class, a student is fitted for a prom gown while another tailors her dress at the sewing machine.

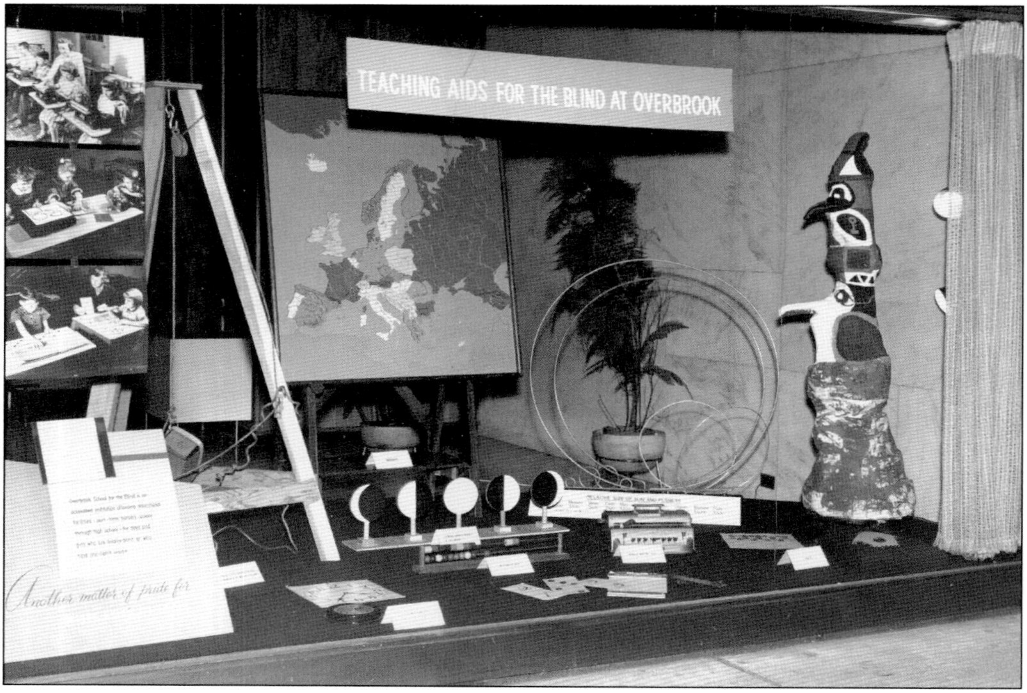

TEACHING AIDS, 1960. Overbrook participates in Philadelphia's Week for the Blind with a display table showing different teaching aids, as well as information about the school.

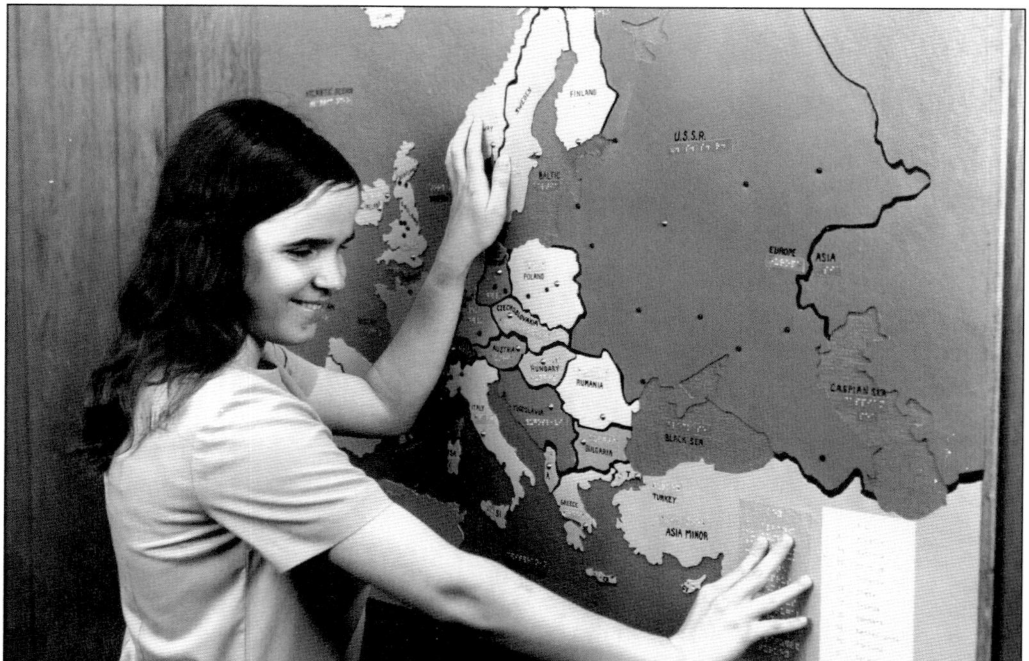

A LESSON IN GEOGRAPHY, 1969. A female student uses this tactile map to identify European countries. Country names are in braille and indicated by a brass tack. Raised lines divide each country.

The Cheetah, 1976. The Touch and Learn Center's collection of mounted and stuffed birds and animals, along with other tactile objects, assists the students in learning concepts and getting close to animals ordinarily out of reach. In this photograph, five students explore a stuffed cheetah.

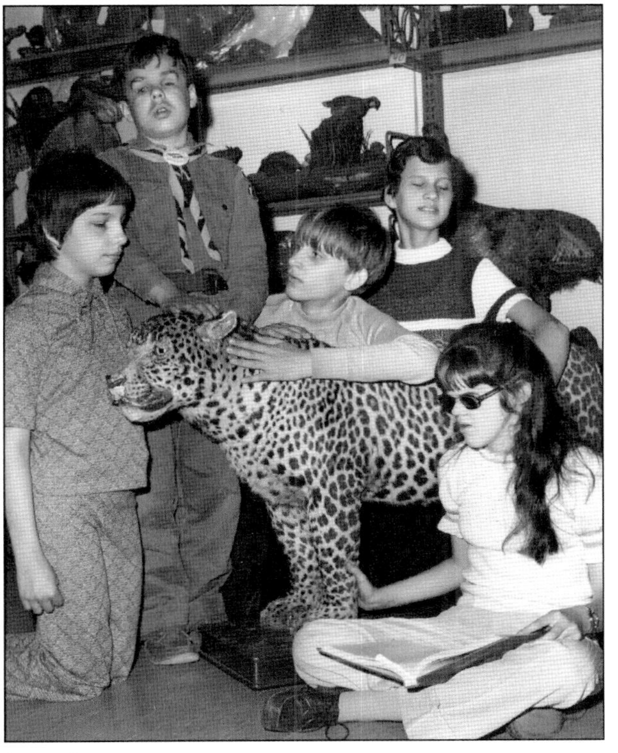

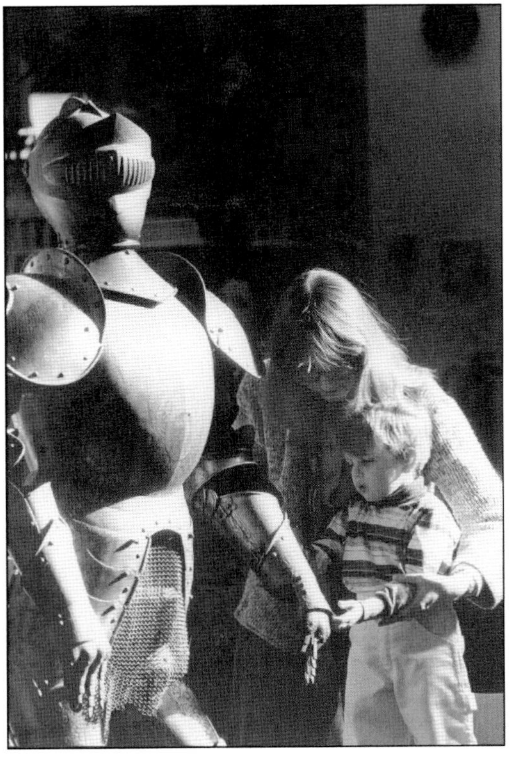

The Knight. A teacher helps her young student examine a suit of armor.

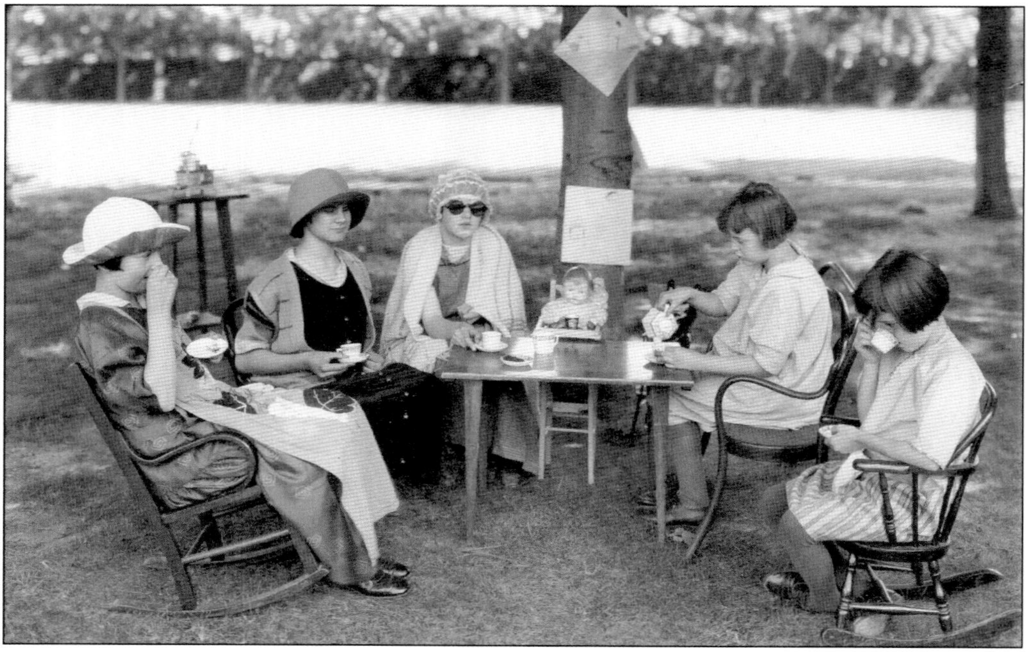

High Tea in Pleasantville, 1926. The girls' school created the imaginary town of Pleasantville, complete with a school, a store, and emergency services. Five young girls wearing dresses and hats sit and sip their tea after a hard day's work. A doll is also seated around the table.

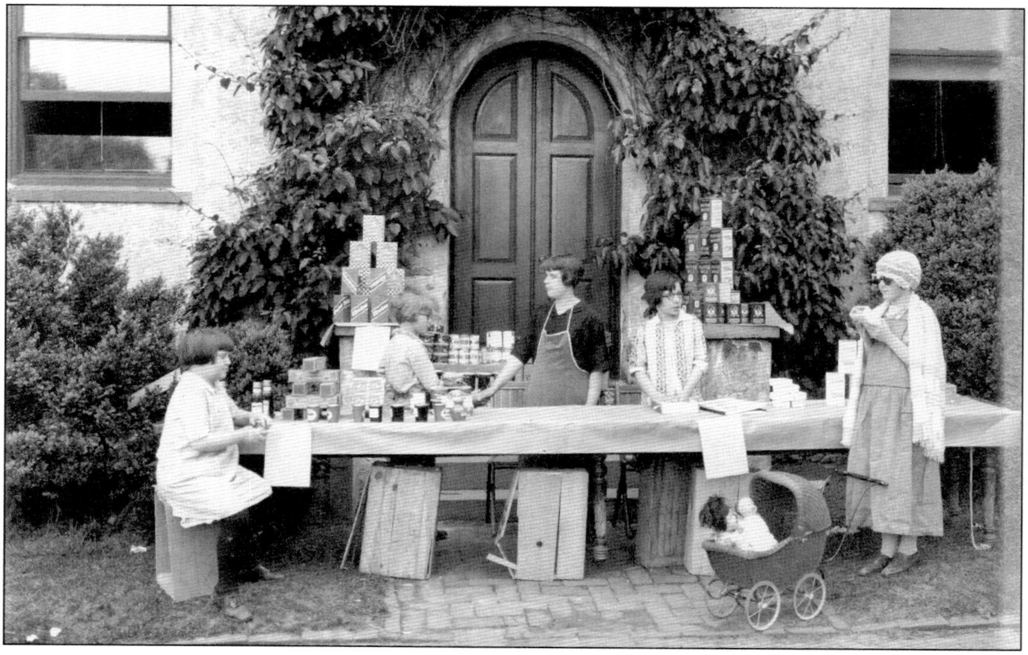

The General Store, 1926. The store in Pleasantville, which was set up outside one of the school buildings, is stocked with puffed wheat, Wheetena, and other boxed and canned goods. Here a student shopper reads the label on a box of tapioca. With her are her "children," two dolls in a carriage.

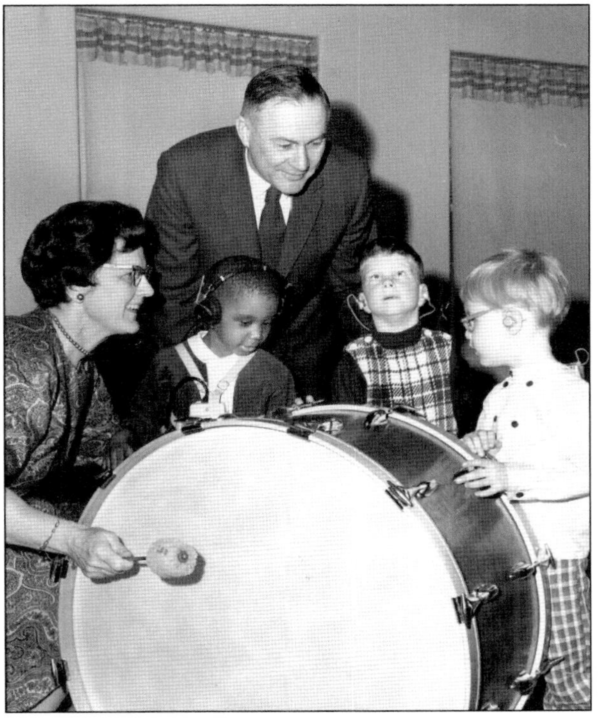

The Beat of a Drum, 1969. David Olson observes deafblind nursery school children react to the vibration of the drum, beat by Harriet Kerr. Olson, the school's 12th principal, announced the launching of the Deafblind Program at the start of the school year in 1969.

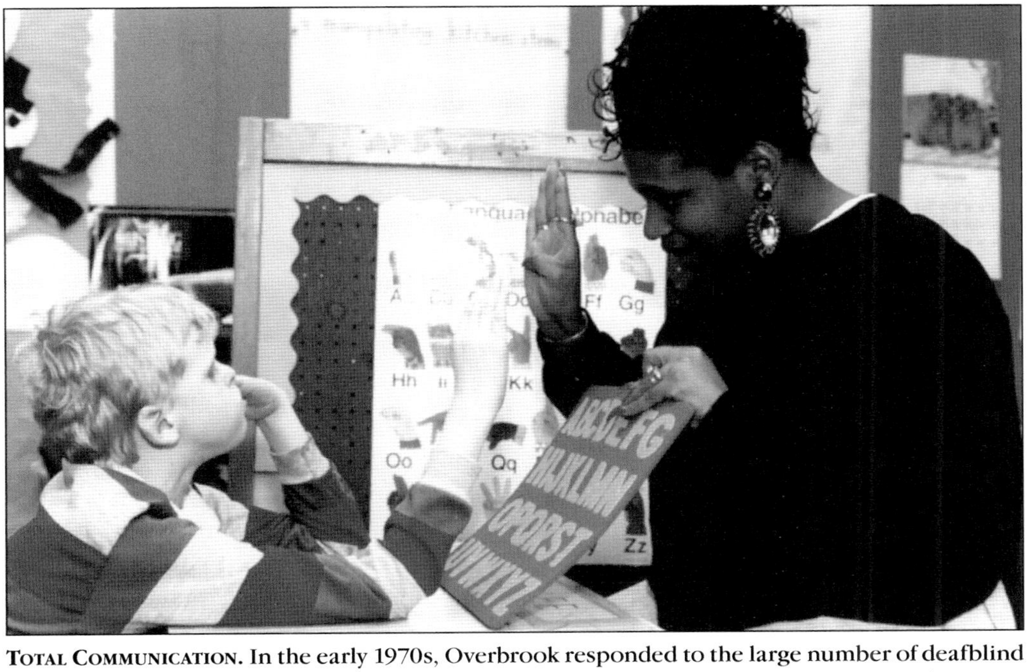

Total Communication. In the early 1970s, Overbrook responded to the large number of deafblind children born as a result of congenital rubella. The Deafblind Program was developed to meet this need and has continued even though rubella is rarely seen today. This boy is congenitally deafblind. He has some usable vision, which helps him communicate with the staff member using American Sign Language.

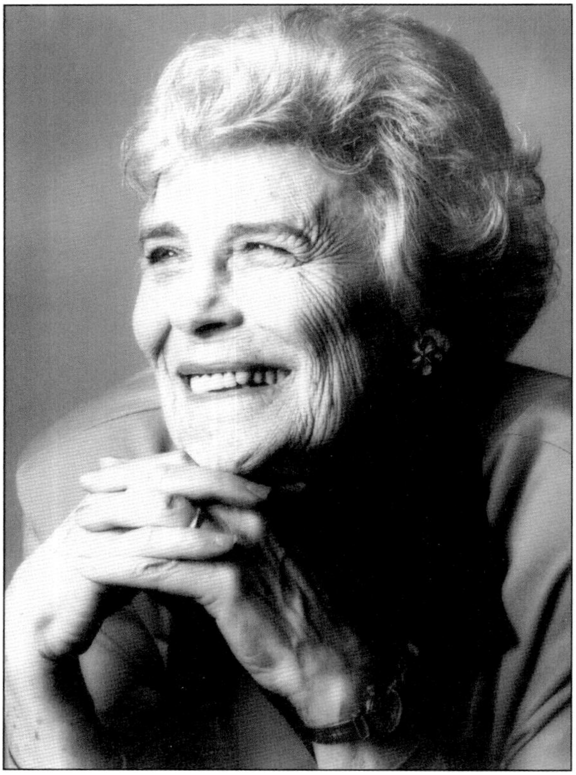

Dr. Mae Davidow. A student, teacher, and member of the board of managers, Dr. Mae Davidow was an ardent advocate for the blind. After earning her bachelor's degree in 1935 from Douglas College for Women in New Jersey, the 1929 Overbrook graduate returned to teach civics and math for 36 years. An expert on the abacus, she used it to teach her classes and, in 1966, wrote the nationally acclaimed book *The Abacus Made Easy*. She pioneered the use of the electronic abacus and worked on the development of the talking calculator. Dr. Davidow was the first blind person to earn both master's and doctoral degrees at Temple University. After her retirement, she served on Overbrook's board of managers. A lifelong athlete, at 75 she won gold medals for swimming and diving in a national competition sponsored by the U.S. Association for Blind Athletes in Long Beach, California. A recipient of numerous awards, she was recognized by the statehouse in 1978 and named a Daughter of Pennsylvania in 1986.

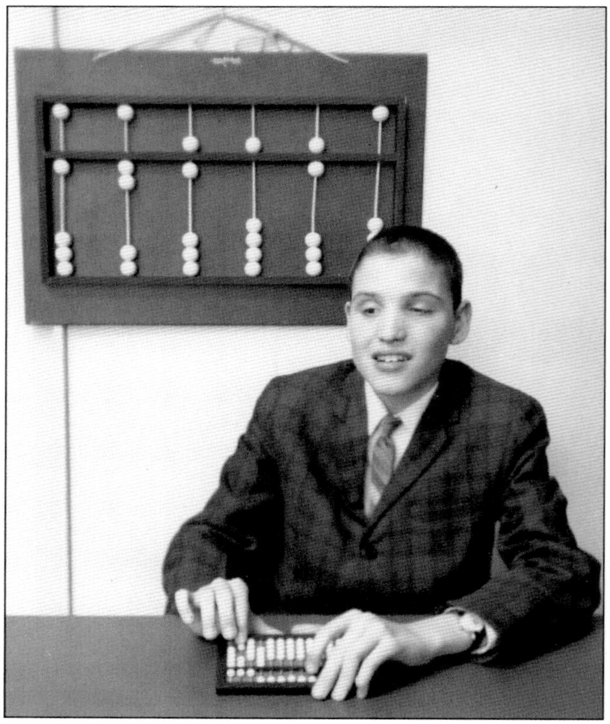

The Abacus. A teenage student uses an abacus to complete his math assignment.

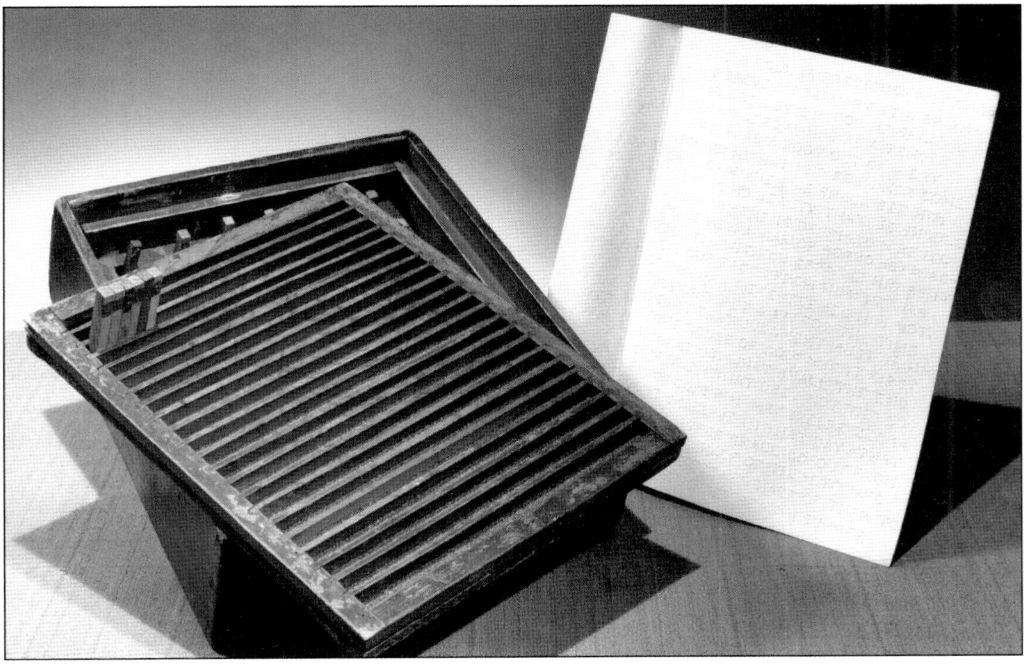

Pinpoint Writing Device. In use throughout the 19th century, pins on wooden blocks pressed messages into paper through a series of dots forming the letters of the English alphabet. The paper was then turned over and read by touching the raised letters.

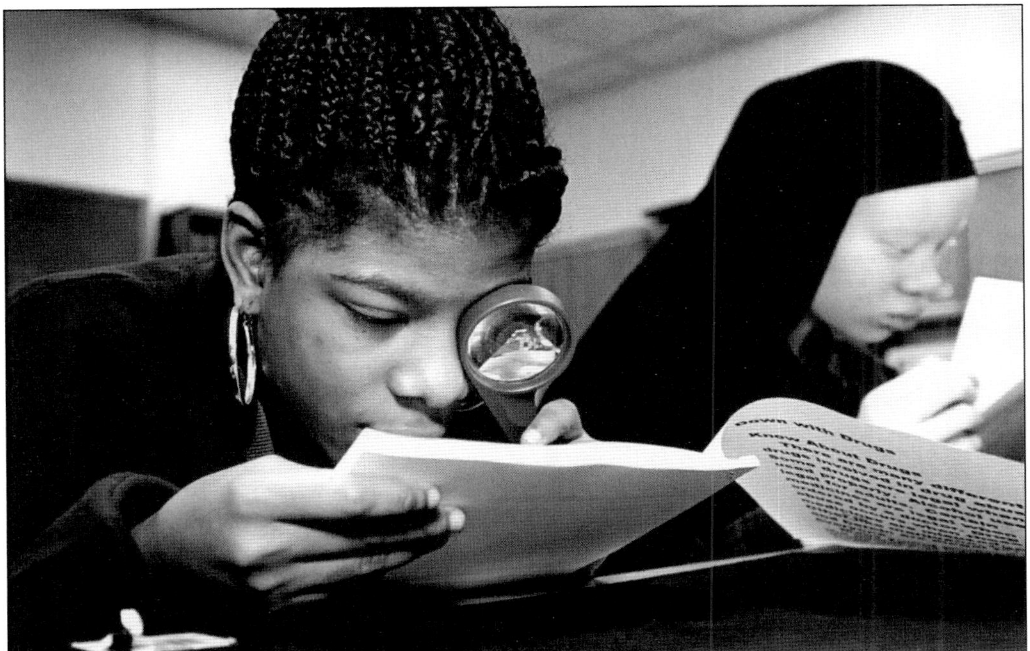

Low-Tech Devices Assist Readers. Large-print documents and a handheld magnifier assist students in reading material for class.

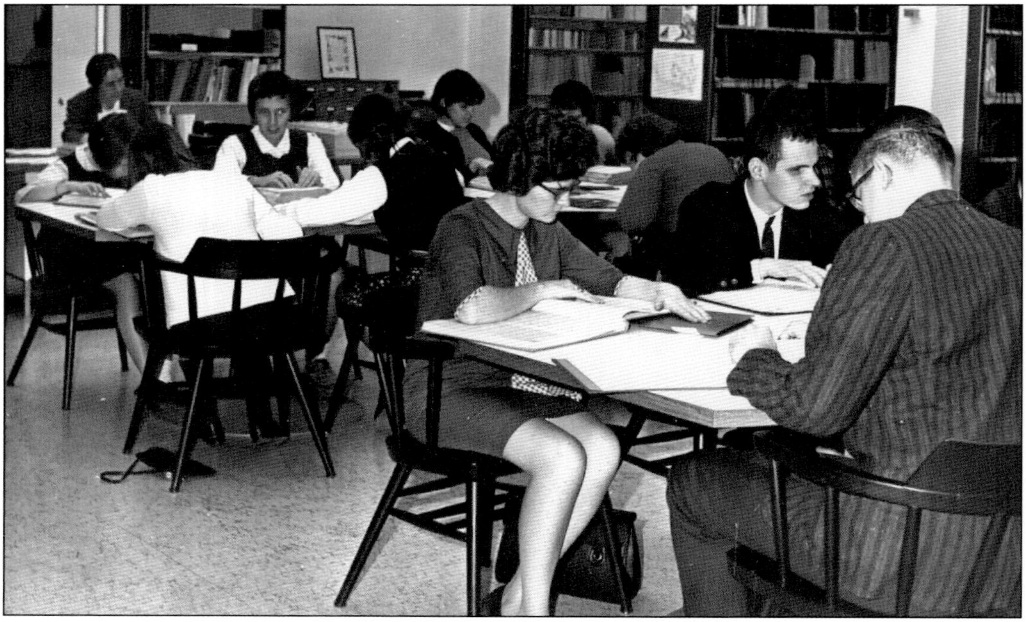

Preparing for Exams, 1960. Boys and girls gather in the library to study and research topics for class projects. As it was in the 1960s, the library today includes a braille collection, large-print books and magazines, children's books, and audio books. The library has stayed current with developing technology, adding Internet-connected computers for student use.

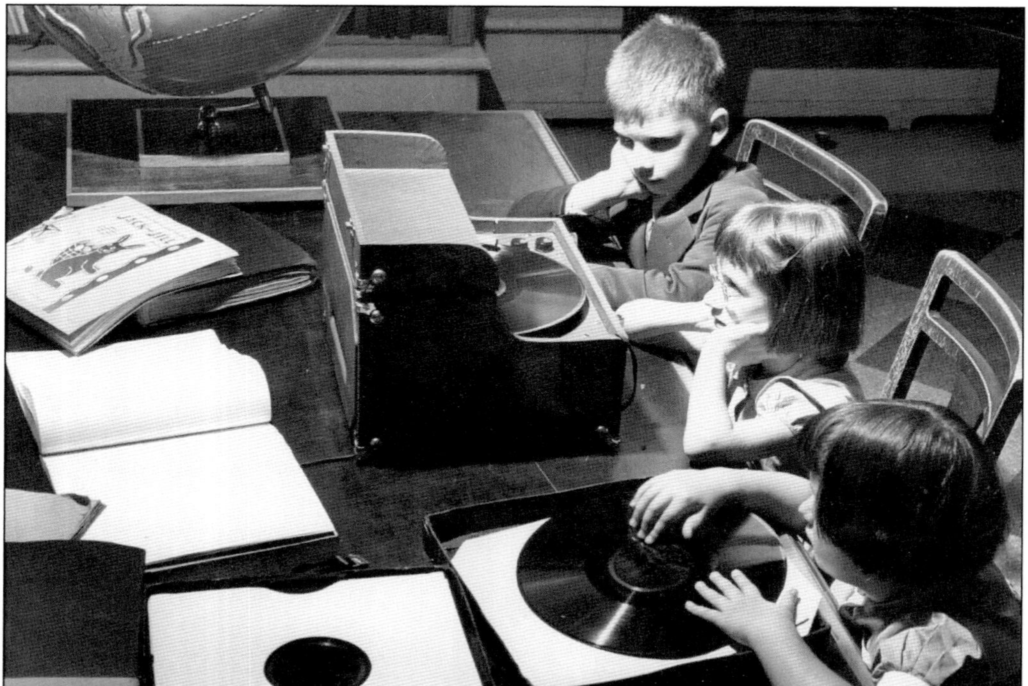

Talking Book, 1954. Two young girls and a boy listen to a talking book being played on a record player.

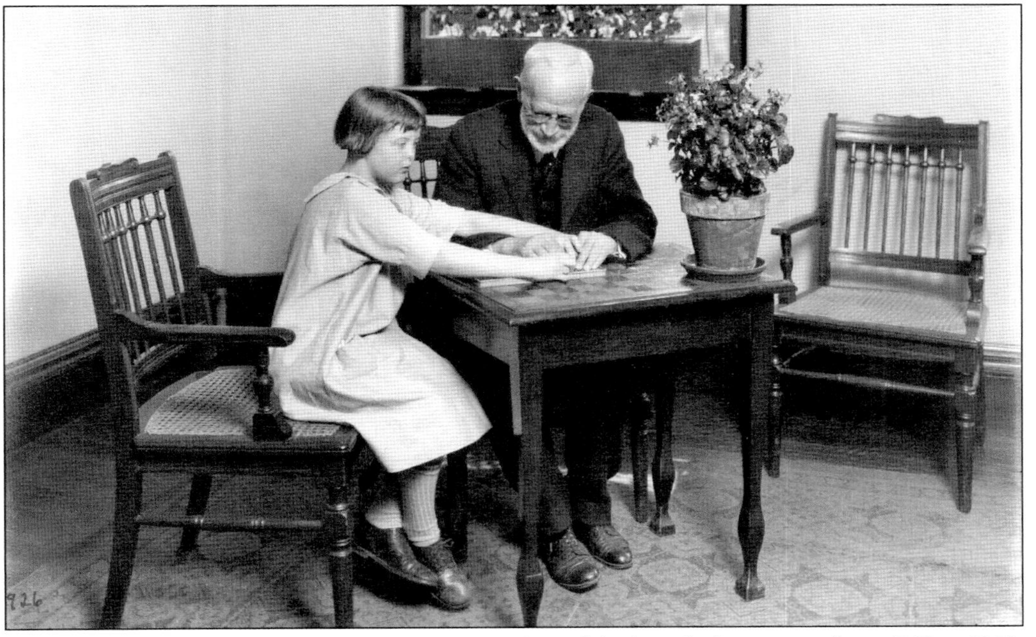

A Skilled Braille Reader. Alexander Gest, a member of the board of managers from 1923 to 1938, works on the type slate with student Katherine McGinty. After Gest retired from the Pennsylvania Railroad, he was a frequent visitor to the classrooms, since he lived near the school. Although sighted, he was able to read braille by touch and embossed over 60 volumes for student use.

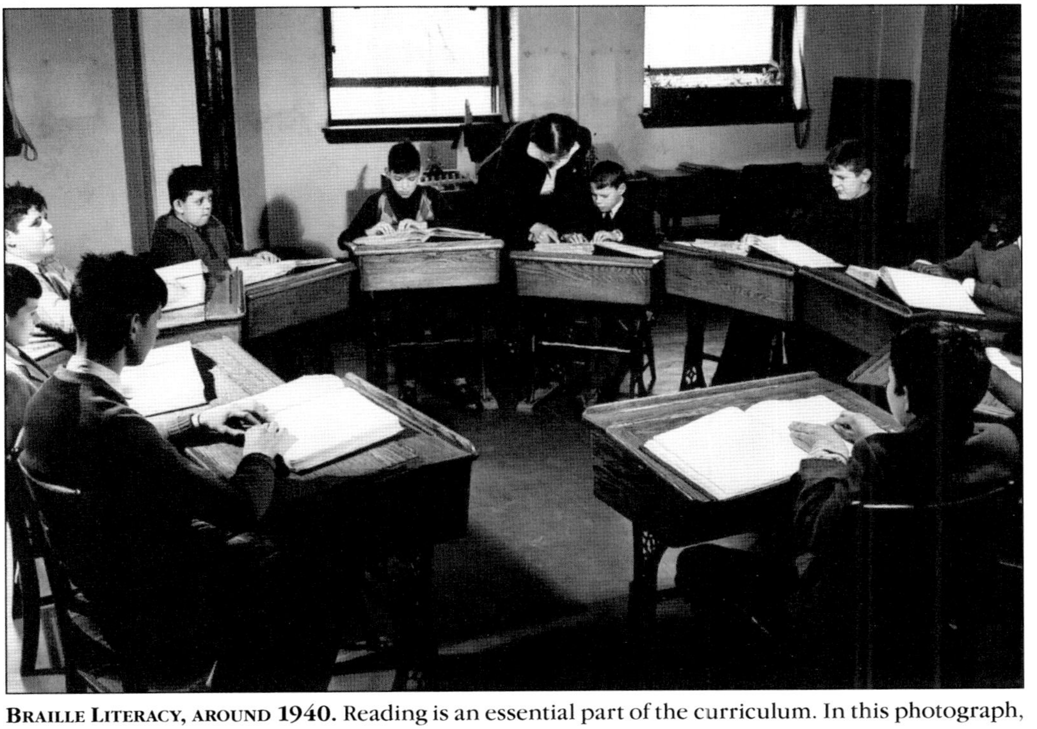

Braille Literacy, around 1940. Reading is an essential part of the curriculum. In this photograph, young students and their teacher read from braille textbooks.

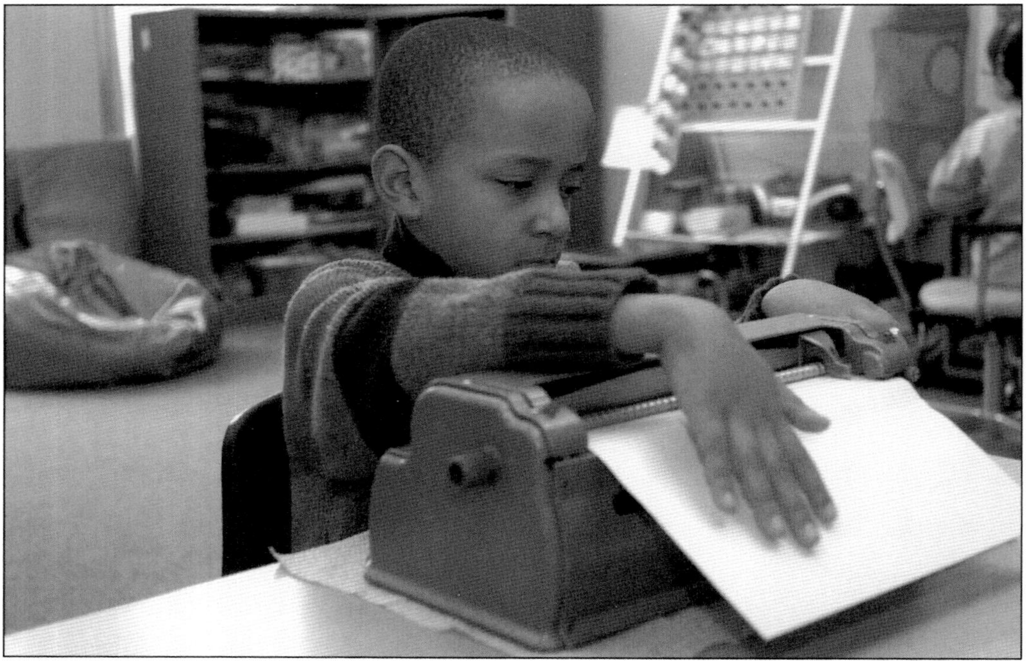

Early Literacy. A preschool student uses the braille writer and checks his writing.

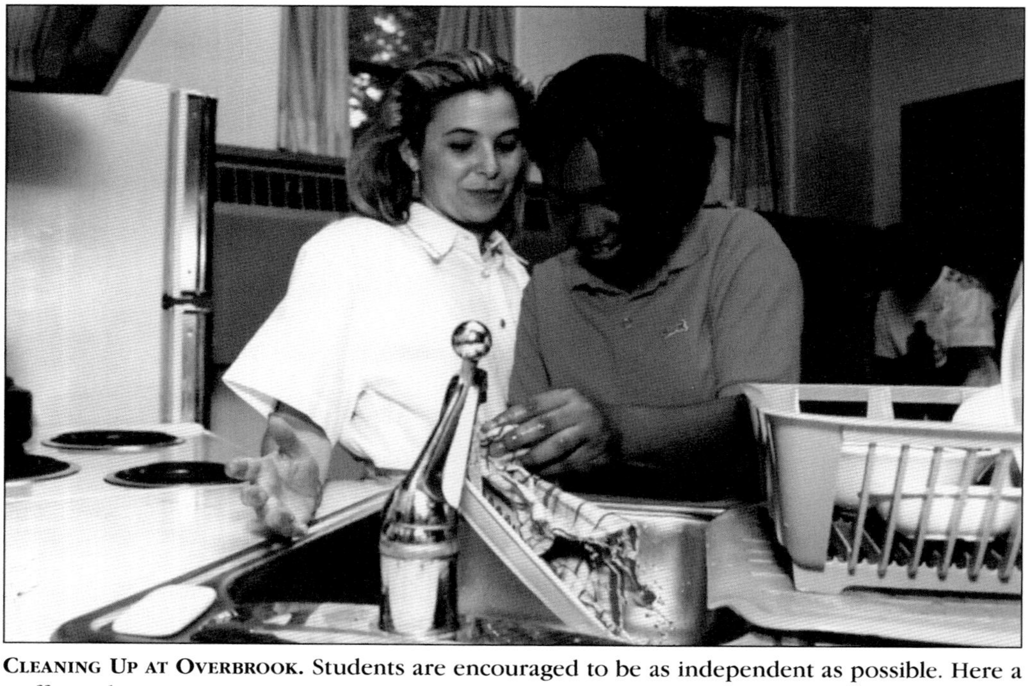

Cleaning Up at Overbrook. Students are encouraged to be as independent as possible. Here a staff member assists a young girl as she washes the dishes.

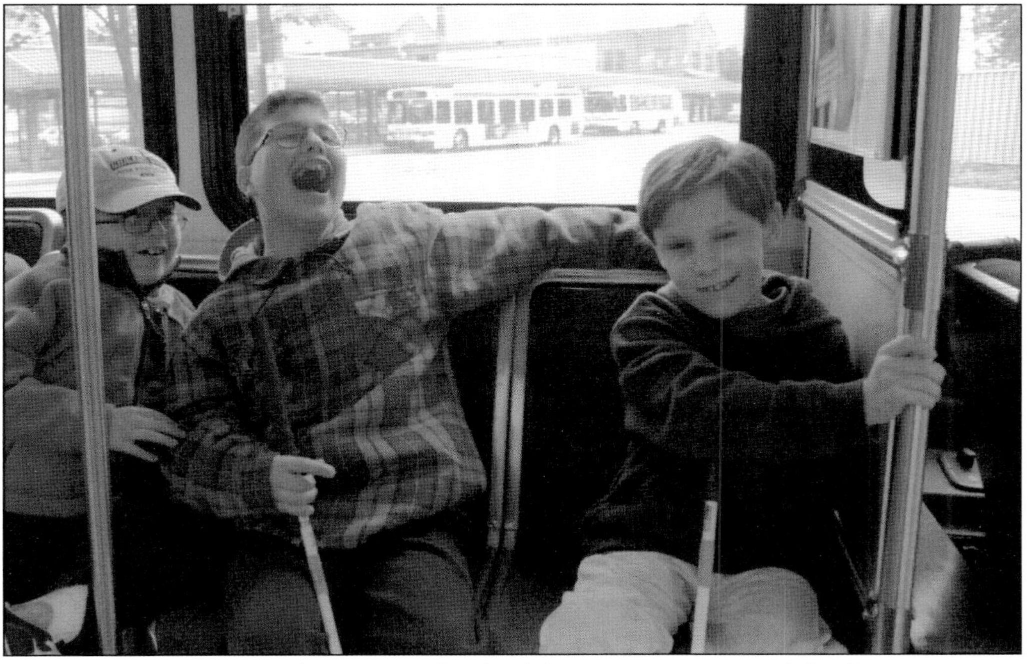

A Fun Day. Elementary-age boys enjoy a laugh while on a community mobility lesson. Learning to travel on public transportation is always a highlight for the students.

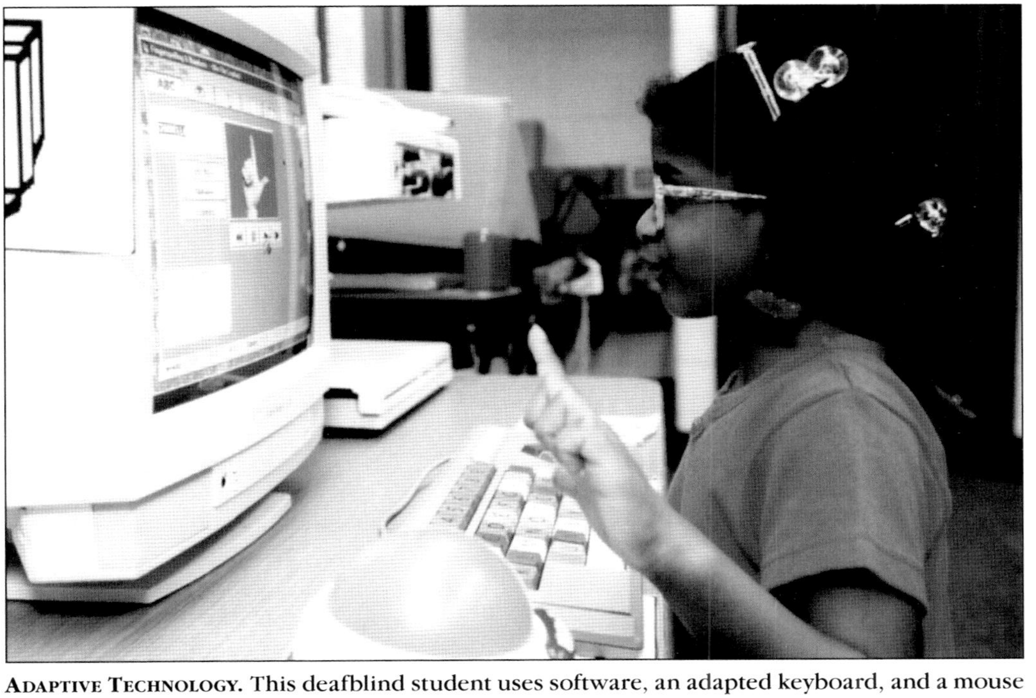

Adaptive Technology. This deafblind student uses software, an adapted keyboard, and a mouse to learn the manual alphabet.

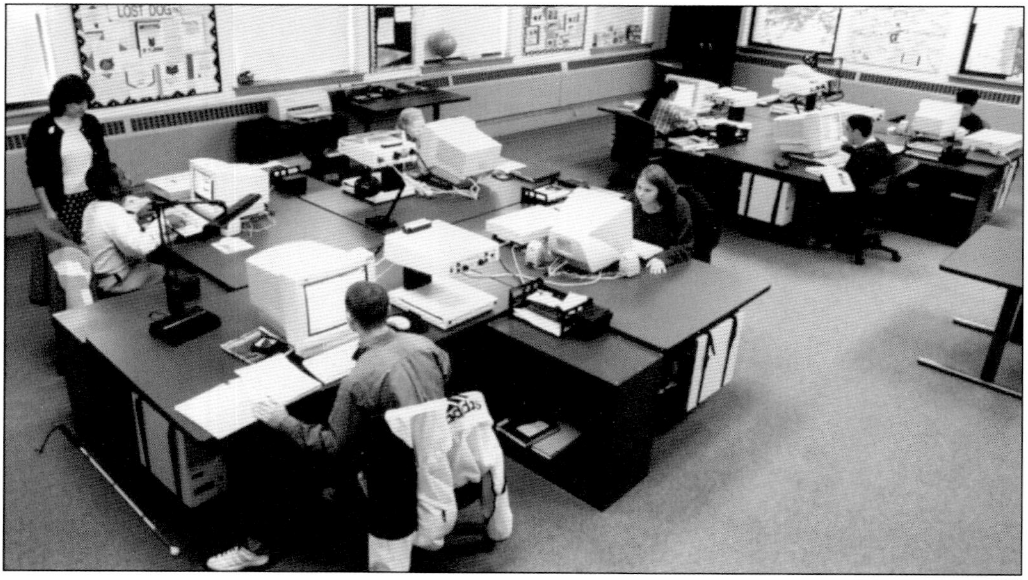

Learning in the 21st Century. Computers are a part of life in the home, in school, and in the workplace. This is also true for students who are blind or visually impaired. The Overbrook 2001 project put appropriate technology into the hands of all the students. The technology was integrated into the daily curriculum and made accessible throughout the day. Here students sit at their personalized workstations. The Overbrook 2001 project was nationally recognized when the school received the 1999 American Foundation for the Blind Access Award.

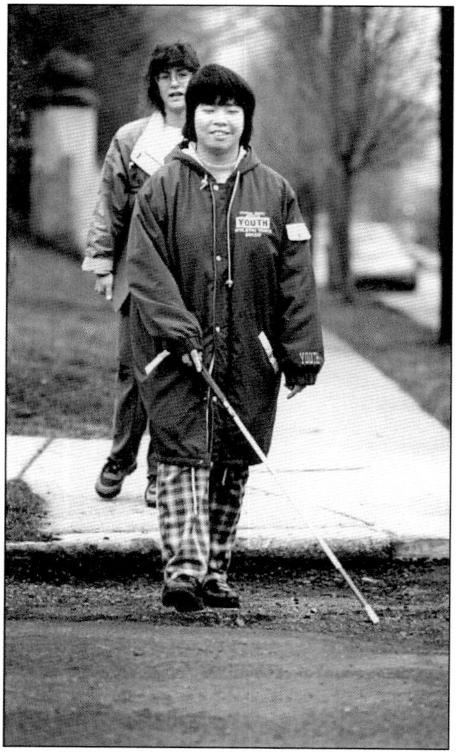

On My Own. Traveling safely and as independently as possible is important for all students. Learning to orient to the environment and moving comfortably in the home begins with infants and toddlers. This student uses the streets around Overbrook to practice outdoor mobility with the assistance of a white cane.

Four

Home Away from Home

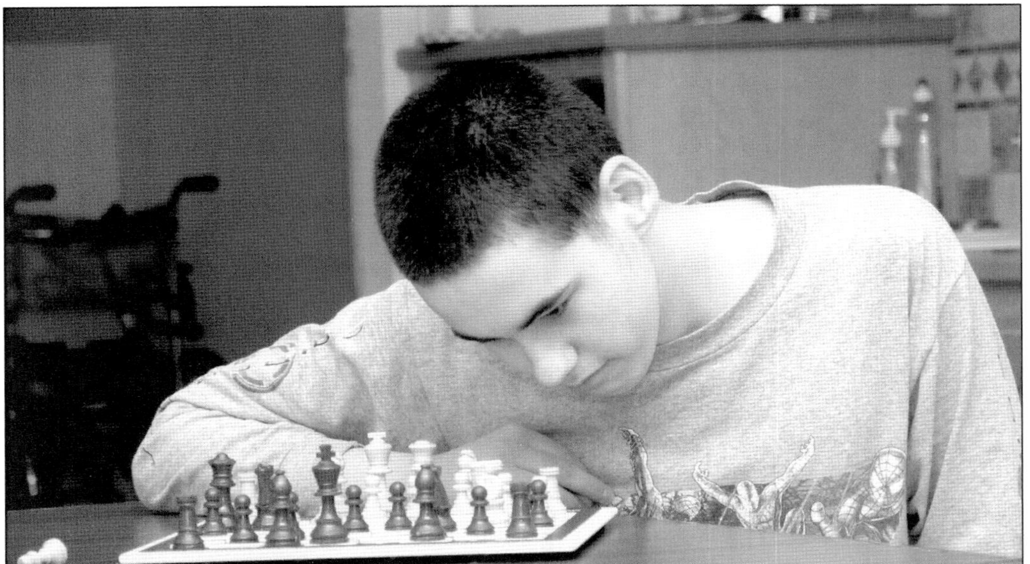

Learning to Be Independent. Since its beginnings, Overbrook has placed emphasis on providing the best possible educational, living, and recreational opportunities for its students. The students of the past, grouped by age and gender, were assisted by houseparents in learning a variety of independent living skills. Today's students live in a modern, coeducational dormitory, but there continues to be emphasis on daily living skills, social interaction, exercise, and recreation. Residents are involved in activities on the campus and spend a great deal of time in the community on field trips and at local restaurants, movie theaters, concerts, and many other events. Being included in the community is an important part of the program at Overbrook.

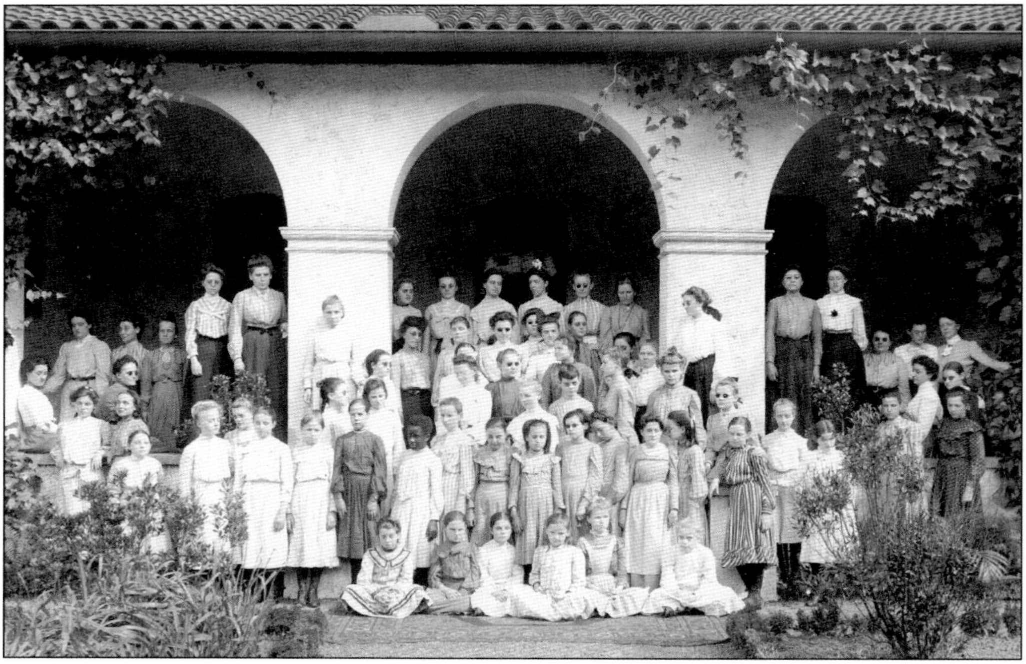

The Girls' School, 1903. The cloisters were designed to provide an outdoor play space and gathering area for students. This photograph depicts the entire girls' school, with the youngest in the first row and the oldest in the last.

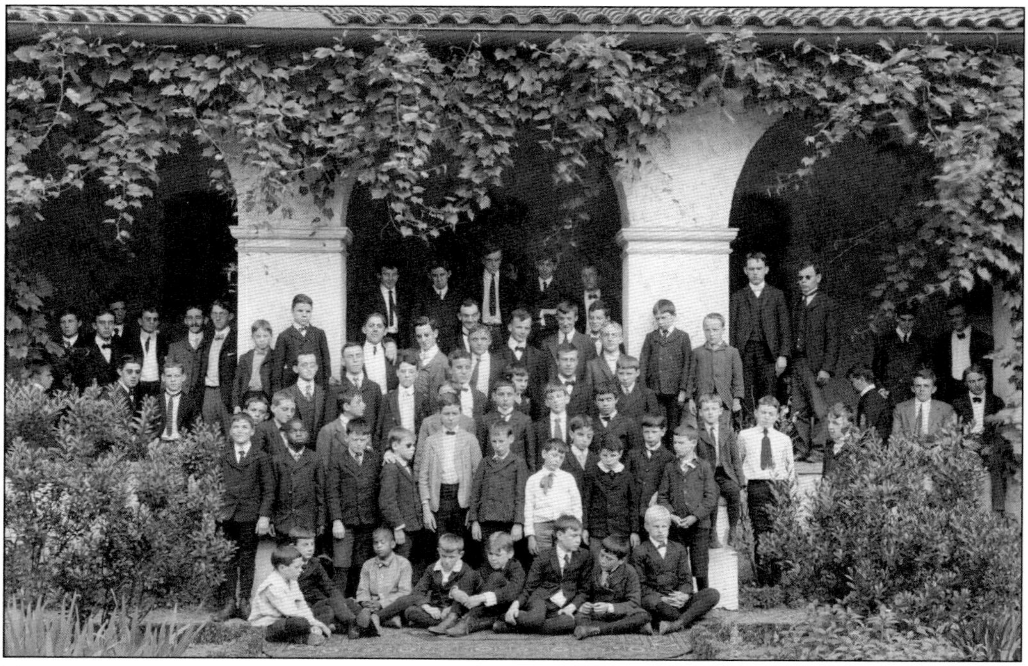

The Boys' School, 1903. The entire boys' school poses here, with the youngest sitting in the first row and the oldest standing in the last. The school was divided into three groups according to age.

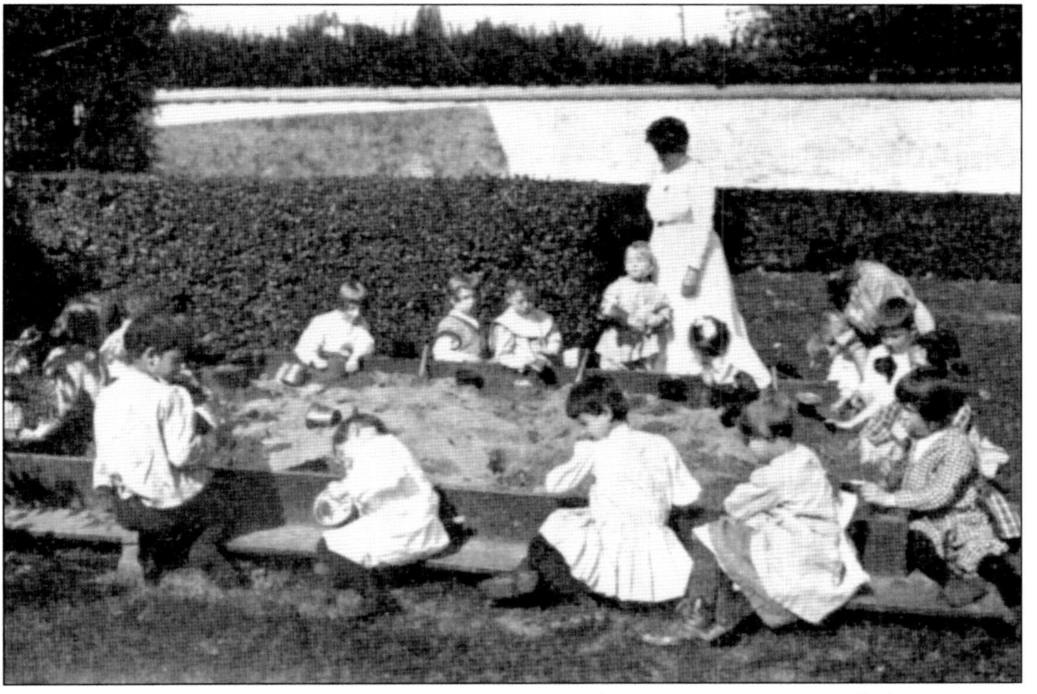

Playing in a Sandbox. Young children were encouraged to participate in typical play activities. Hands-on experiences are essential for good concept development. Here kindergartners enjoy an outdoor sandbox.

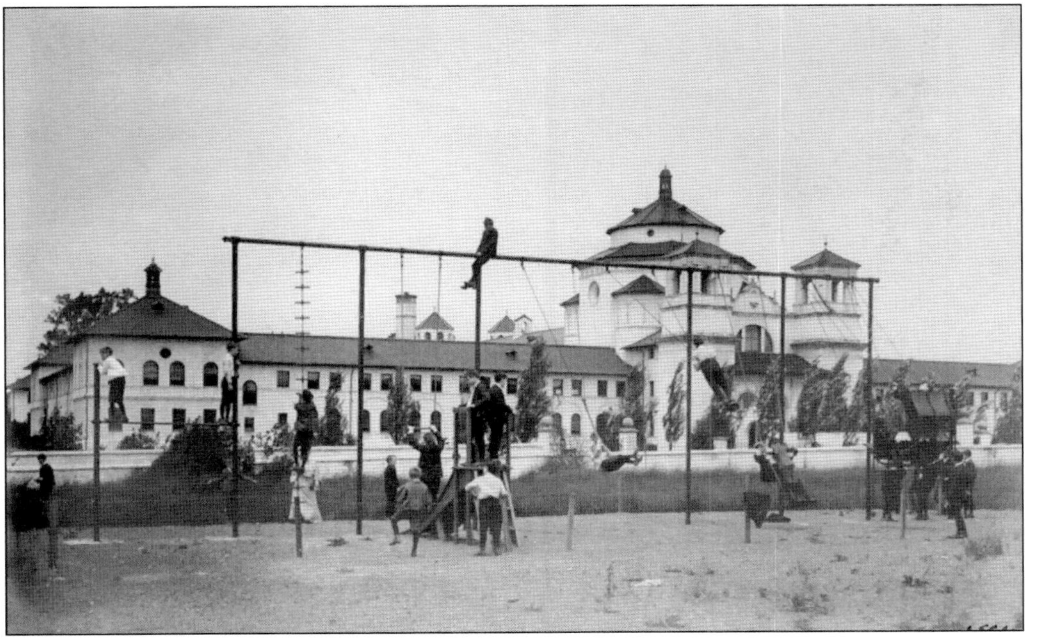

Outdoor Fun. The design of the campus offered children many opportunities to take part in physical activities. These students playfully climb, swing, and balance on playground equipment.

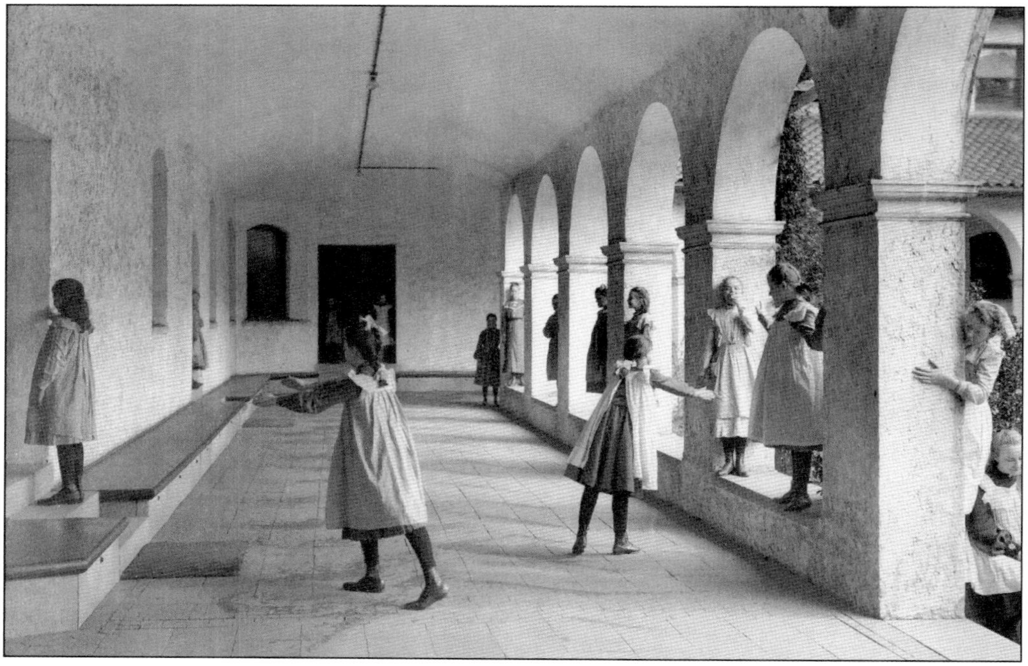

BLINDMAN'S BLUFF, 1907. A group of girls plays blindman's bluff in the girls' cloister. Since they were covered, the cloisters provided a nice alternative for students to play games and exercise during inclement weather.

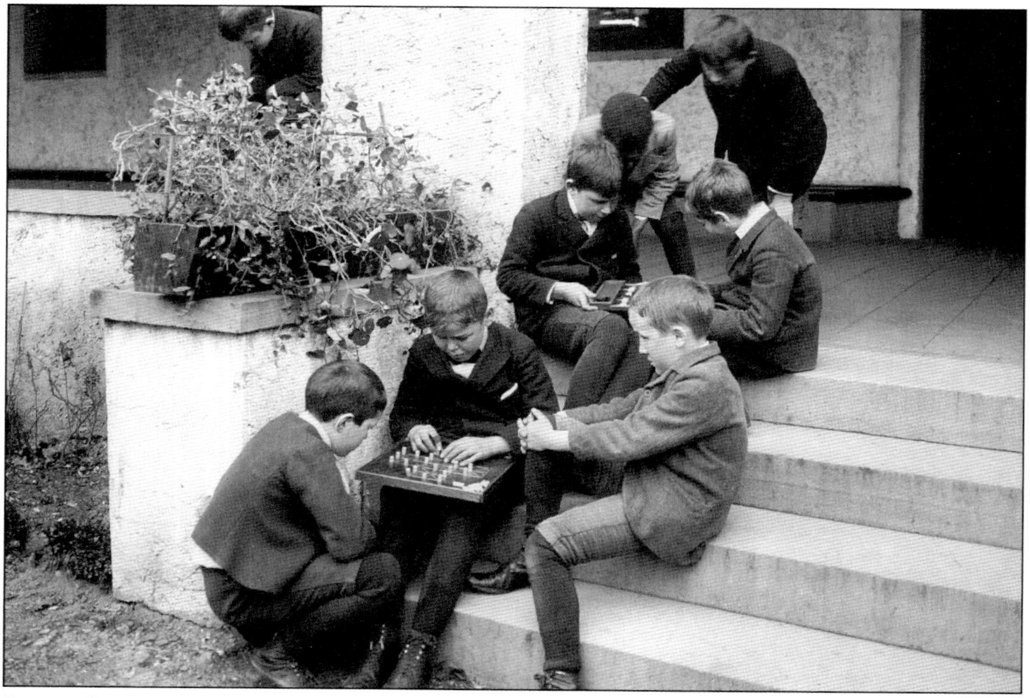

BOARD GAMES, 1907. Several boys take a break from their studies to play board games on the steps in the cloister.

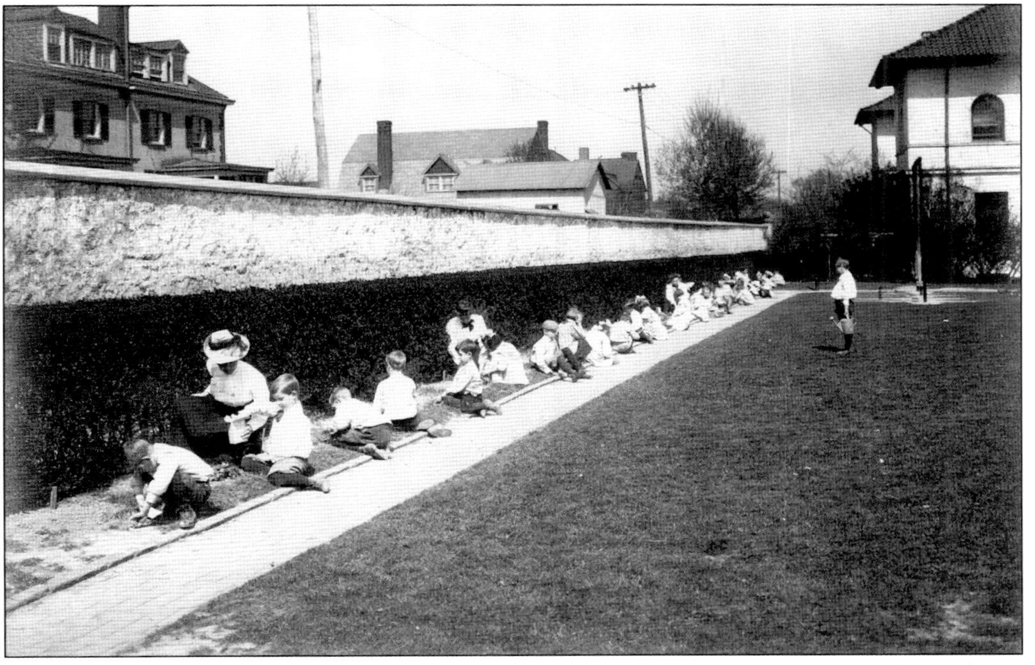

Planting a Garden, 1910. Developing leisure skills has always been a part of the day for students. Here young children plant a garden along the wall that surrounds the school's campus. One boy stands back with a watering can, waiting to water the newly planted flowers.

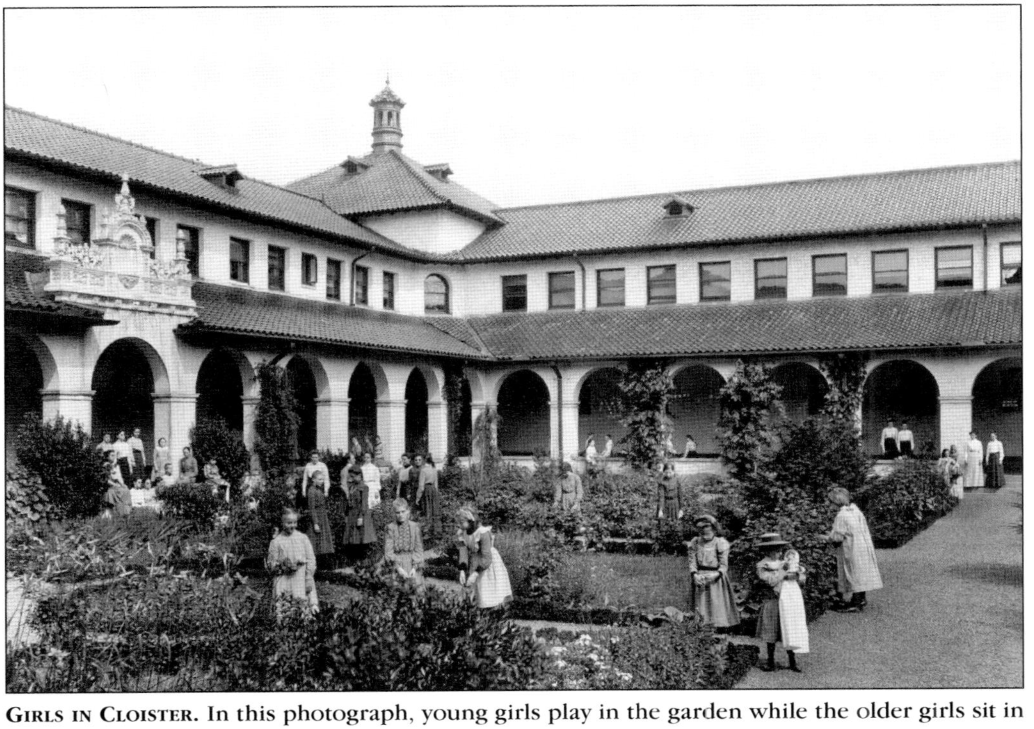

Girls in Cloister. In this photograph, young girls play in the garden while the older girls sit in the archways.

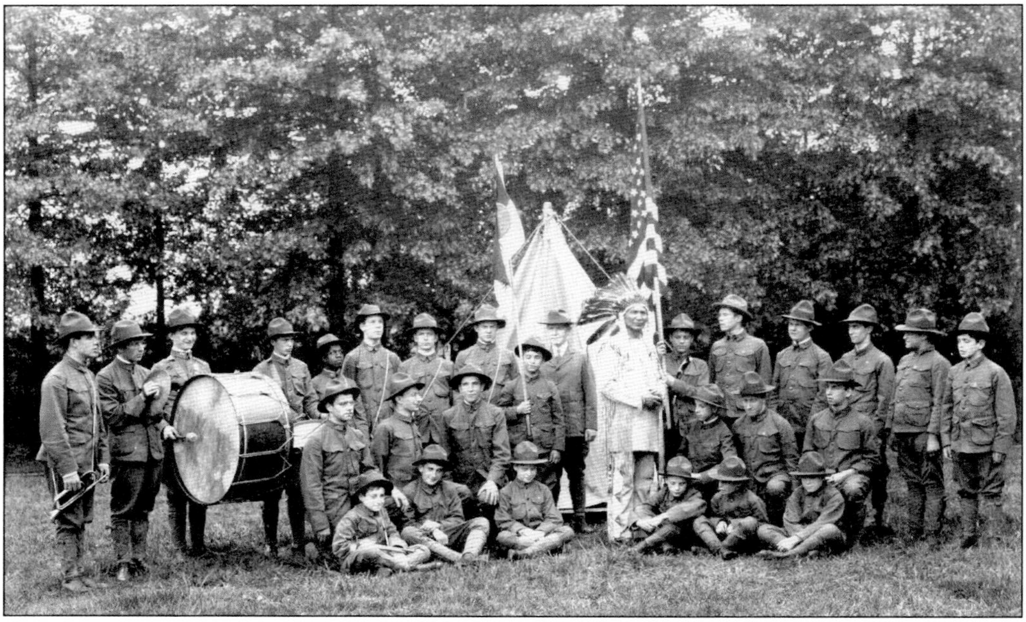

Troop 118. On a camping trip, Boy Scout Troop 118 poses with Charles Eastman, a Native American whose many accomplishments include helping to establish the Boy Scouts.

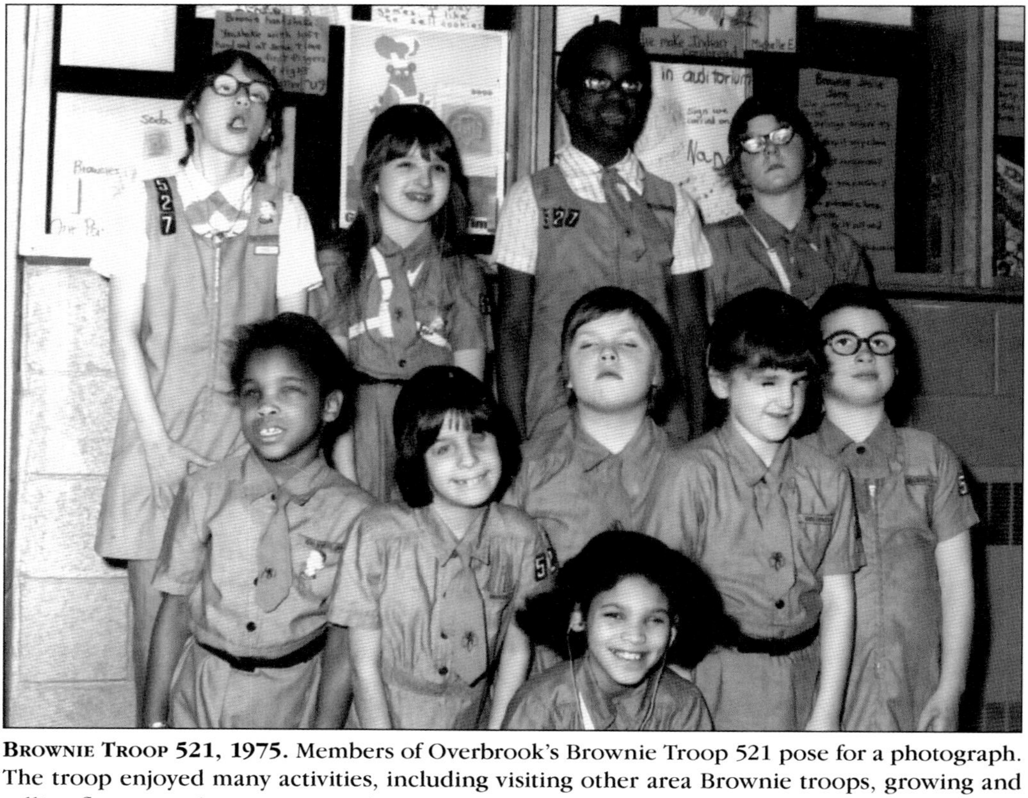

Brownie Troop 521, 1975. Members of Overbrook's Brownie Troop 521 pose for a photograph. The troop enjoyed many activities, including visiting other area Brownie troops, growing and selling flowers at the May Fair, and camping overnight.

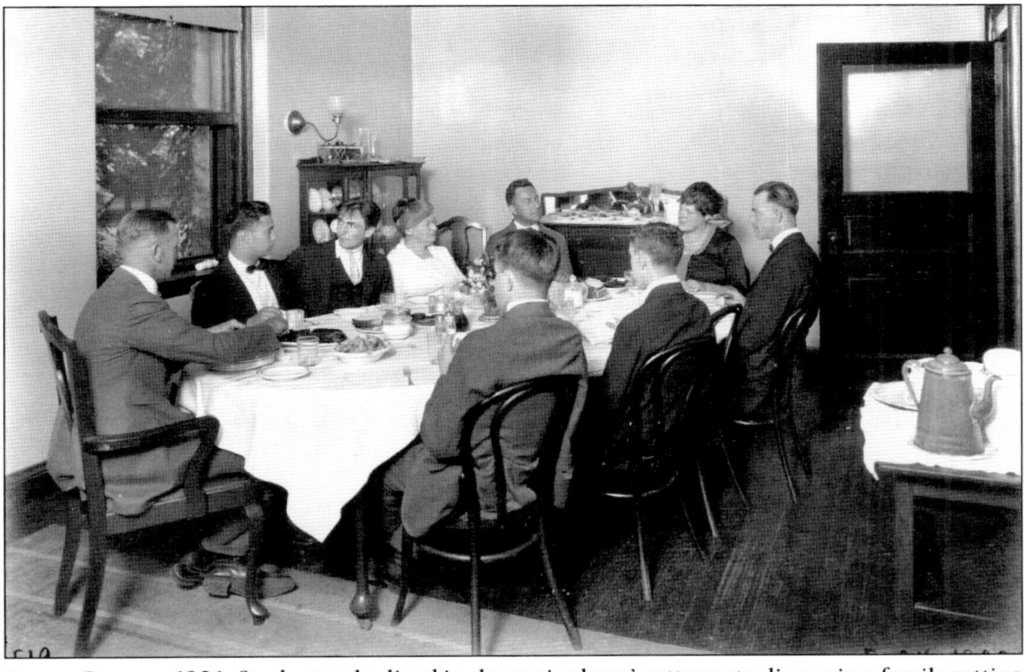

Eating Dinner, 1921. Students who lived in the senior boys' cottage ate dinner in a family setting to learn etiquette in a home atmosphere. Houseparents were seated with the students at the table as examples.

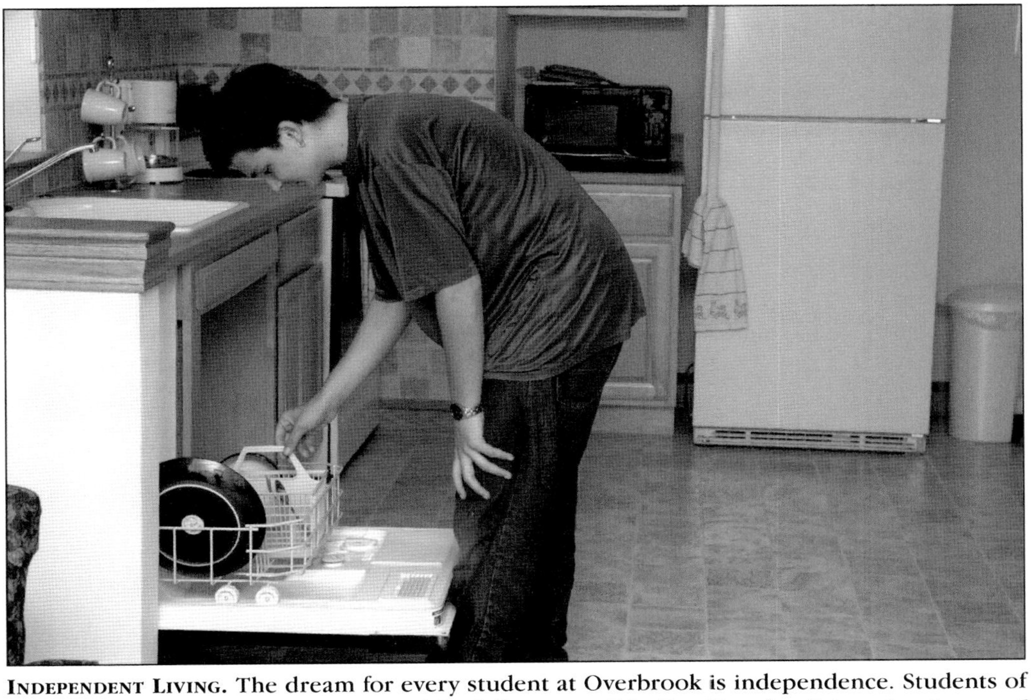

Independent Living. The dream for every student at Overbrook is independence. Students of all ages take classes to learn as many life skills as possible. Loading the dishwasher is one of these skills.

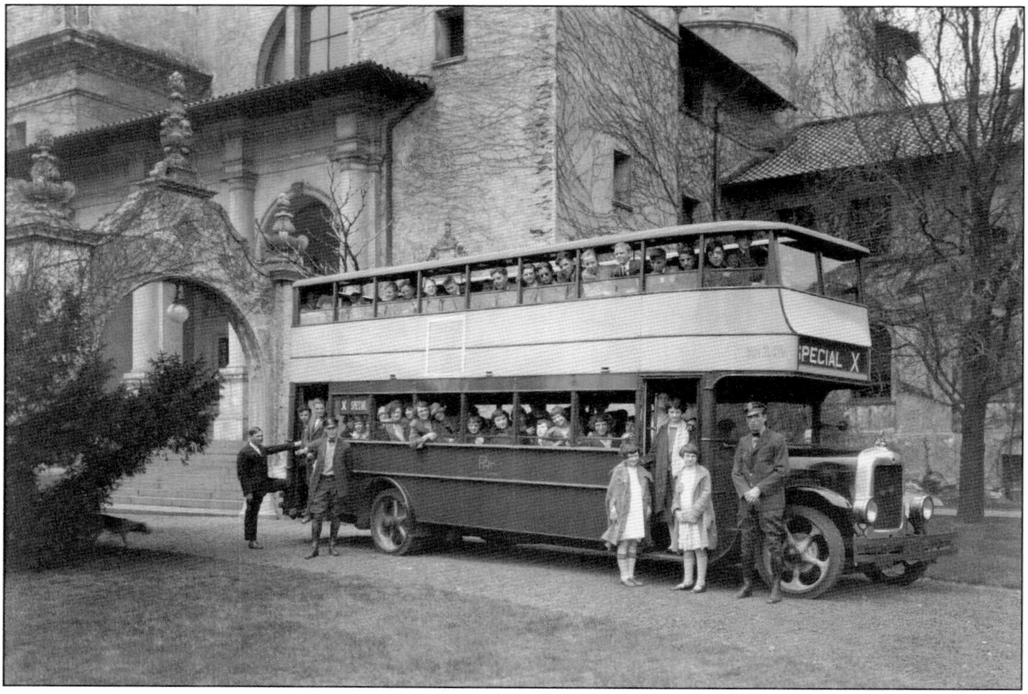

FIELD TRIP, 1926. Girls and boys look out the windows of a double-decker bus on their way to the circus.

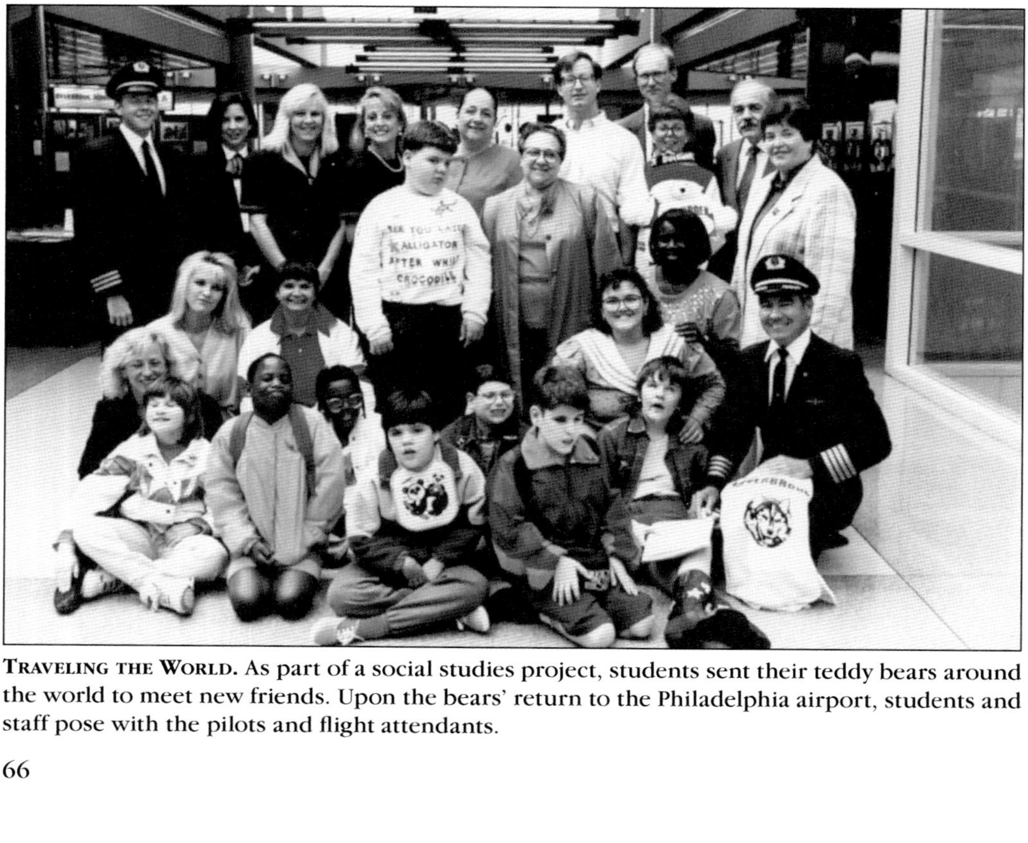

TRAVELING THE WORLD. As part of a social studies project, students sent their teddy bears around the world to meet new friends. Upon the bears' return to the Philadelphia airport, students and staff pose with the pilots and flight attendants.

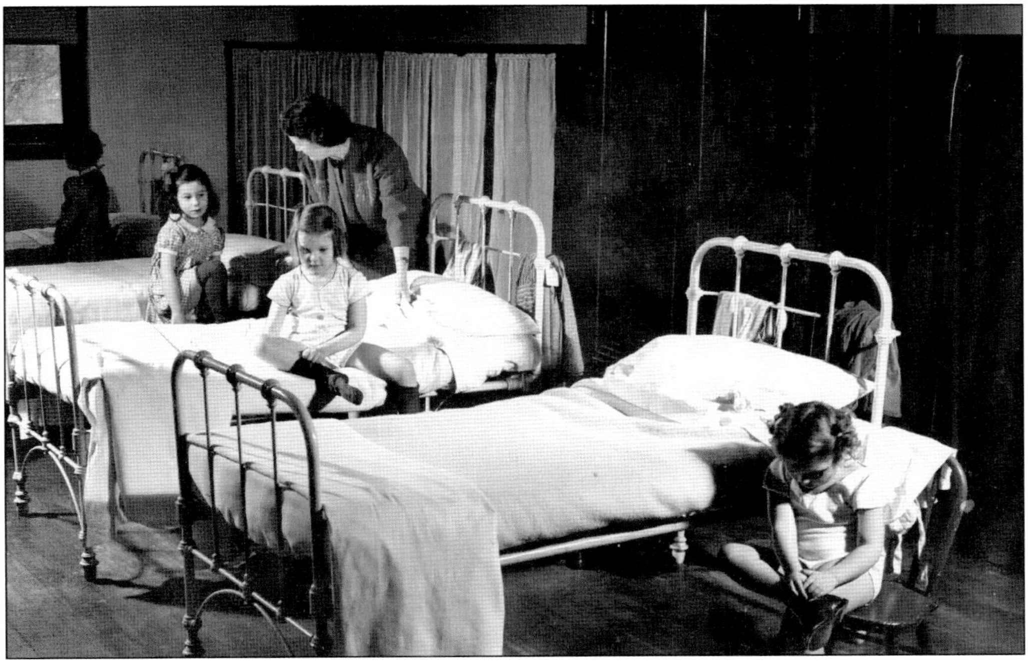

Bedtime, 1959. Each group of students was housed in a cottage with a housemother in charge. There were open dormitories for the younger boys and girls and the cubicle system for the older ones. In this photograph, four girls prepare for bed in their kindergarten dormitory.

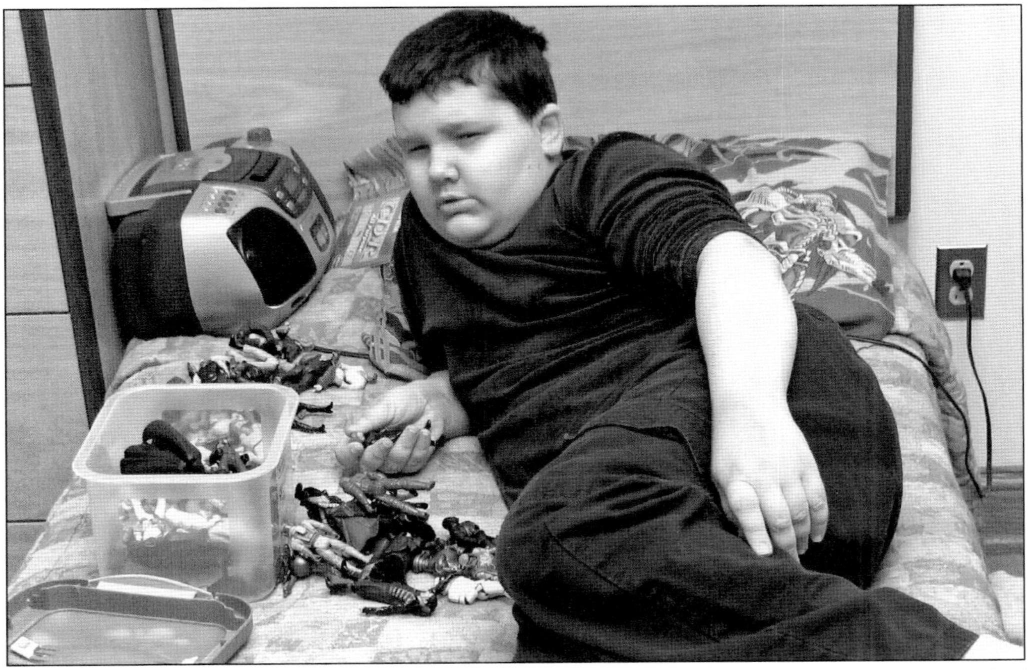

Dormitory Living. Although only a small number live on campus today, students are made to feel as though it is their second home. Here a young boy plays with action figures on his bed while listening to his boom box.

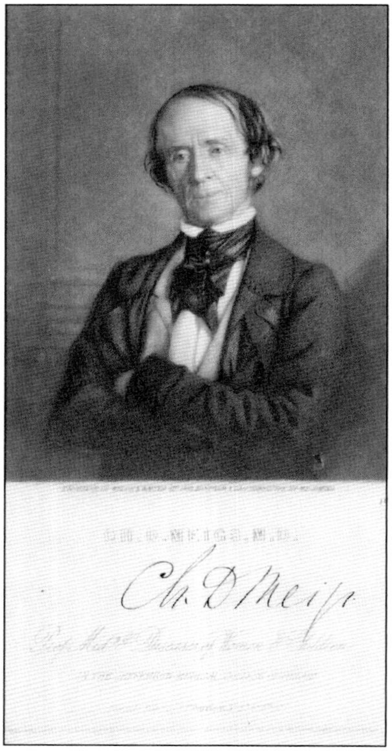

DR. CHARLES DELUCENA MEIGS, BOARD MEMBER AND SCHOOL PHYSICIAN (1792–1869). Serving on the original board of managers, Dr. Charles Delucena Meigs became the school's consulting physician in 1838 and participated on the Committee of Instruction. He was born in St. George, Bermuda, but attended school in Athens, Georgia. He studied medicine at the University of Pennsylvania, specializing in obstetrics. He was a master of many languages. In 1841, Dr. Meigs was elected professor of obstetrics and diseases of women at Jefferson Medical College and remained there until retiring in 1861.

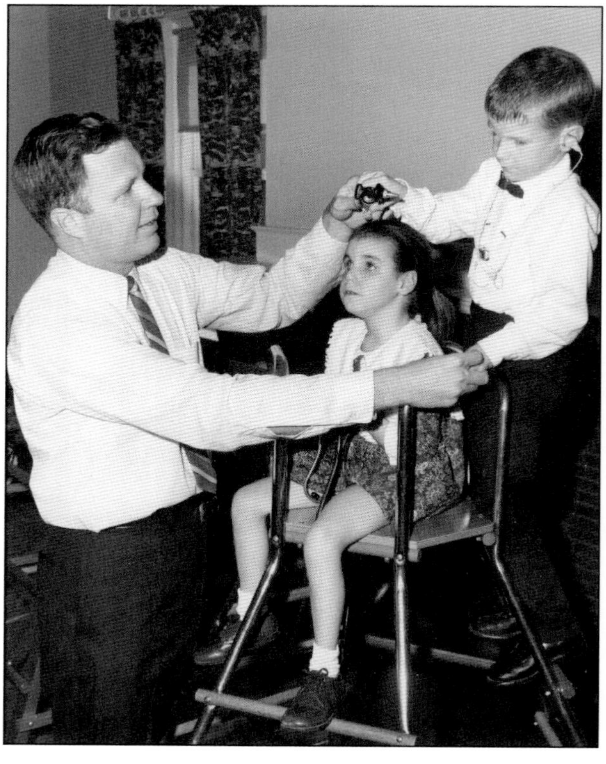

PLAYING DOCTOR, 1970. Dr. Robert E. Weibel, the school's consulting physician, assists students in the Deafblind Program in playing doctor.

Five

ATHLETICS AND MUSIC

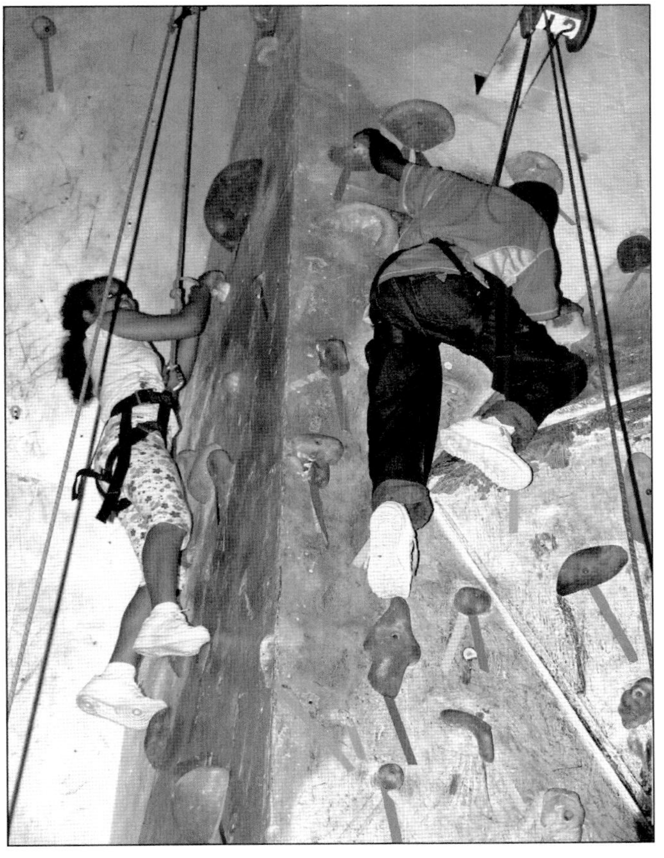

EXTRACURRICULAR ACTIVITIES. Along with their education, Overbrook students become involved in extracurricular activities including sports and music. Whether they participate individually or on a team, sports help students develop self-esteem, teamwork, independence, and socialization skills. Overbrook's music program gives students many opportunities to explore sound through singing, moving, listening, and playing instruments. Through groups like the choir and bell choir, they experience sharing music with one another and making music together.

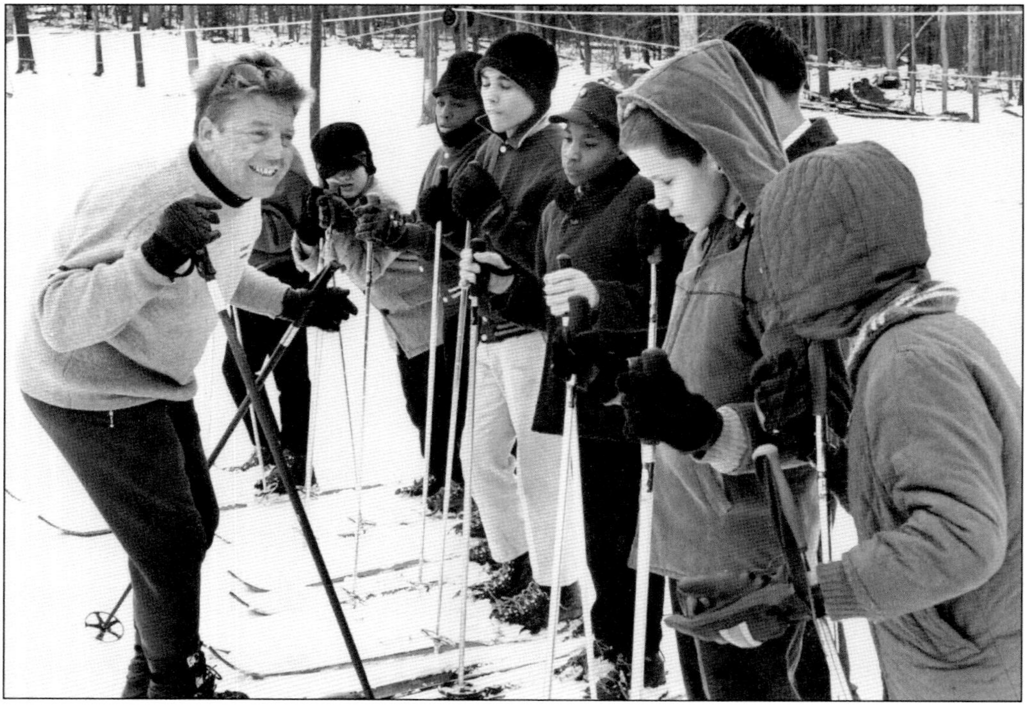

Ski Lessons, 1960. Bundled up in winter coats and hats, students line up side by side for a ski lesson.

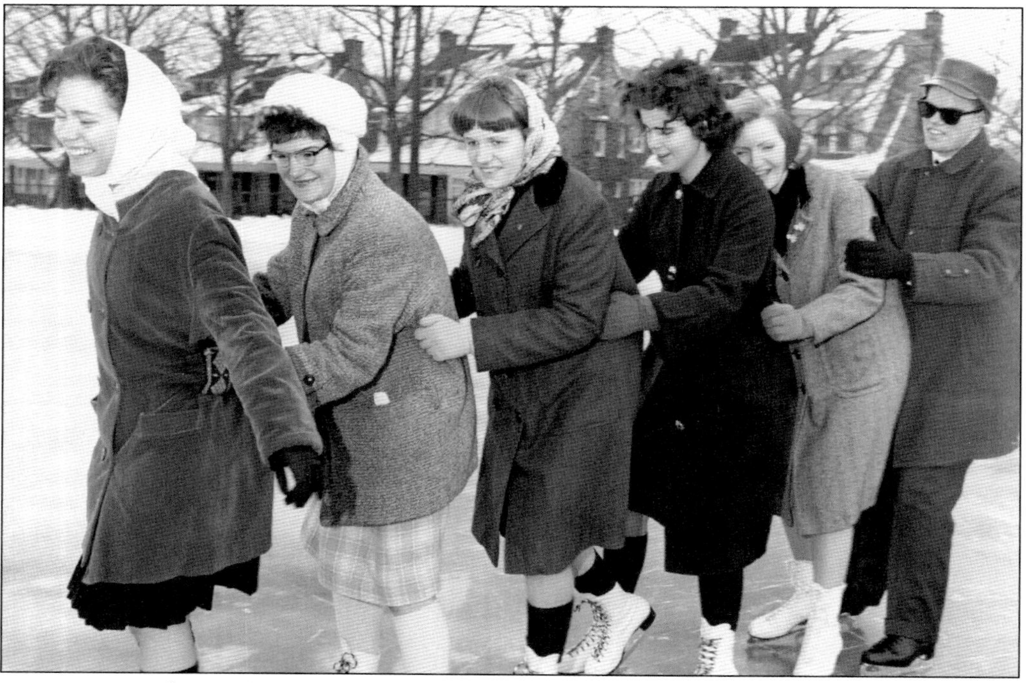

Ice-skating, 1965. Students take advantage of the new ice-skating rink in back of the Nevil Field House. The six students form a train for their first time around.

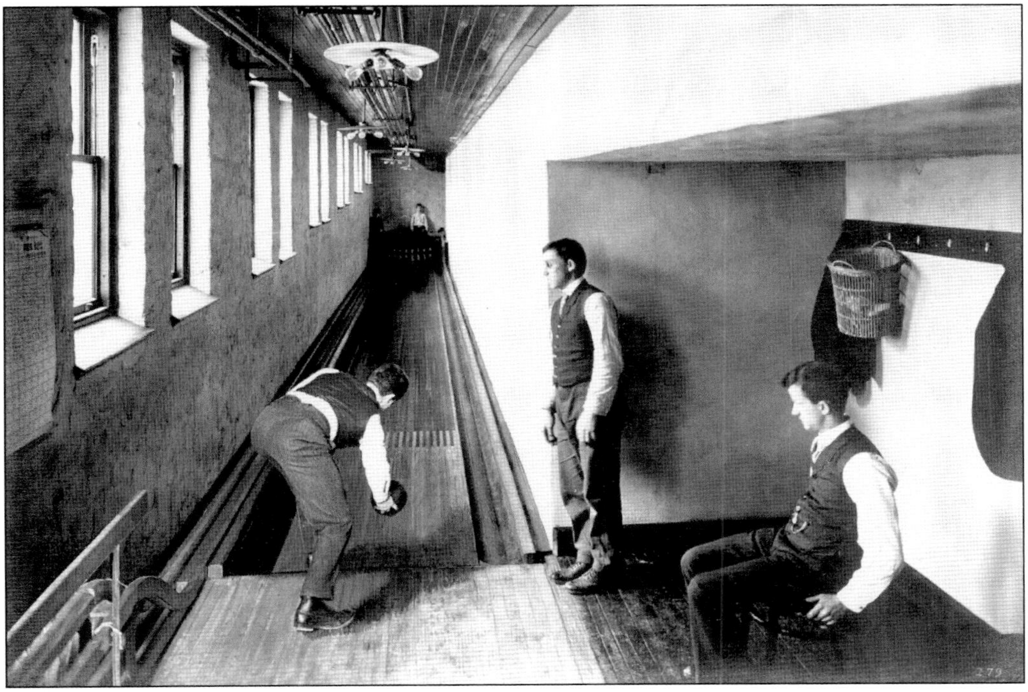

Recreational Bowling, 1910. The original bowling alley was located under the swimming pool. Here three male students take turns on this single alley.

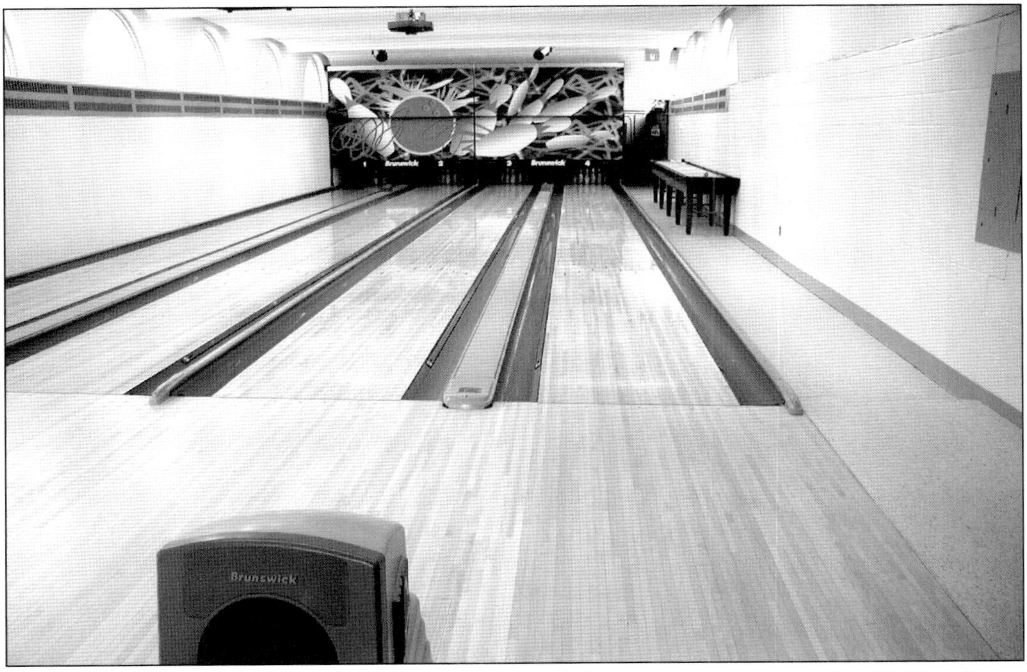

High-tech Bowling. The bowling alley in the Nevil Field House was renovated in 2003 and now features an automated scoring system, Technicolor lights, and a new sound system, which all make it a fun place for students to bowl and socialize.

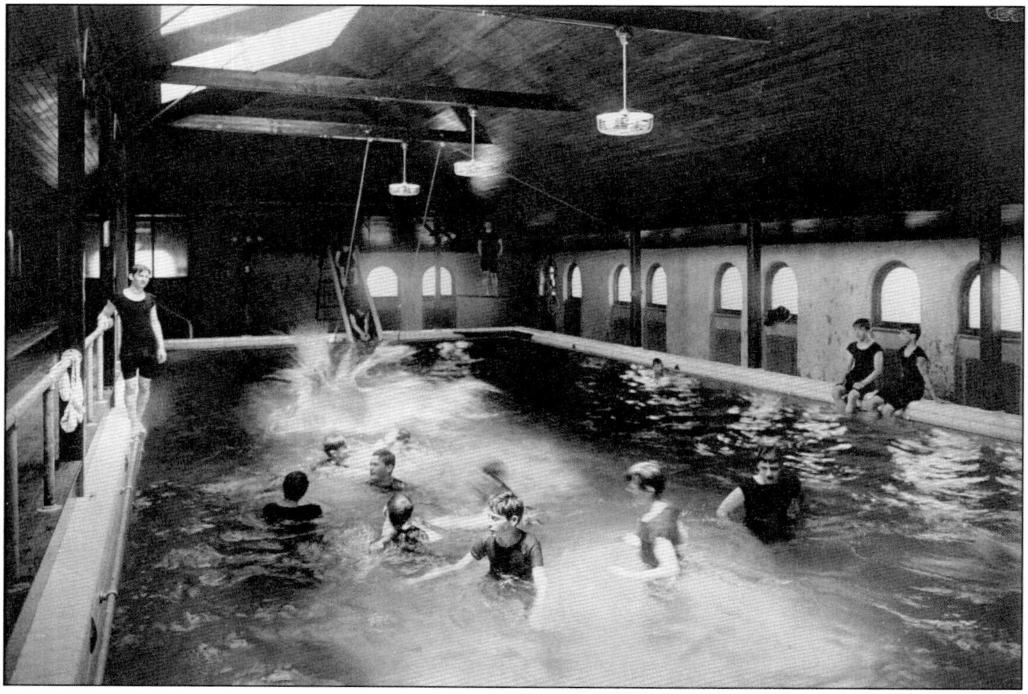

Swimming, 1907. Boys splash in the newly opened pool in February 1907.

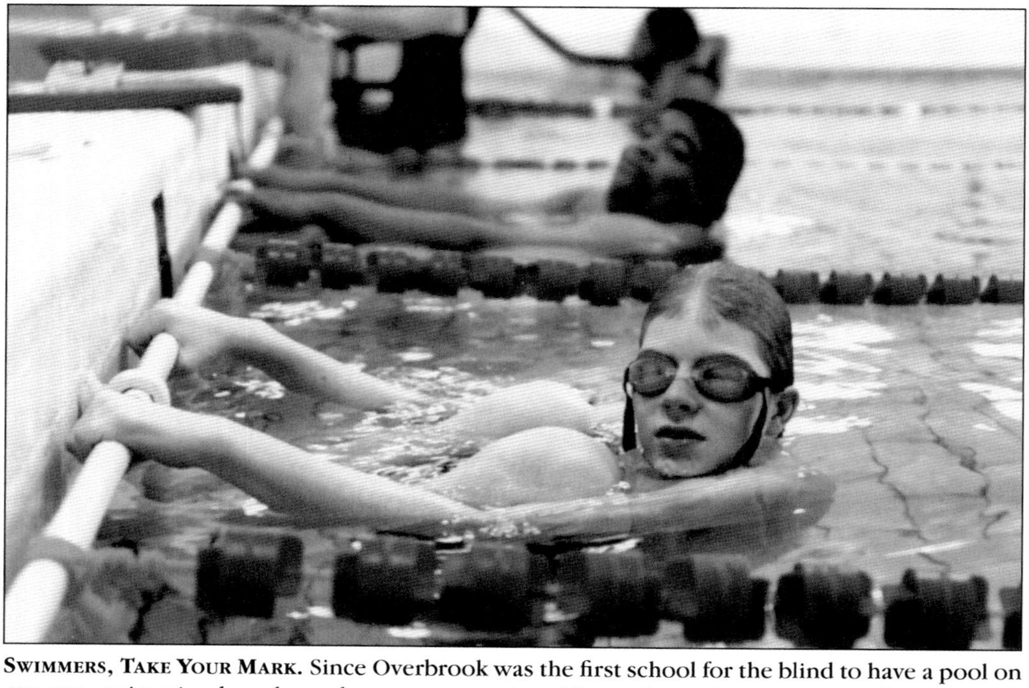

Swimmers, Take Your Mark. Since Overbrook was the first school for the blind to have a pool on campus, swimming has always been a sport enjoyed by students. Here a teenage boy prepares for the start of competition at a swim meet.

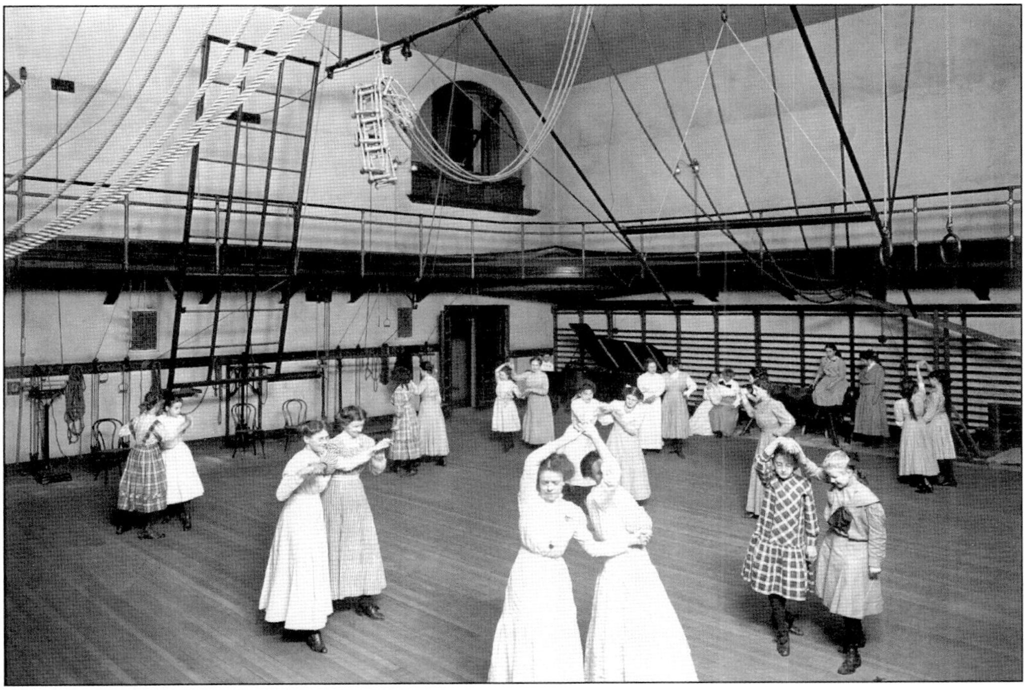

Ballroom Dancing, 1911. Girls learn to ballroom dance by partnering up in the gymnasium.

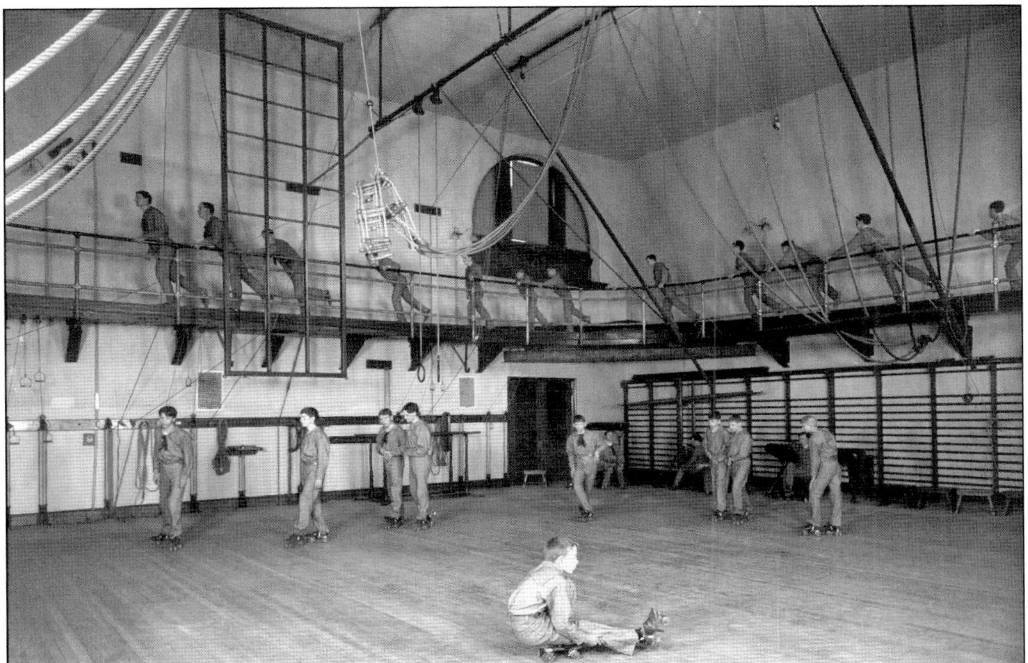

Roller-skating, 1911. A group of boys roller-skate in the gymnasium while others walk around the elevated indoor track. The boys are all dressed in gym uniforms of long pants and long-sleeved shirts.

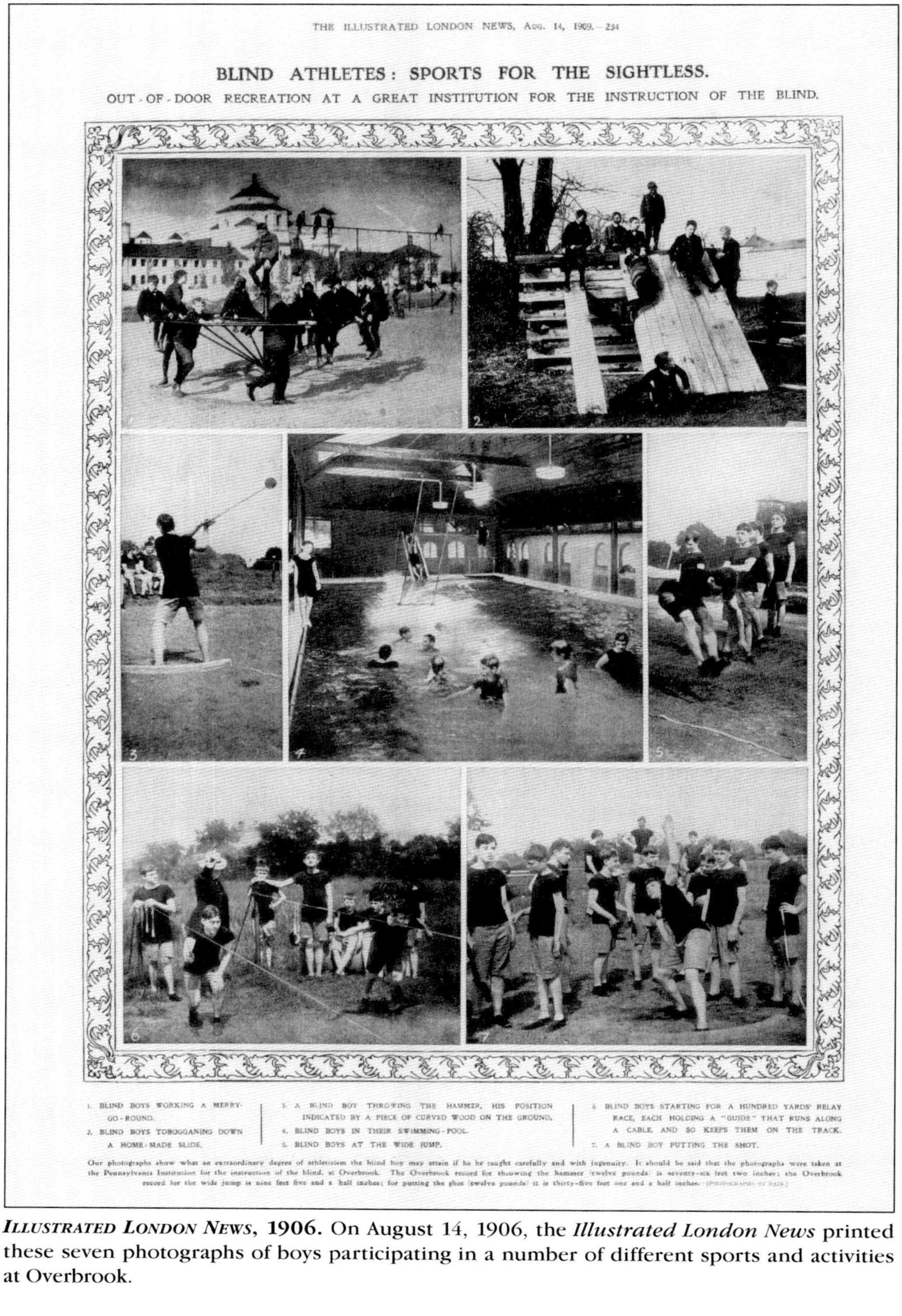

THE ILLUSTRATED LONDON NEWS, Aug. 14, 1909.—234

BLIND ATHLETES: SPORTS FOR THE SIGHTLESS.

OUT-OF-DOOR RECREATION AT A GREAT INSTITUTION FOR THE INSTRUCTION OF THE BLIND.

1. BLIND BOYS WORKING A MERRY-GO-ROUND.
2. BLIND BOYS TOBOGGANING DOWN A HOME-MADE SLIDE.
3. A BLIND BOY THROWING THE HAMMER, HIS POSITION INDICATED BY A PIECE OF CURVED WOOD ON THE GROUND.
4. BLIND BOYS IN THEIR SWIMMING-POOL.
5. BLIND BOYS AT THE WIDE JUMP.
6. BLIND BOYS STARTING FOR A HUNDRED YARDS' RELAY RACE, EACH HOLDING A "GUIDE" THAT RUNS ALONG A CABLE AND SO KEEPS THEM ON THE TRACK.
7. A BLIND BOY PUTTING THE SHOT.

Our photographs show what an extraordinary degree of athleticism the blind boy may attain if he be taught carefully and with ingenuity. It should be said that the photographs were taken at the Pennsylvania Institution for the instruction of the blind, at Overbrook. The Overbrook record for throwing the hammer (twelve pounds) is seventy-six feet two inches; the Overbrook record for the wide jump is nine feet five and a half inches; for putting the shot (twelve pounds) it is thirty-five feet one and a half inches.—(PHOTOGRAPHS BY BAIN.)

***ILLUSTRATED LONDON NEWS*, 1906.** On August 14, 1906, the *Illustrated London News* printed these seven photographs of boys participating in a number of different sports and activities at Overbrook.

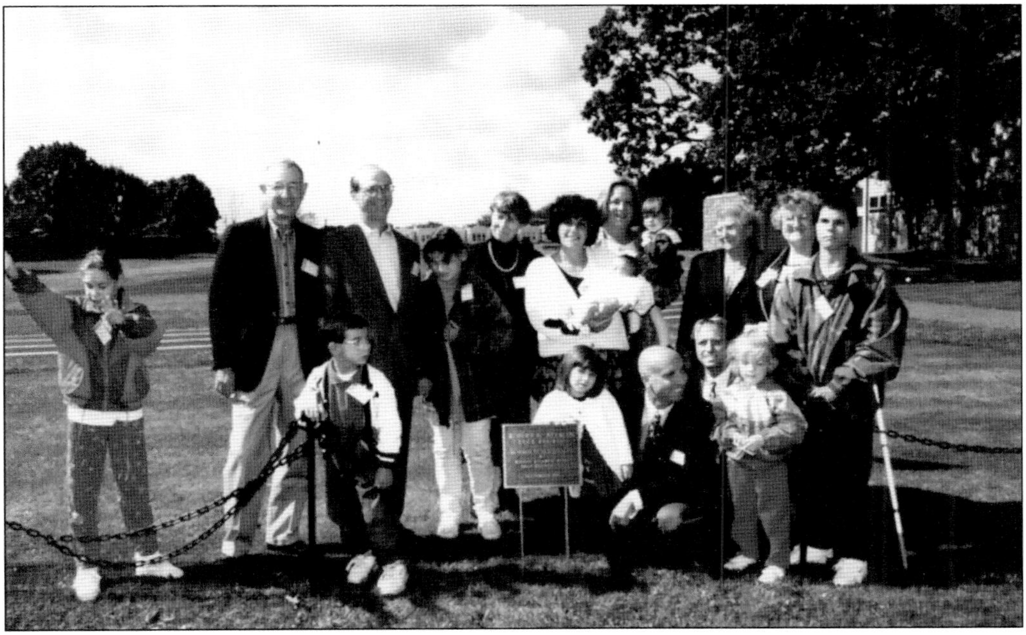

Never Too Young to Tee Off. Athletics and recreation have always been a part of the extracurricular activities at Overbrook. Students gather with members of the Mid-Atlantic Blind Golf Association for the dedication of a nine-hole chip and putt course in memory of Robert Allman, a 1935 graduate, outstanding wrestler, attorney, and avid golfer.

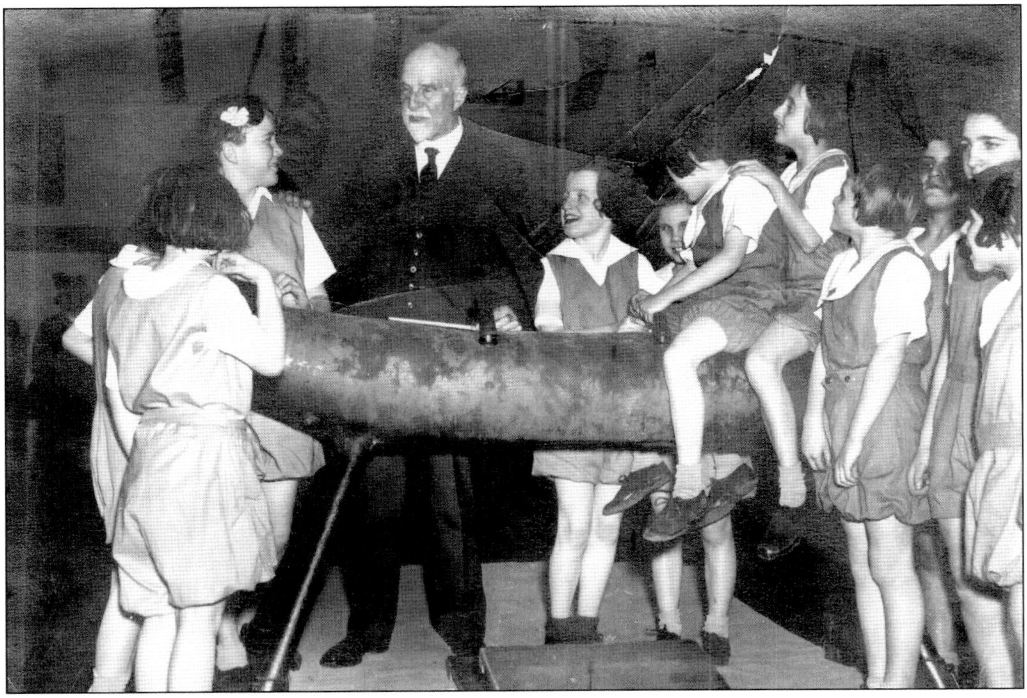

Girls' Gym Class, 1939. Dr. Edward Allen, the eighth principal of the school, visits a girls' gym class.

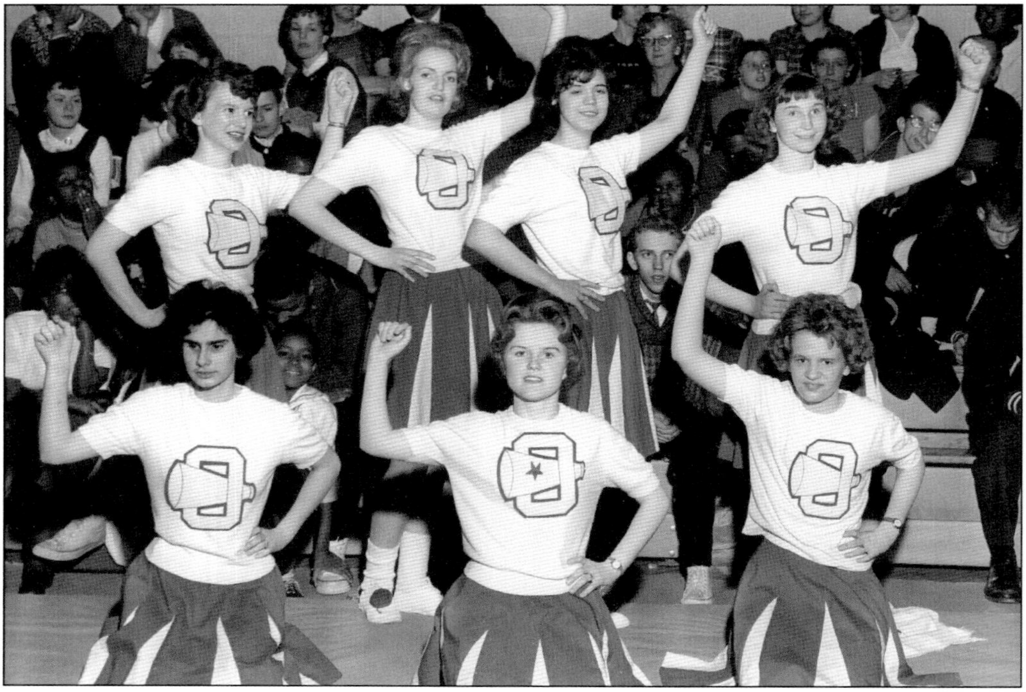

Cheering on the Huskies, 1963. These seven high school cheerleaders cheer for their team while wearing skirts and T-shirts embellished with an *O* and a megaphone.

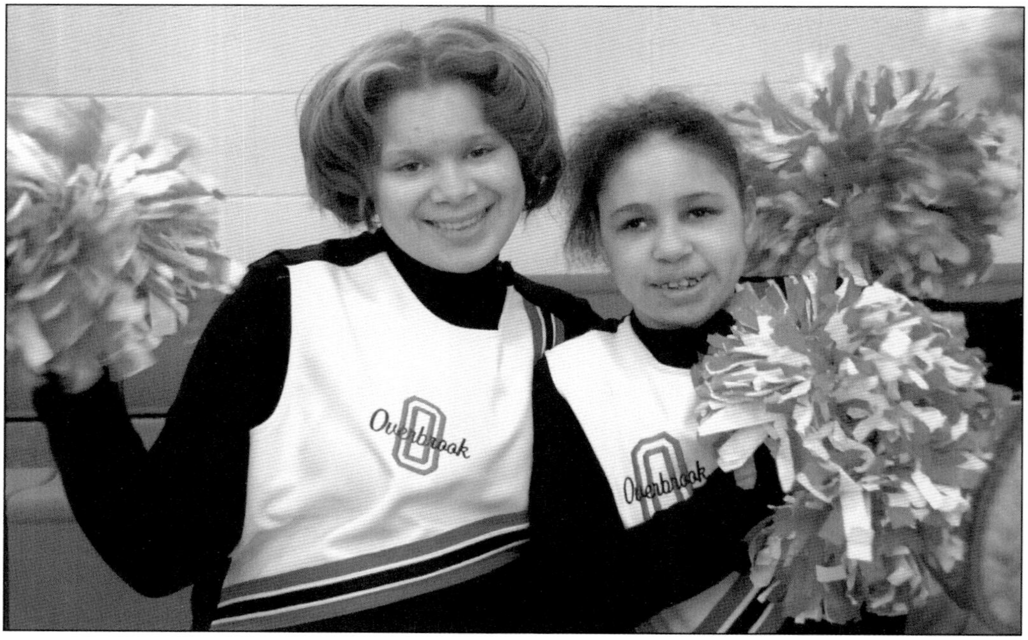

The Tournament. The early founders stressed the importance of sports and recreation. Since the beginning of the school, students have enjoyed competing with schools in the area as well as other schools for the blind. These two cheerleaders carry on the Overbrook tradition during a 2006 tournament.

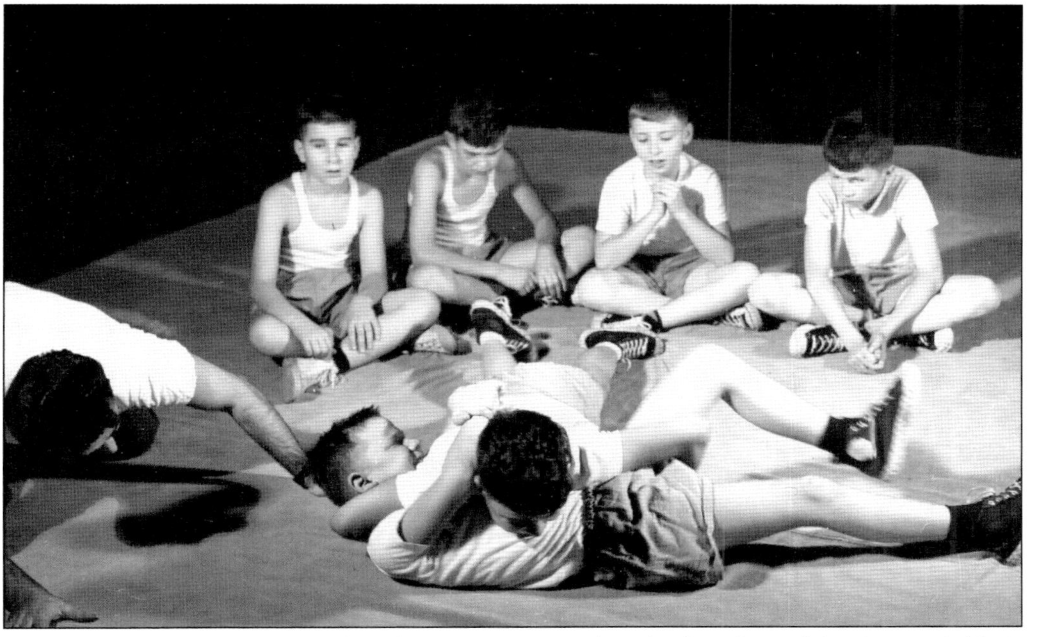

Pinned on the Mat, 1957. Overbrook was instrumental in the founding of the Eastern Athletic Association for the Blind. For over 60 years, this organization has offered students from schools for the blind an opportunity to compete in several sports. In this photograph, one student pins another while classmates cheer them on.

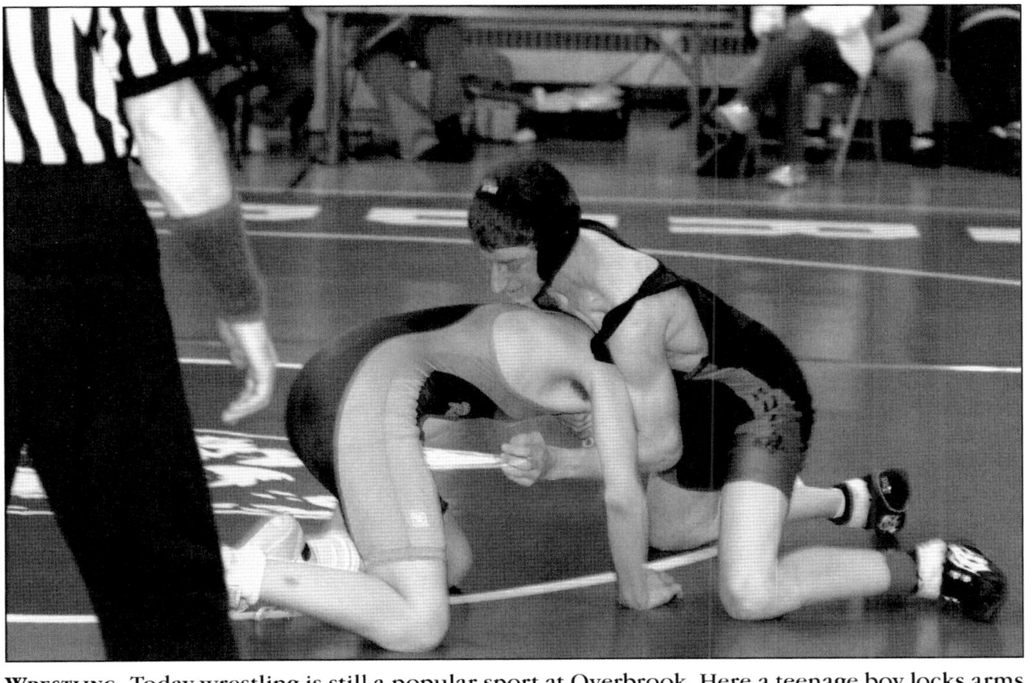

Wrestling. Today wrestling is still a popular sport at Overbrook. Here a teenage boy locks arms with an opponent during a wrestling match.

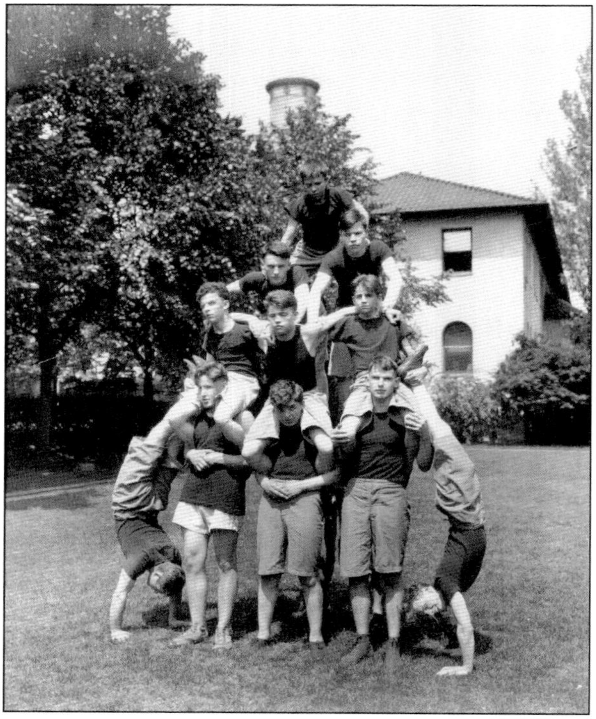

The Pyramid, 1922. These 11 boys form a pyramid by sitting on each other's shoulders.

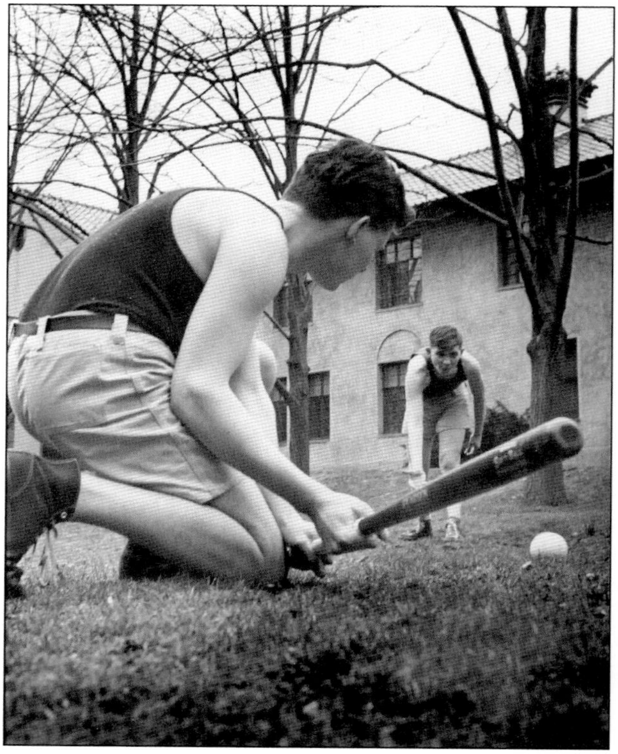

Batter Up, 1950. Two high school boys dressed in shorts and tank tops play ground baseball, a sport that was part of the physical education program.

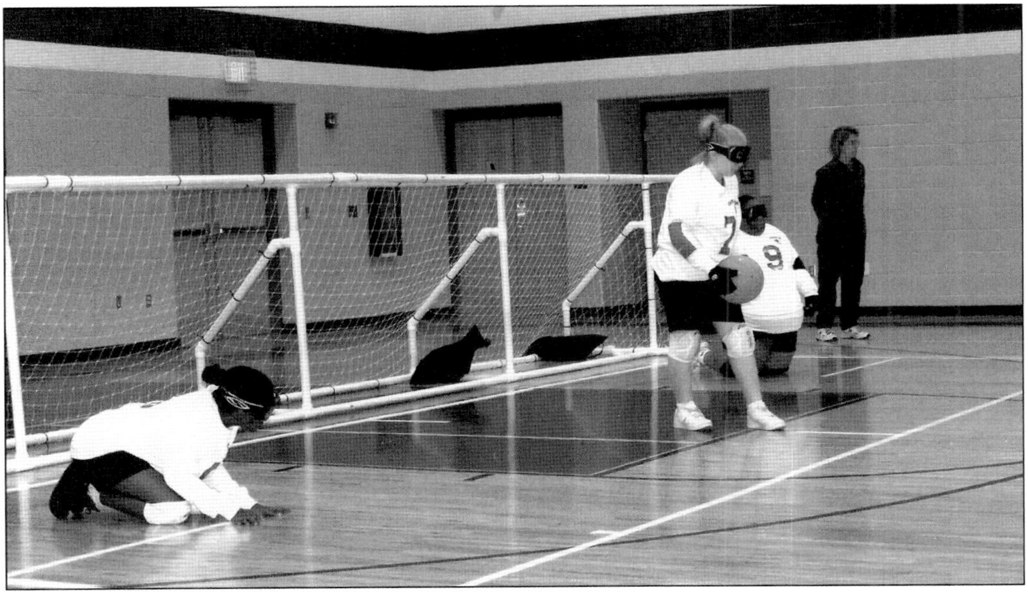

Goalball. In this photograph, Overbrook students compete in a goalball match. Goalball is a highly competitive sport played three against three and indoors on a gymnasium floor, primarily by athletes who are blind or visually impaired. Two teams play on either end of the 60-by-40-foot court. Players are blindfolded to make the game fair to all. The object is to throw a three-pound goalball, which is like a heavy basketball with a bell inside, past the opposing team.

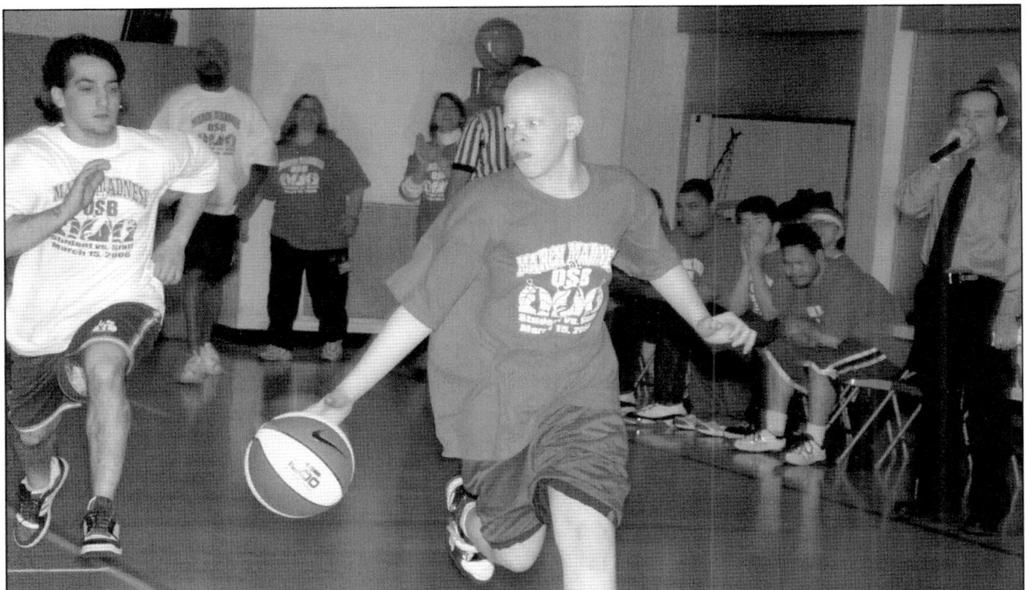

March Madness. The students' interest and skill in basketball is demonstrated at a yearly basketball game between the students and staff. The student players proudly take the court, and the entire student body cheers for them. Here a student dribbles the basketball while a staff member tries to catch up to him.

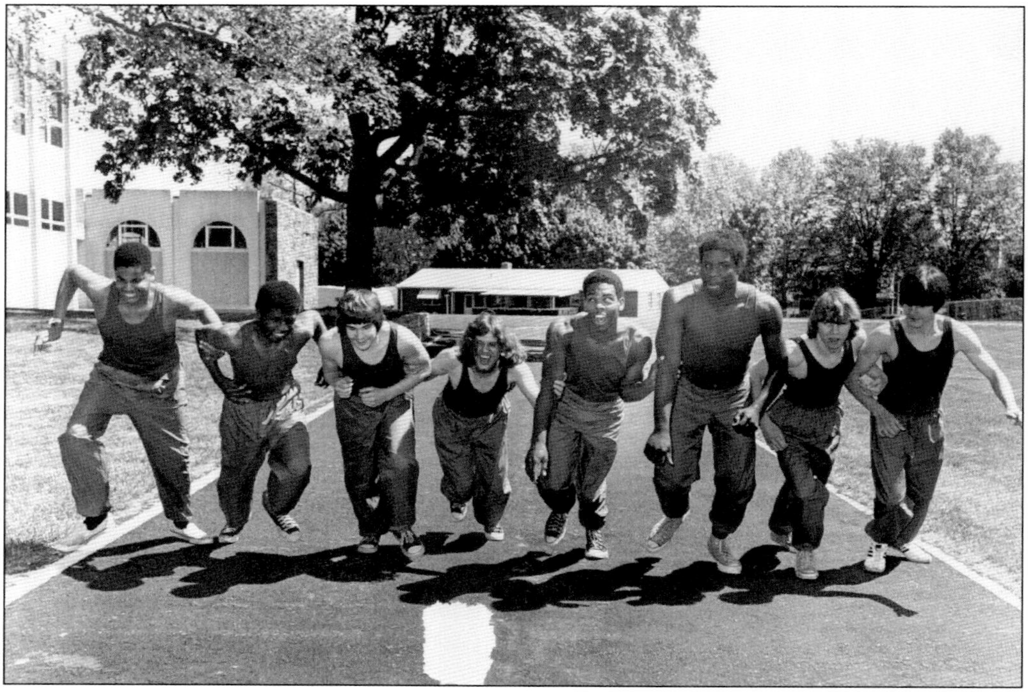

The Track Team, 1965. These eight members of the boys' track team run around the track with their arms linked, side by side.

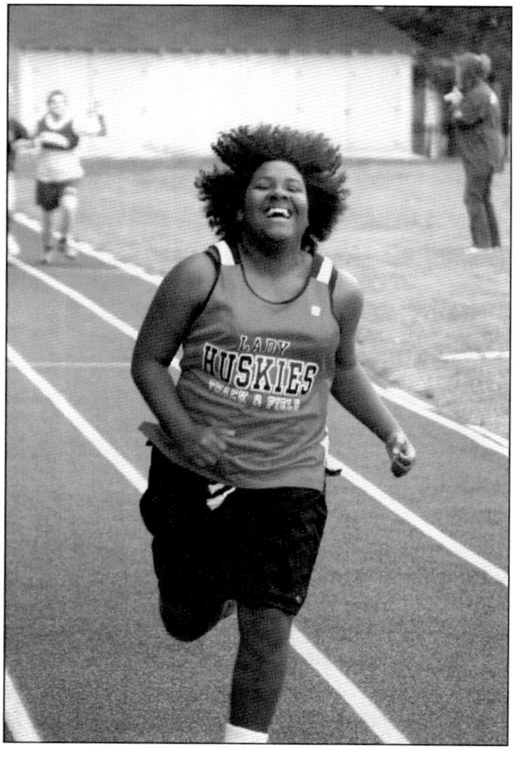

Sprint to the Finish. Tethered guide wires for sprint competitions and sighted guides for longer races make track a sport that is accessible for people who are blind or visually impaired. Here an Overbrook student dashes to the finish line.

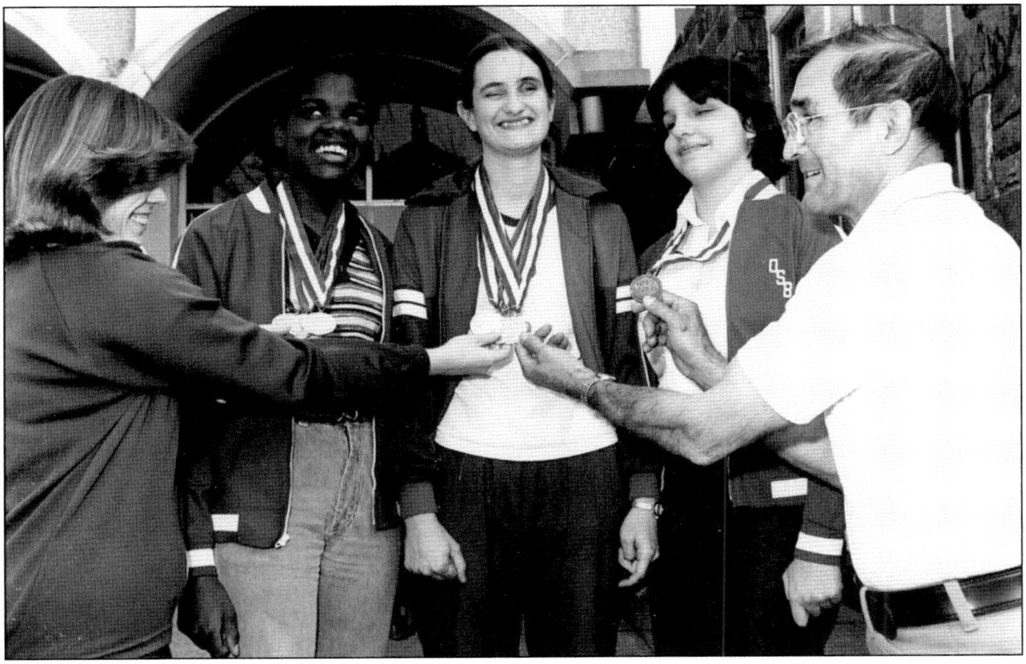

Medal Presentation, 1979. Overbrook students Carmella Lovitt, Donna Brown, and Licinda Morelli, from left to right, proudly display medals won at the third national championships of the U.S. Association for Blind Athletes in Seattle, Washington.

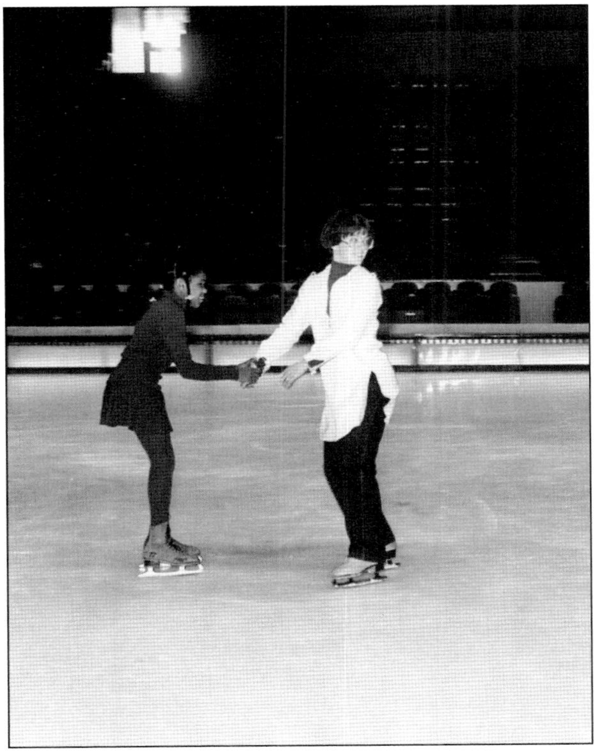

Ice-skating with an Olympian, 1979. A lucky Overbrook student has the unique opportunity to ice-skate with Olympic legend Dorothy Hamill.

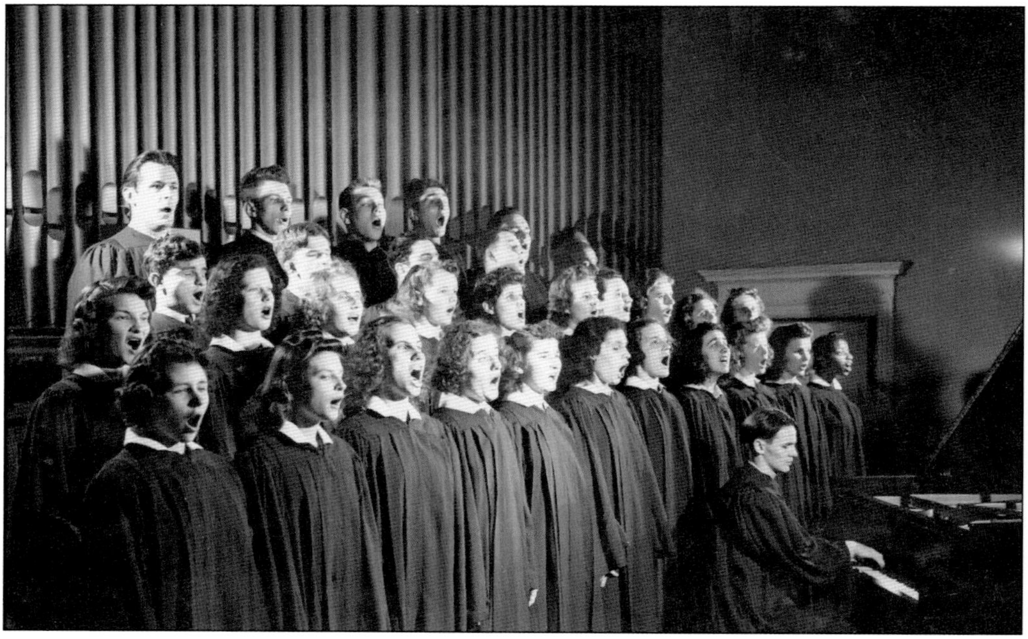

Girls' Choir, 1948. Students' interest in music was formally developed in a variety of classes. In this photograph, Overbrook's Senior Choir performs in front of the organ pipes under the direction of Henry N. Becker.

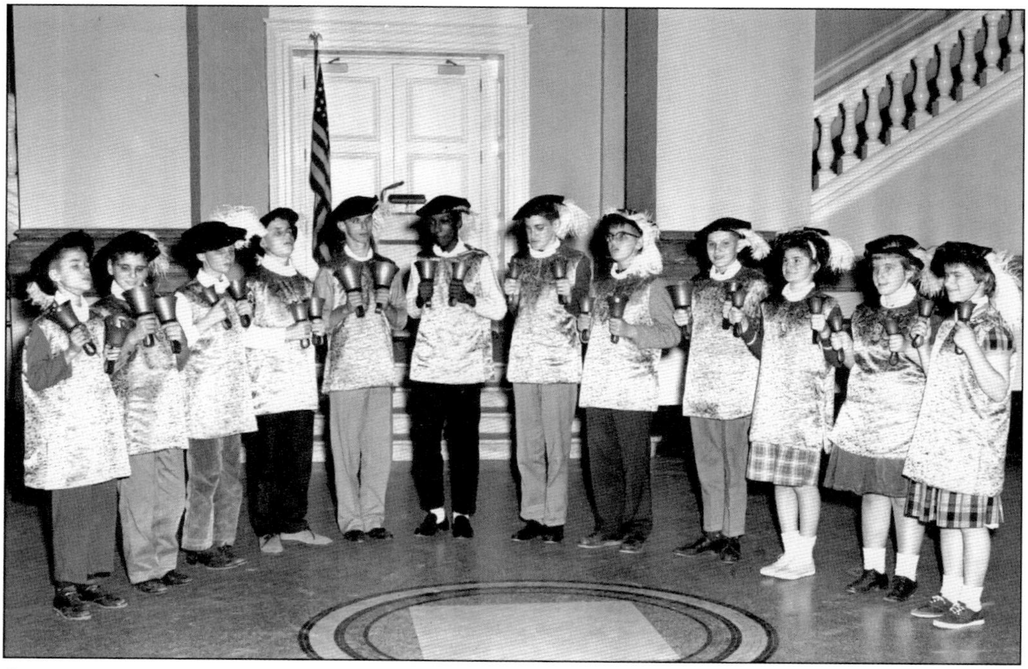

Children's English Hand Bell Choir, 1961. Young members of the Children's English Hand Bell Choir ring their bells in the rotunda. The handbell choir was started in 1960 under the direction of Dorothy Cage.

DR. DAVID DUFFLE WOOD (1838–1910). Born in western Pennsylvania and blind by age two, Dr. David Duffle Wood was sent to the Pennsylvania Institution for the Instruction of the Blind on a canal boat at age five in the care of a traveling merchant. By 1853, he was an assistant music teacher and, in 1887, was promoted to director of music. For 46 years, he served as organist and choirmaster of St. Stephen's Church in Philadelphia. Dr. Wood was known during his life as an organist and organ teacher. He was a prolific composer and is probably best remembered for the hymn "There Shall Be No More Night."

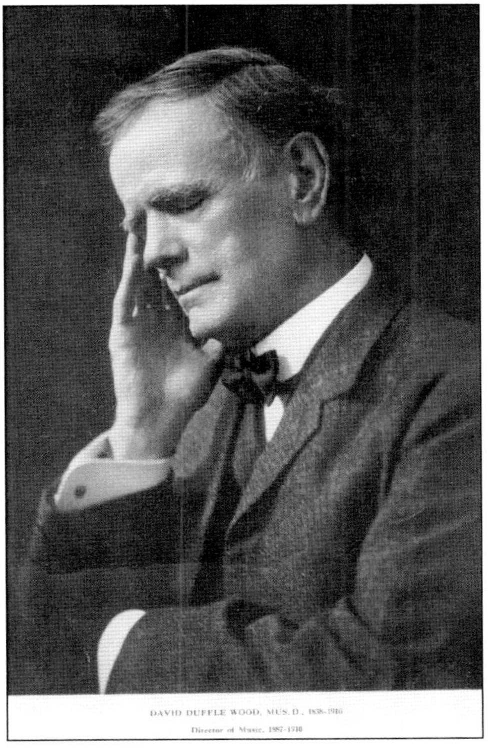

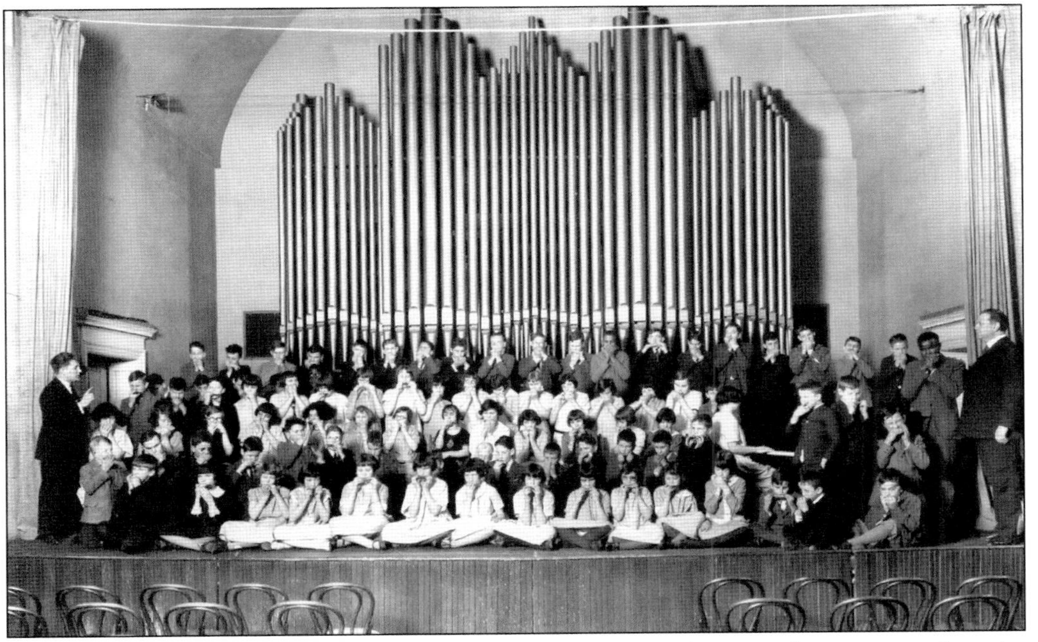

HARMONICA BAND, 1926. The harmonica was one of the most popular musical instruments from the 1920s through the 1940s. Its cheapness made it an ideal instrument for teaching music to children during the Depression. Harmonica youth bands were influential in instilling discipline. In this photograph, Overbrook's Harmonica Band is on stage in the auditorium, ready to perform.

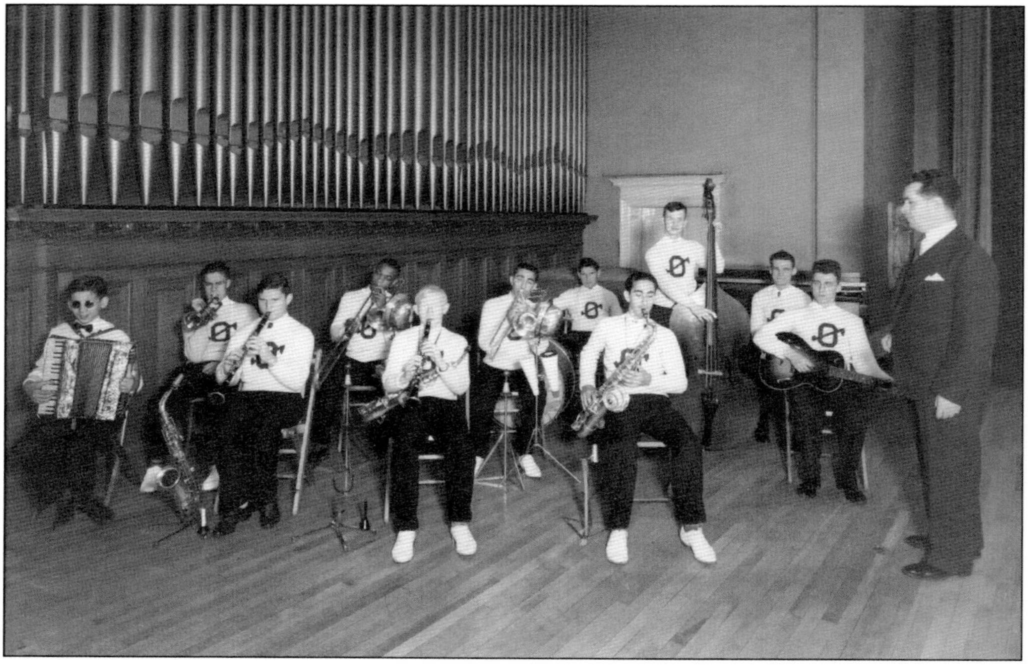

The Swing Band, 1939. Dressed in their Overbrook sweaters, the boys in the Overbrook Swing Band make music with the saxophone, clarinet, accordion, trumpet, trombone, guitar, and upright bass under the direction of William R. Currlin.

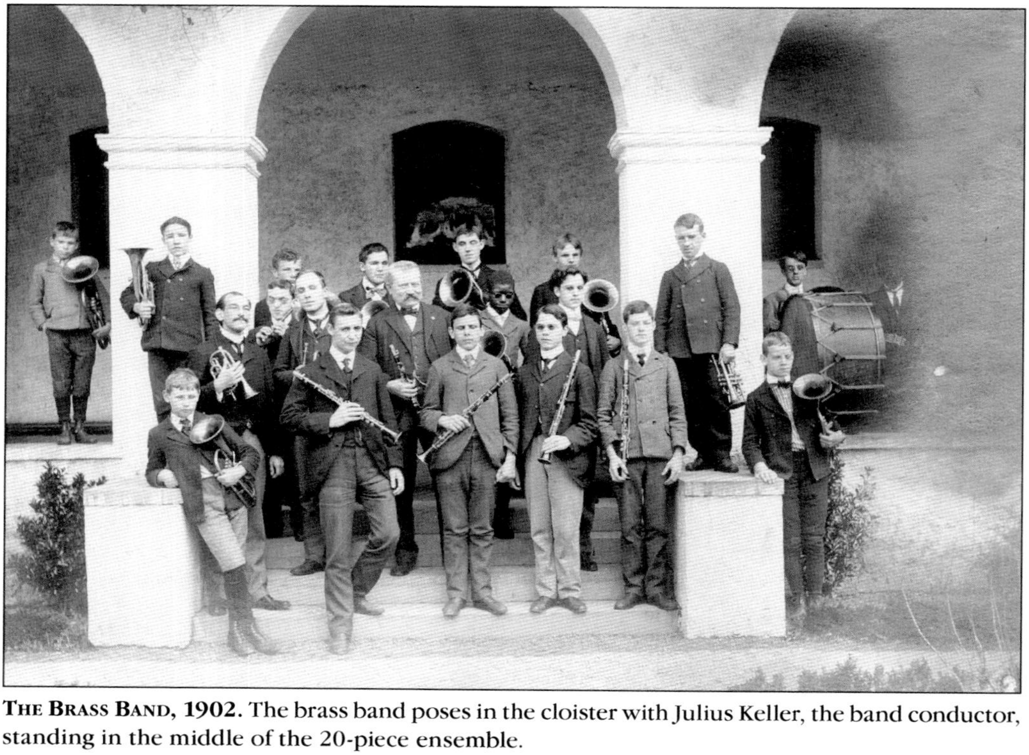

The Brass Band, 1902. The brass band poses in the cloister with Julius Keller, the band conductor, standing in the middle of the 20-piece ensemble.

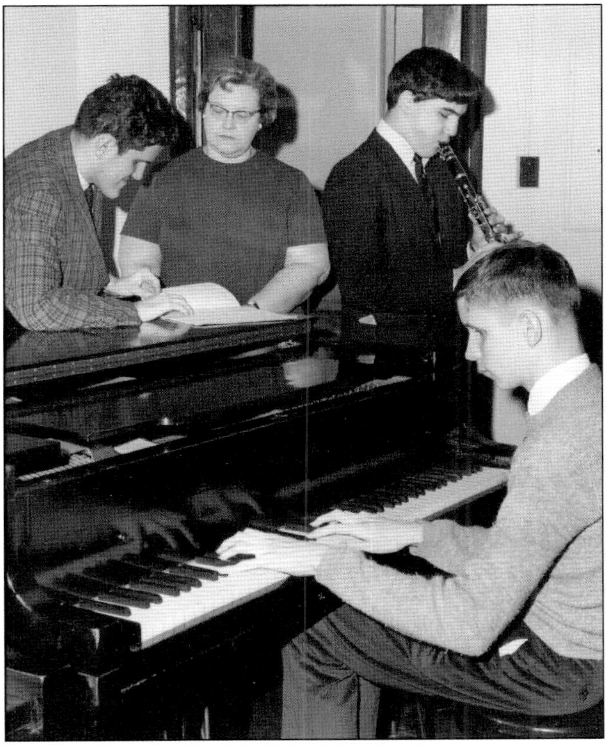

Making Music, 1968. While one teenage boy plays the piano and another the clarinet, music teacher Edith Murray helps a student read braille music.

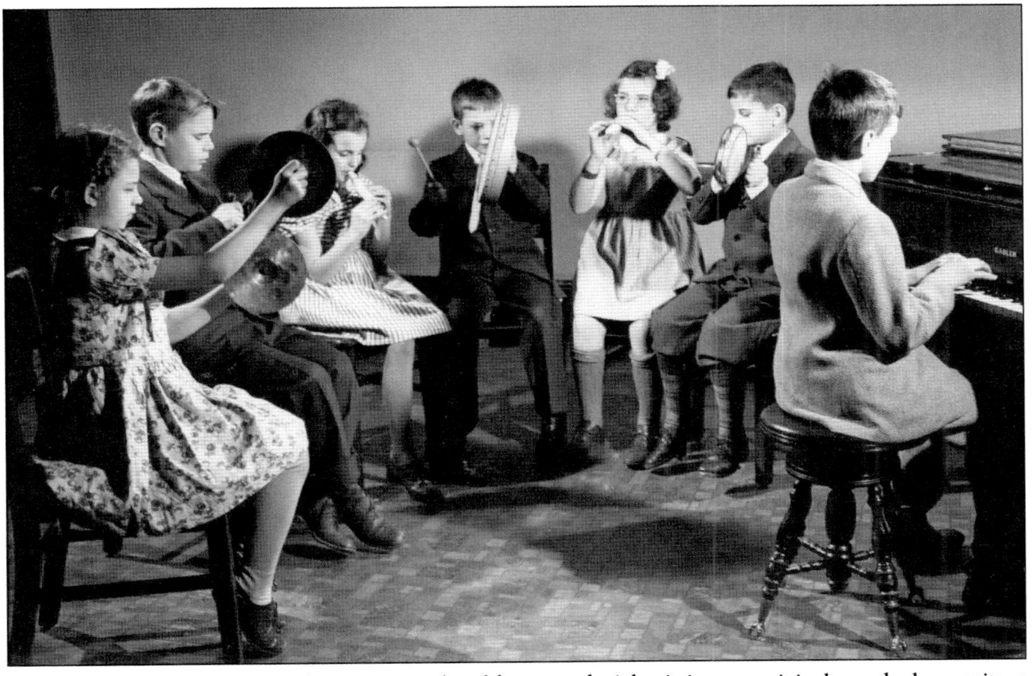

The Rhythm Band, 1970. Elementary school boys and girls sit in a semicircle and play various instruments, including the cymbals, tambourine, and kazoo. One of their classmates accompanies on the piano.

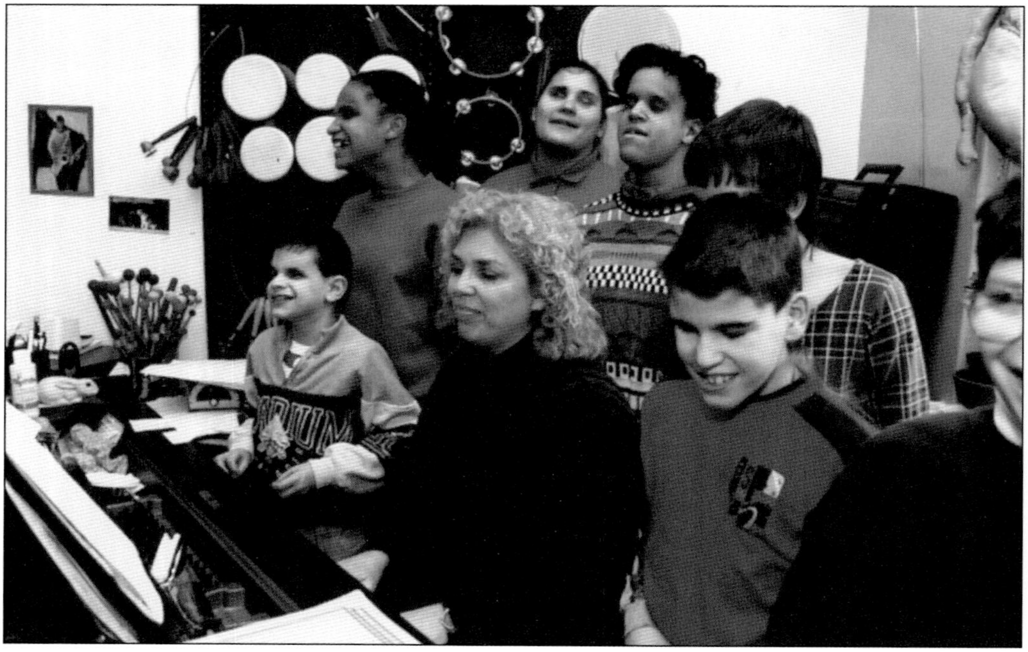

YOUNG PERFORMERS. Singing is a favorite activity at Overbrook. In formal music classes, students learn to use their talents in a group.

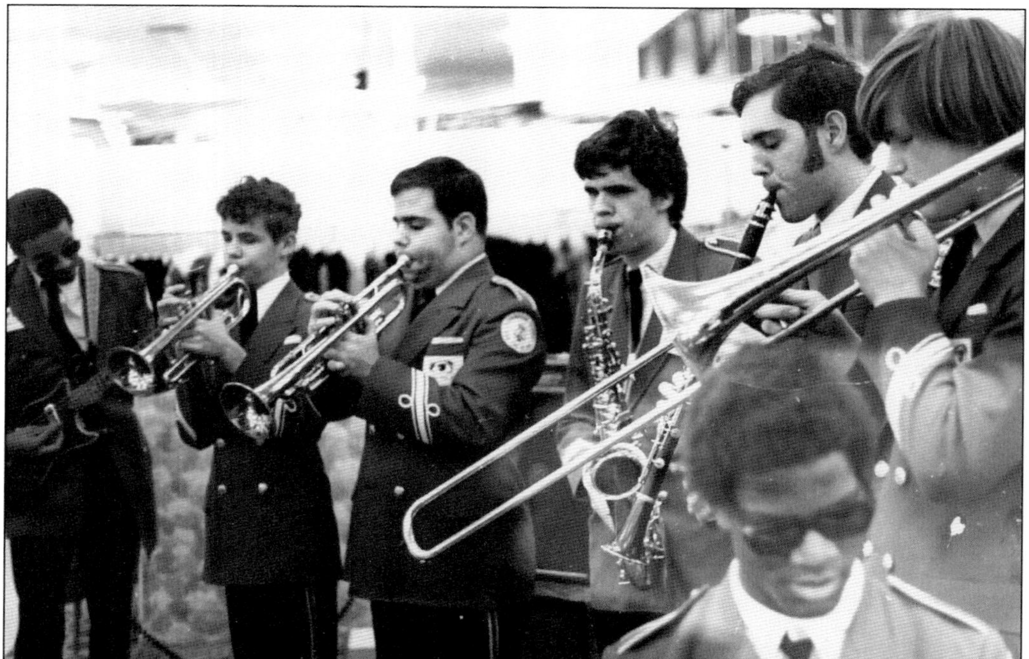

COMMUNITY PERFORMANCE. Julius Friedlander often brought the students to different community events. In the 1960s, the boys' brass band played at many different venues, including this one, a local department store.

Six

PLAY AND CELEBRATION

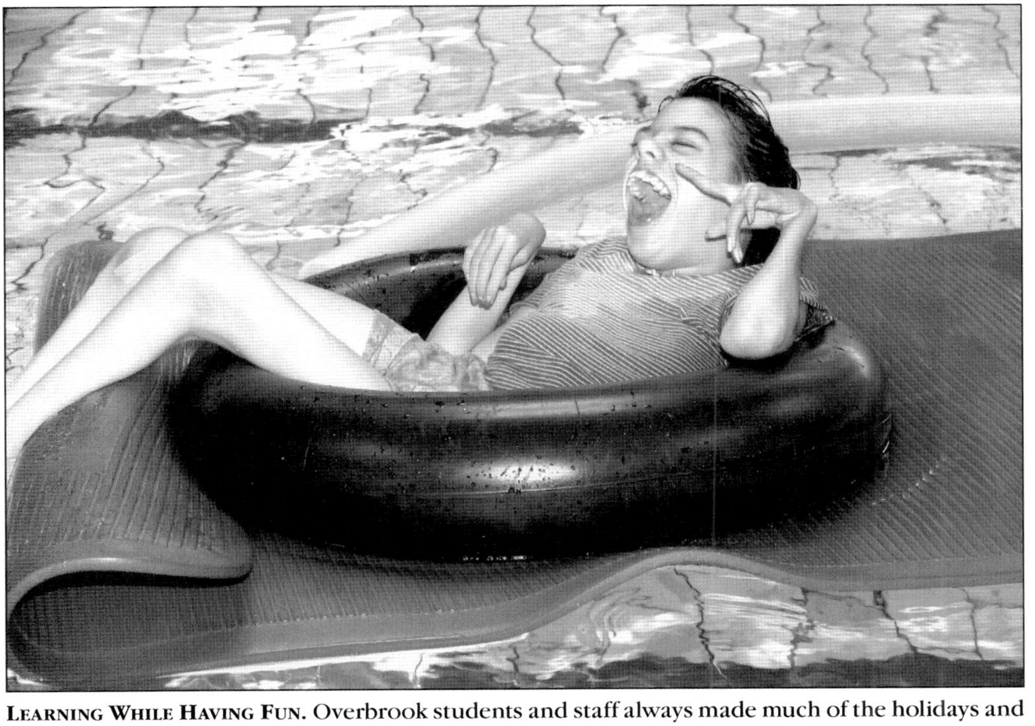

LEARNING WHILE HAVING FUN. Overbrook students and staff always made much of the holidays and special events. Each spring, students in the Deafblind and Early Childhood Programs hunted for beeping Easter eggs provided by the Telephone Pioneers of America. Over the years, students on the campus eagerly awaited dances for various holidays, participated in athletic tournaments, learned to play games in the dormitories, and entertained people in the community. A favorite holiday observance is still Halloween. Staff and students dress for the annual parade, and excitement mounts to hear who has won the award for best costume in a variety of categories. The alumni remember the fun events as they gather on the campus.

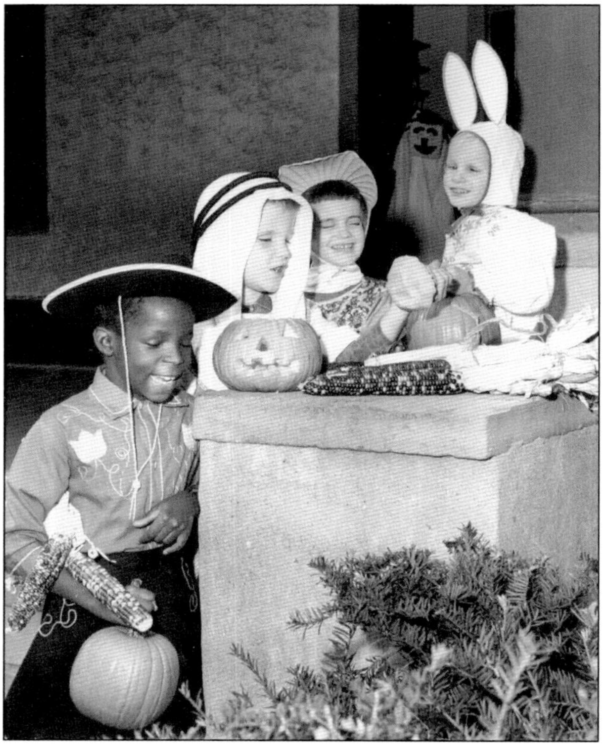

Halloween, 1964. Young students wearing costumes enjoy seasonal decorations, including Indian corn and pumpkins. They are dressed as a cowgirl, shepherd, Little Bo Peep, and a bunny.

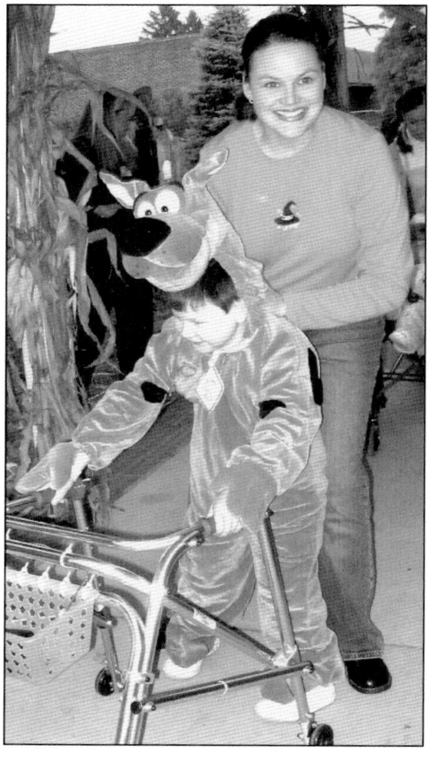

The Halloween Parade. Halloween has always been a big day for students. The tradition continues with this student dressed as Scooby Doo for the annual parade.

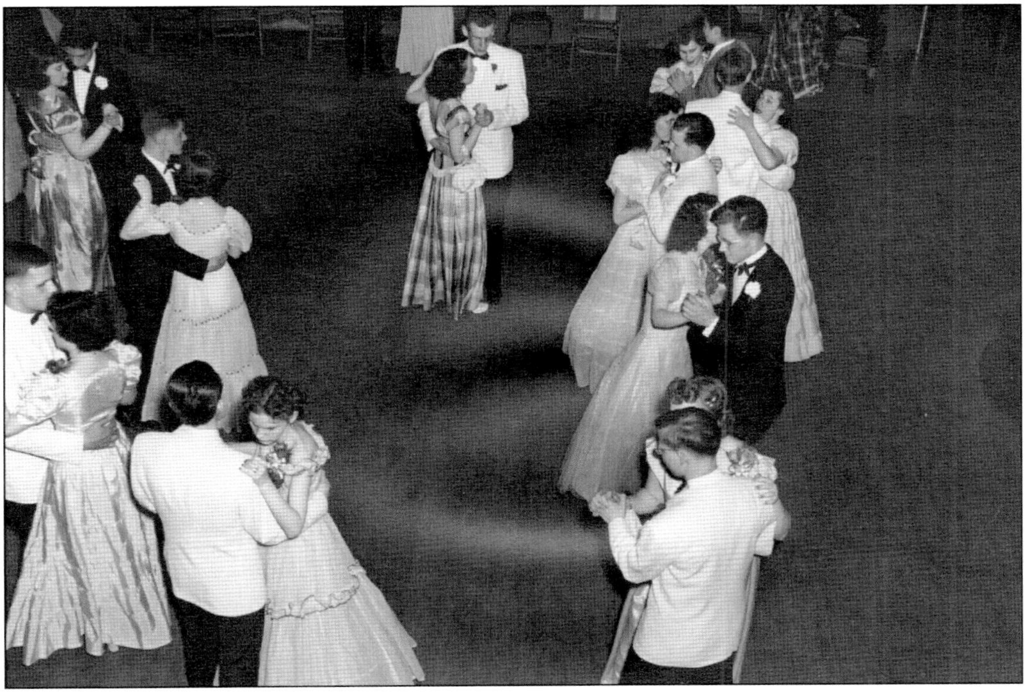

Prom Night, 1947. Dressed in tuxedos and gowns, older boys and girls slow dance together at their prom.

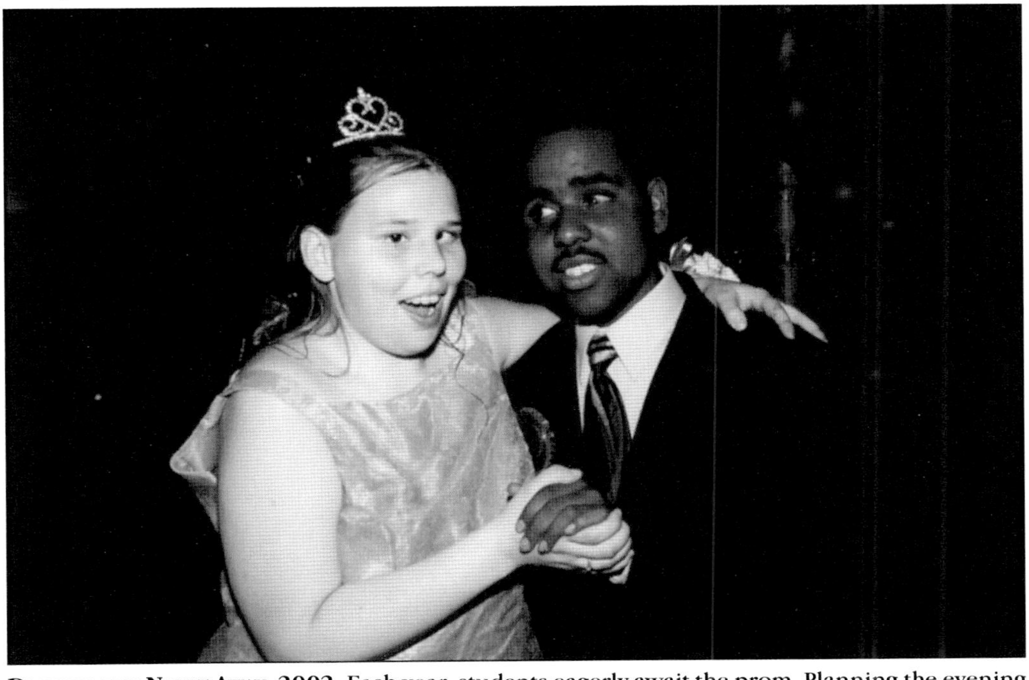

Dancing the Night Away, 2002. Each year, students eagerly await the prom. Planning the evening and selecting the perfect outfit are parts of becoming a young adult. This photograph shows a young man dancing with the prom queen.

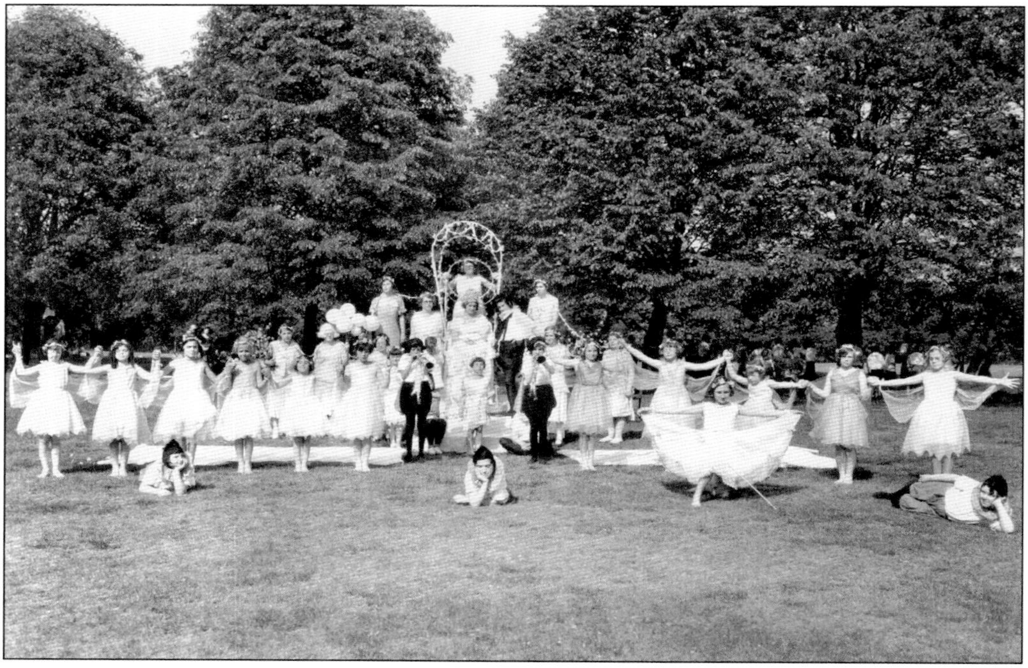

Historical Pageant, 1915. In this pageant, young flower girls line up side by side clad in white dresses. The queen of the pageant stands in the middle wearing her crown. The pages, standard bearers, and ladies-in-waiting are in the background.

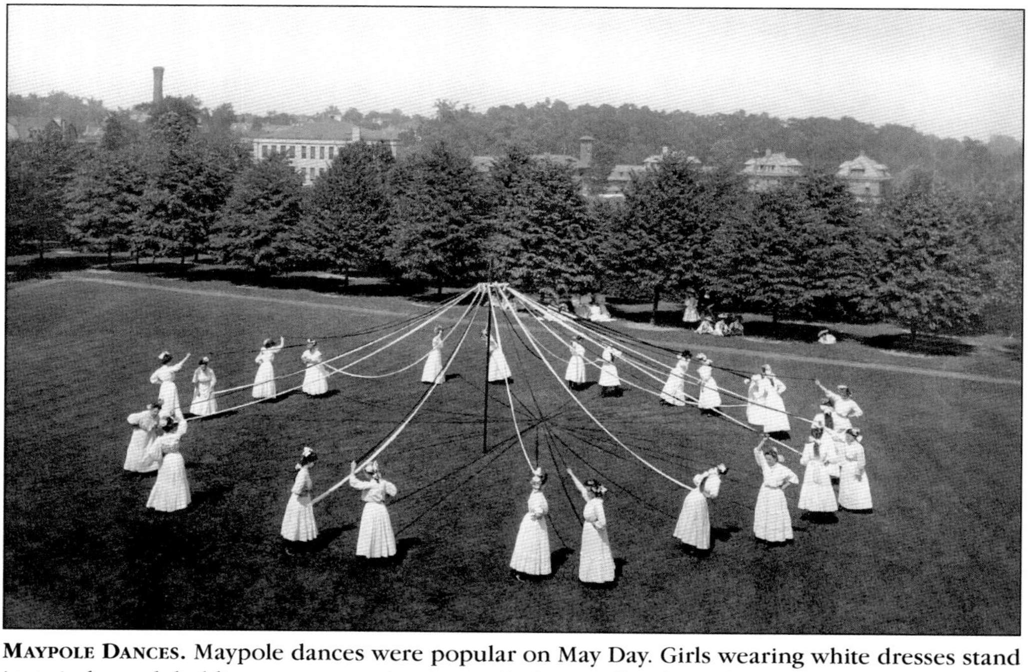

Maypole Dances. Maypole dances were popular on May Day. Girls wearing white dresses stand in a circle, each holding a streamer that is attached to a tall pole in the center. The girls perform choreographed dances using their streamers. In the background, houses from the surrounding neighborhood are visible.

May Day Celebration, the 1960s. Donning spring dresses and floral headpieces, five young girls stand in front of maypole streamers holding a long flower arrangement.

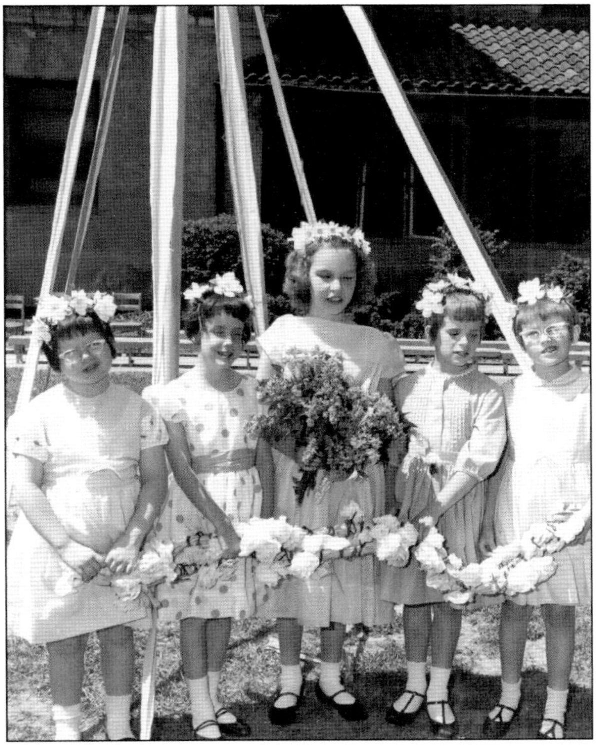

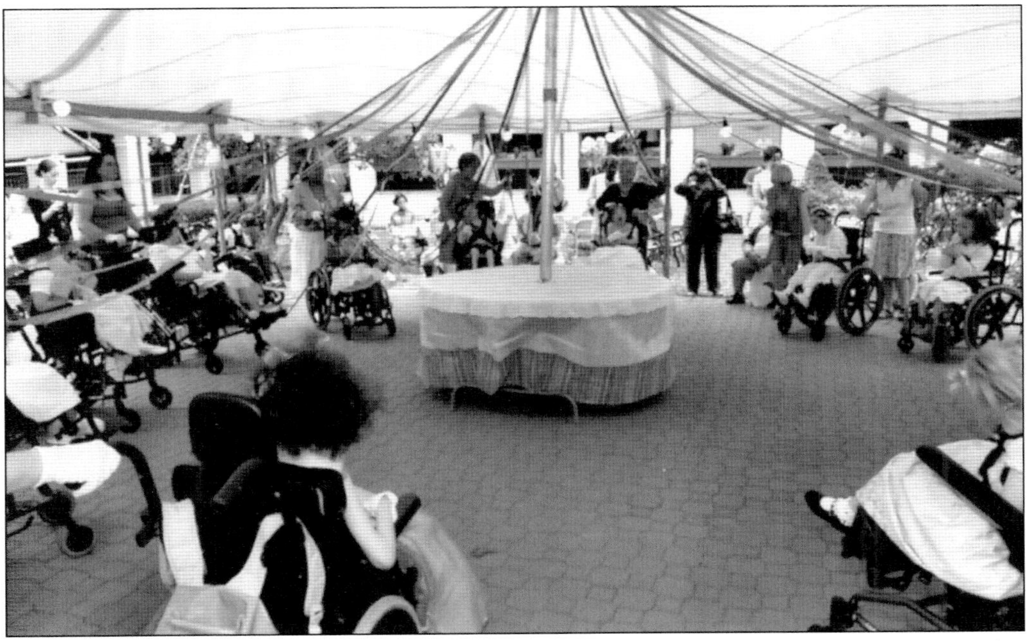

The Cotillion, 2006. The tradition of the May Day celebration continues at Overbrook. In this photograph, the maypole dance is adapted for wheelchair users. Streamers are attached to a pole in the center of a table, and students in wheelchairs are pushed around the table as they hold onto their streamers.

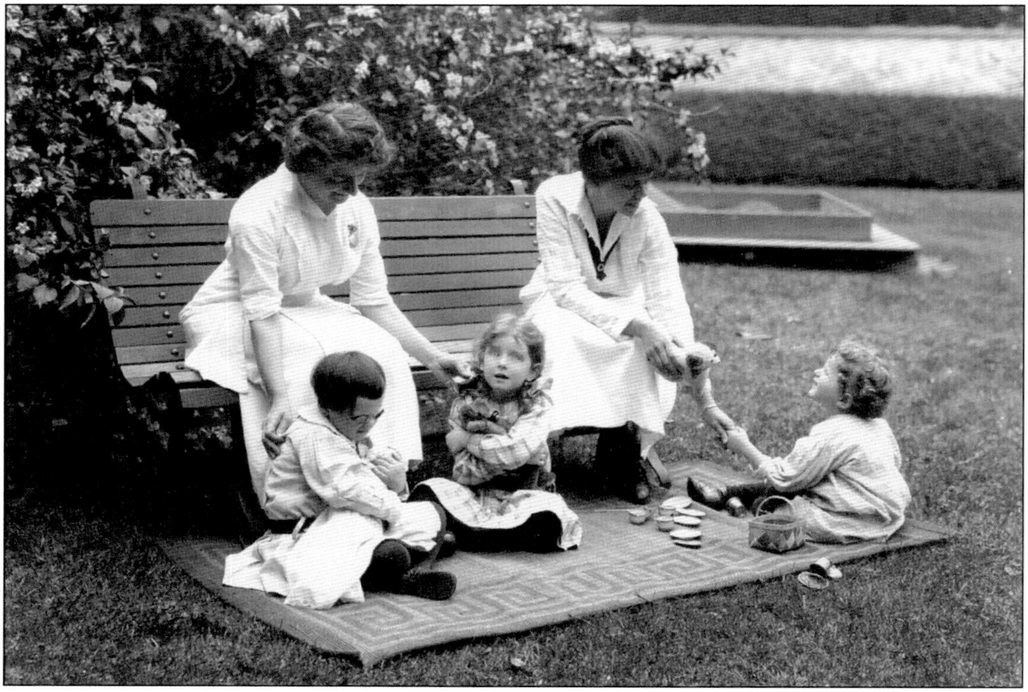

Afternoon Tea. Three kindergarten students and two teachers have an afternoon tea party on the grass. Adding to the fun atmosphere are china cups and a woven carpet.

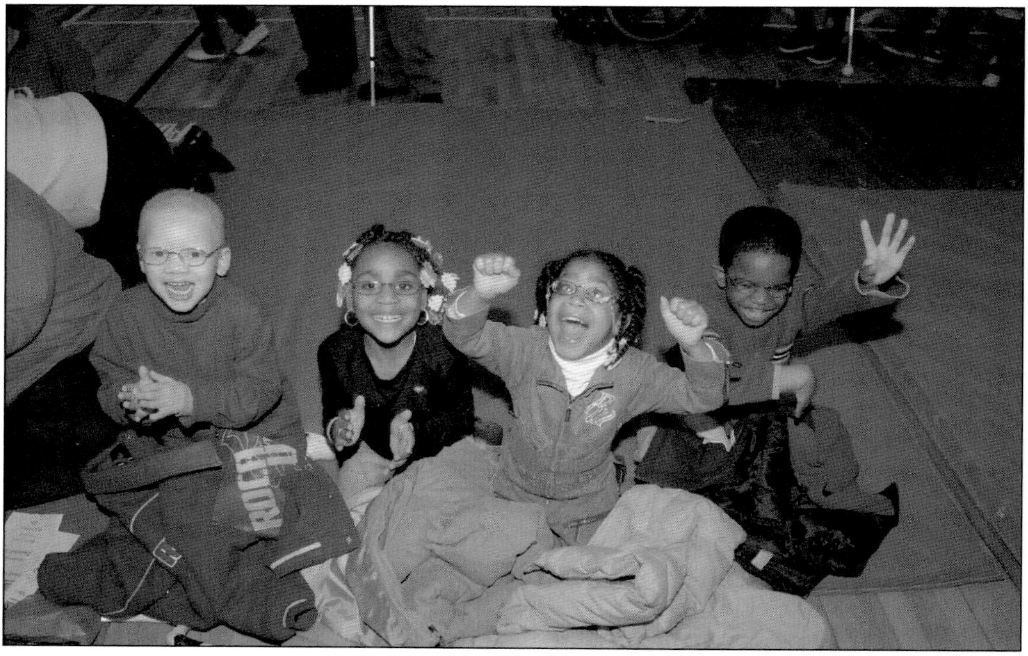

Yeah, Overbrook! Several times during the year, students come together to celebrate various events and to just have fun. At this assembly, preschoolers cheer for their friends.

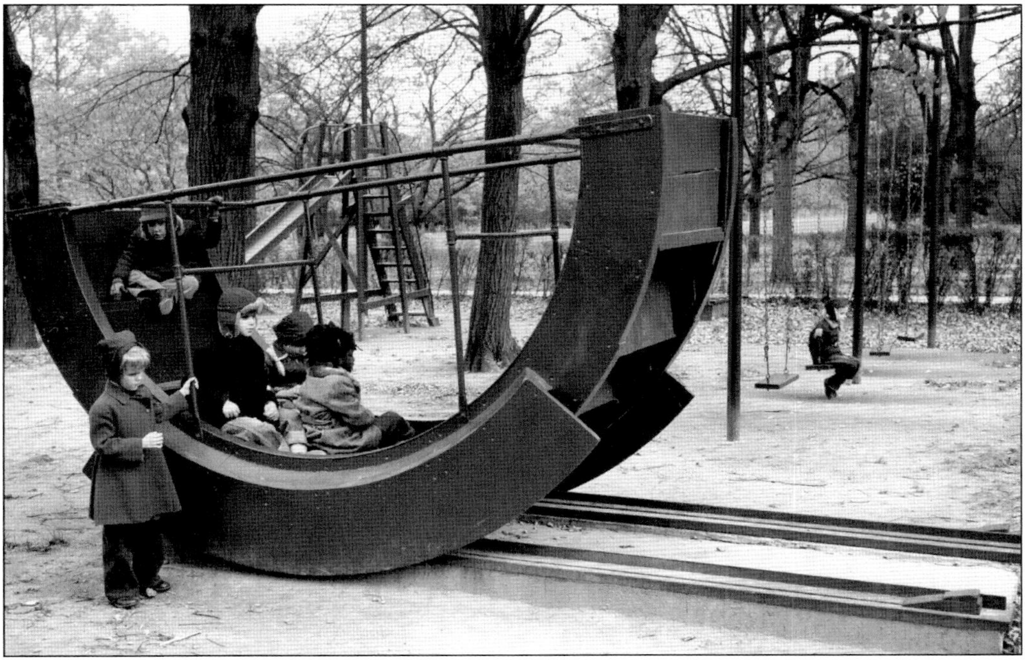

ROCKING BOAT, 1950. Three young children play inside a rocking boat while another waits for her turn. The rocking boat was a popular outdoor activity for the students. The sensation of rocking to as high as six feet put smiles on many faces.

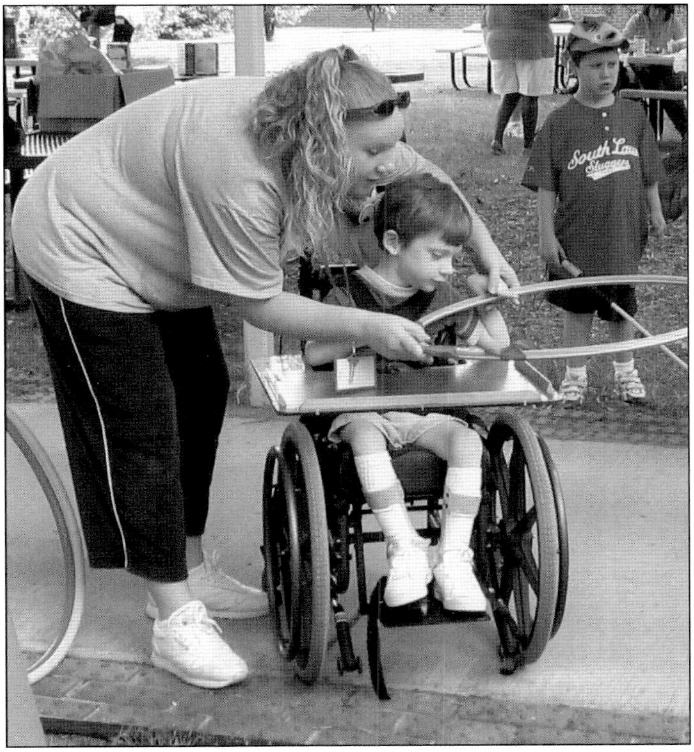

FUN DAY. Overbrook held an annual May Fair for many years. Students played carnival games, bought food, and participated in a variety of competitive activities. In the late 1990s, this special day was renamed Fun Day. The day takes on a particular theme, and all the festivities are coordinated around that theme. The children in this photograph use a hula hoop as a lasso during a Wild West–themed Fun Day.

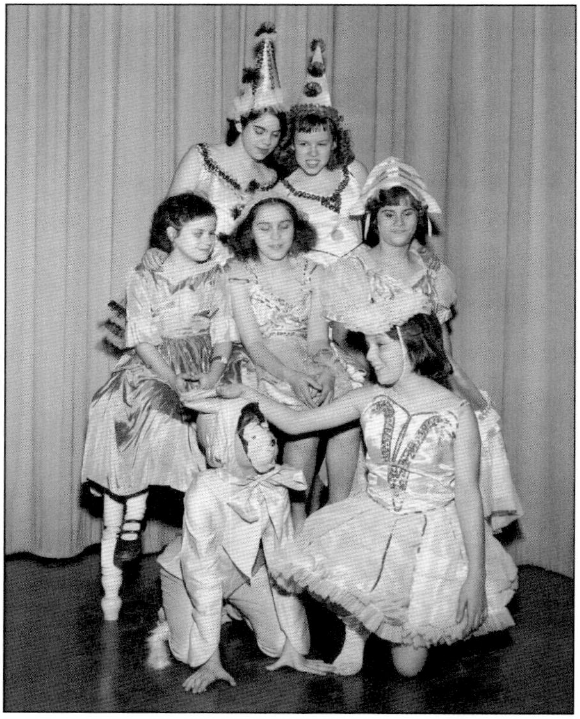

The Toy Shop, 1956. During a Christmas performance, these girls wear shiny dresses and clown hats and form a pyramid.

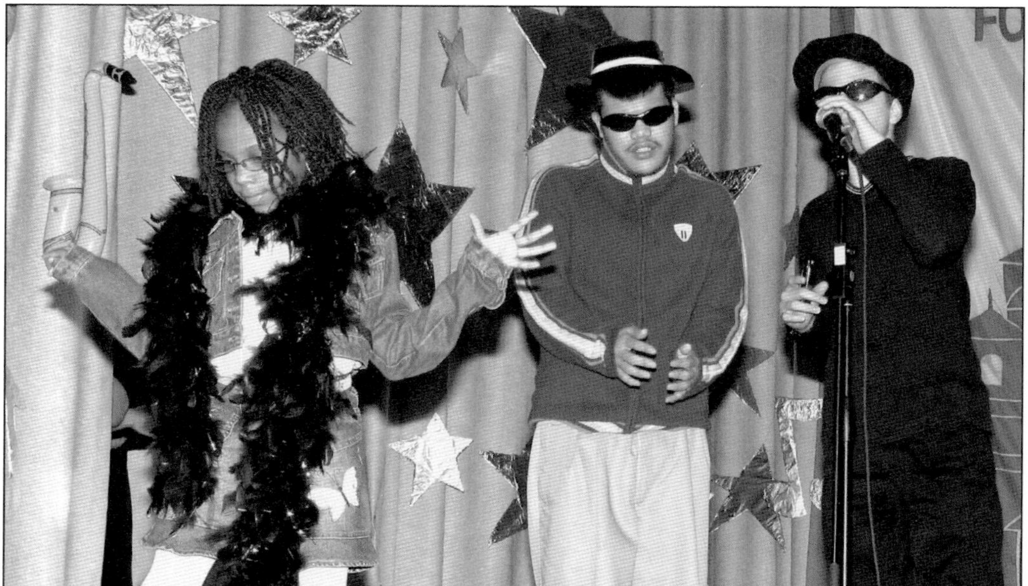

Showcasing Talent. Just as young people around the country wanted to show off their talent on the popular show *American Idol*, the students at Overbrook created their own contest. From preschool to high school, the students sang and entertained their friends, the staff, and family members. Clad in costumes related to their songs, these three performers work hard to win the title of Overbrook Idol.

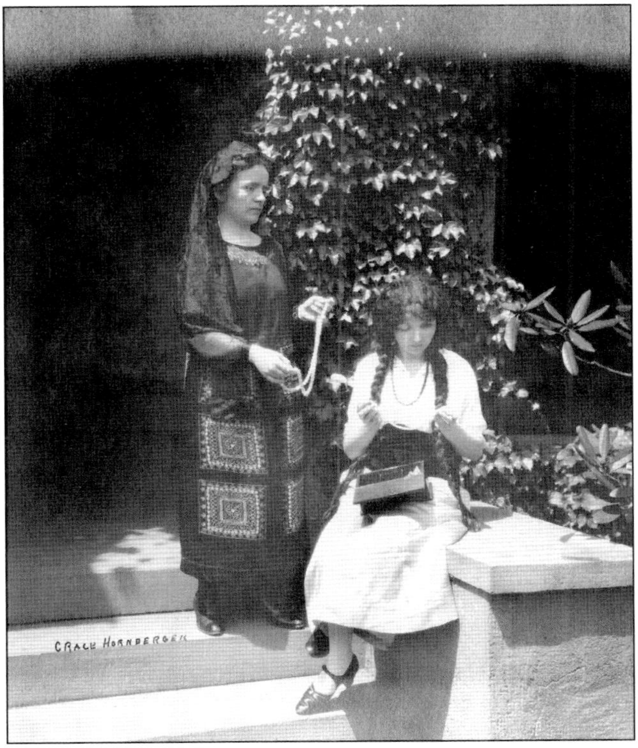

***RAMONA*, 1926.** Theatrical performances gave the students an opportunity to learn about different cultures and periods in history. The performances were held on the Overbrook stage as well as settings around the campus. Elaborate costumes were used in all the plays. For their production of *Ramona*, two girls look at their jewelry as they rehearse.

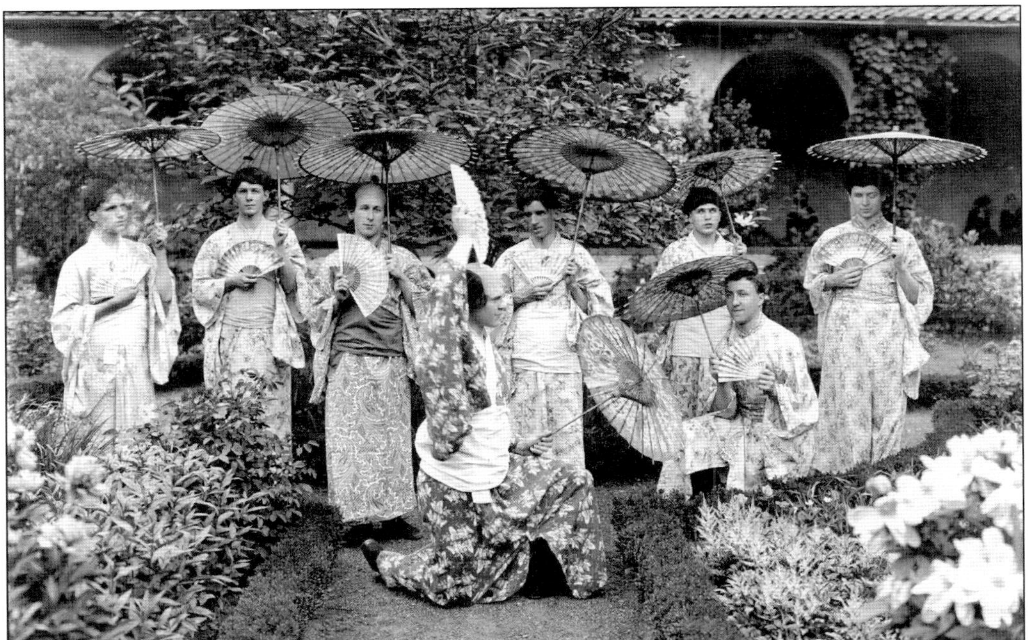

***THE MIKADO*.** The Boys' Glee Club performance of *The Mikado* at the LuLu Temple earned them money that was divided between the Uniform Type Committee and the Graduates' Loan Fund. In this photograph, the boys pose in kimonos and hold umbrellas.

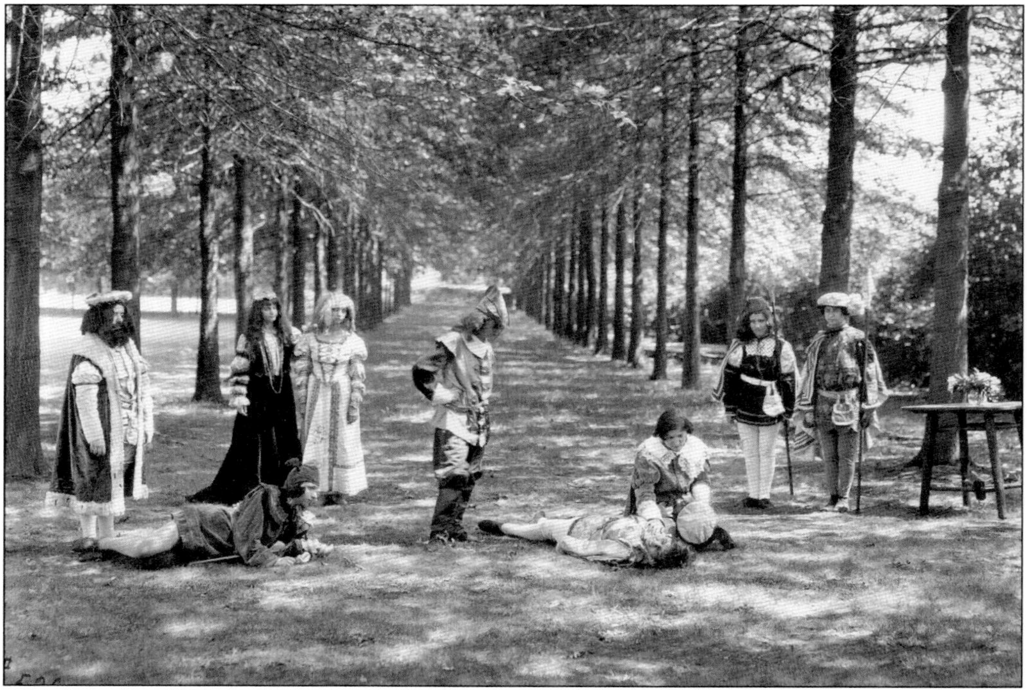

***THE MERCHANT OF VENICE*, 1911.** Dressed in period costumes, students from the boys' school stage an outdoor performance of a Shakespearean classic.

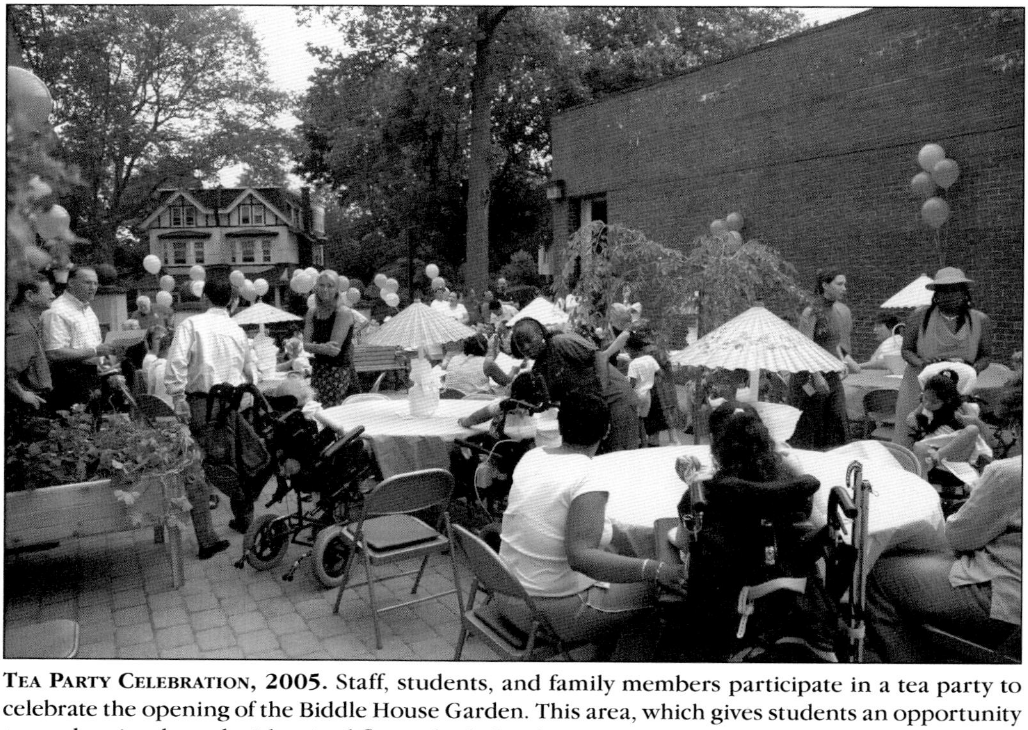

TEA PARTY CELEBRATION, 2005. Staff, students, and family members participate in a tea party to celebrate the opening of the Biddle House Garden. This area, which gives students an opportunity to garden, is adapted with raised flower beds for those in wheelchairs.

Two Graduates, 1917. Students at Overbrook have always been happy to congratulate each other for academic success, athletic achievement, or other types of personal recognition. Bessie Elinor Kulp (right) and Virginia Whitaker share a moment after receiving diplomas in music.

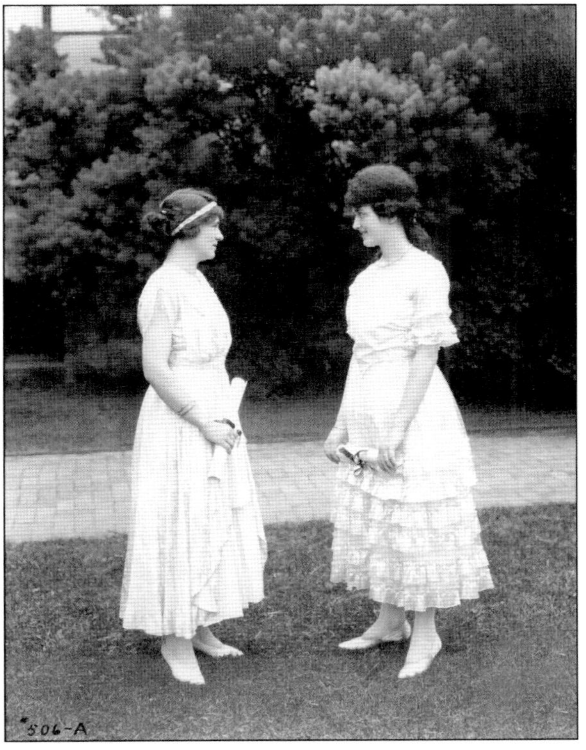

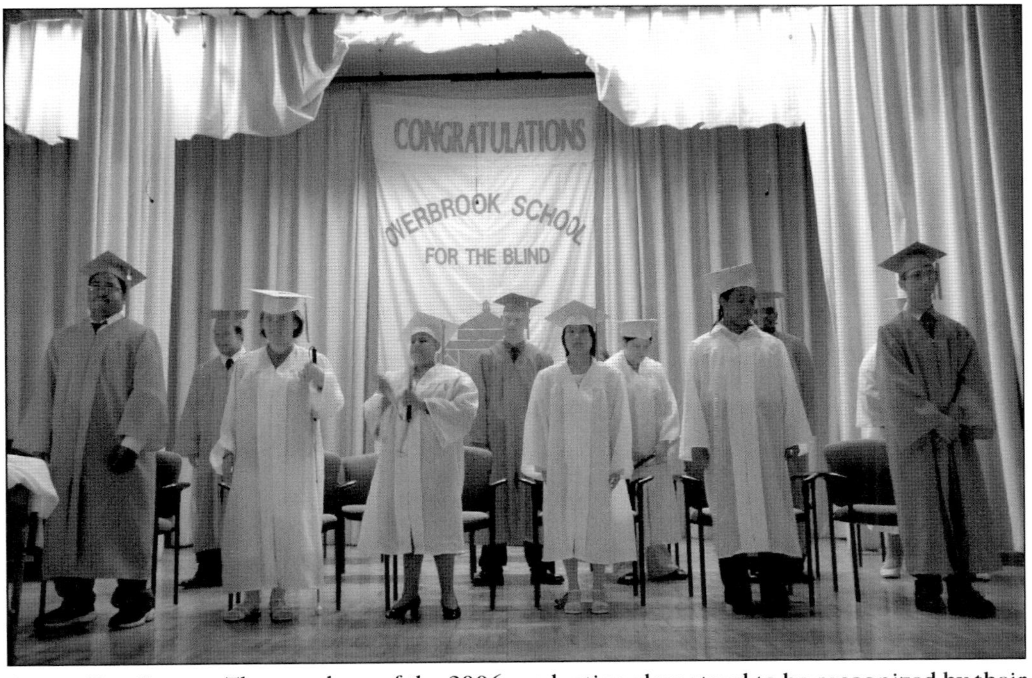

Off to New Places. The members of the 2006 graduating class stand to be recognized by their teachers, family, and friends. Turning their tassels signals the beginning of the journey to college, work, or a training program.

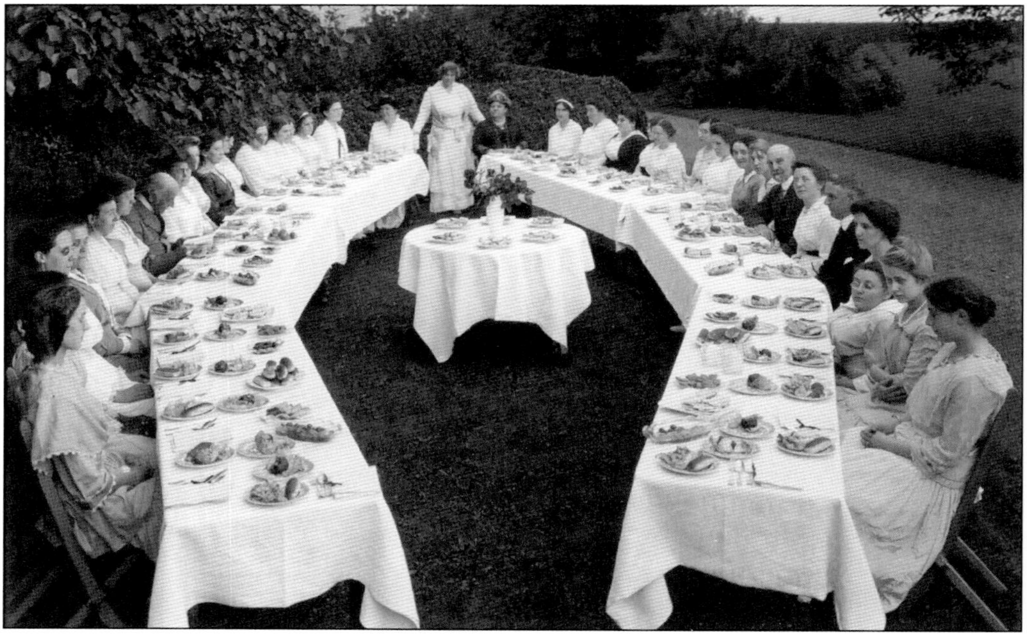

Overbrook Alumni. Since 1906, Overbrook School for the Blind has been fortunate to have an active alumni association. The group is made up of graduates and former students of all ages. At alumni association events, members have the opportunity to get together with their former classmates and share memories of their school days at Overbrook. Also, the association supports campus programs and activities. Members volunteer their time for activities, and the association presents an annual gift to the school. In the photograph above, alumnae celebrate the association's 10th anniversary with a luncheon on the green. Below, Overbrook alumni enjoy a game of bingo at a gathering in 2000.

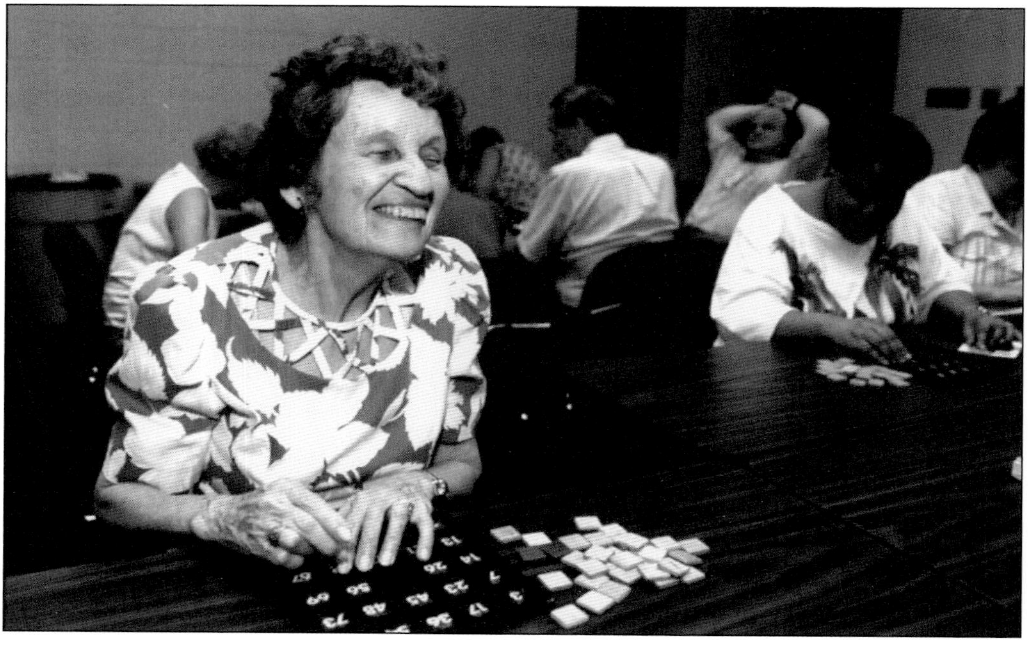

Seven

WORKING TOWARD INDEPENDENCE

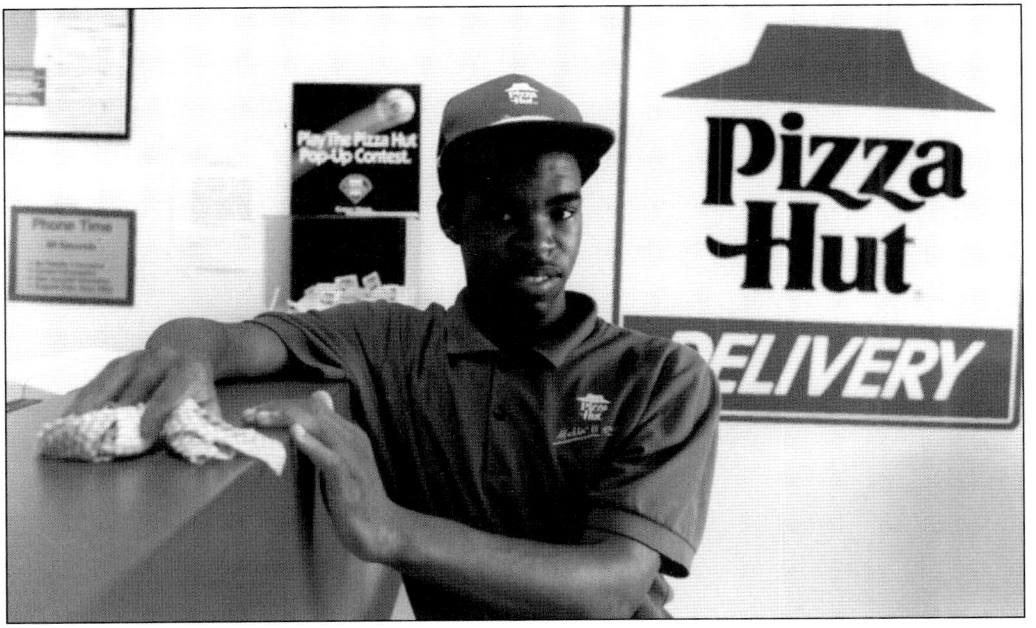

SKILLS FOR EMPLOYMENT. Preparing for the future has always been an important concern in establishing the curriculum. Whether it is through classroom lessons or actual job experiences, students leave Overbrook prepared for the work world they will enter after graduation. Specially trained staff members work with each student individually to determine appropriate goals and structure the sequential learning experiences that will best help him reach those goals. Career awareness courses, prevocational classes, the production workshop, on-campus employment, and off-campus employment provide for a wide range of needs and varying student abilities.

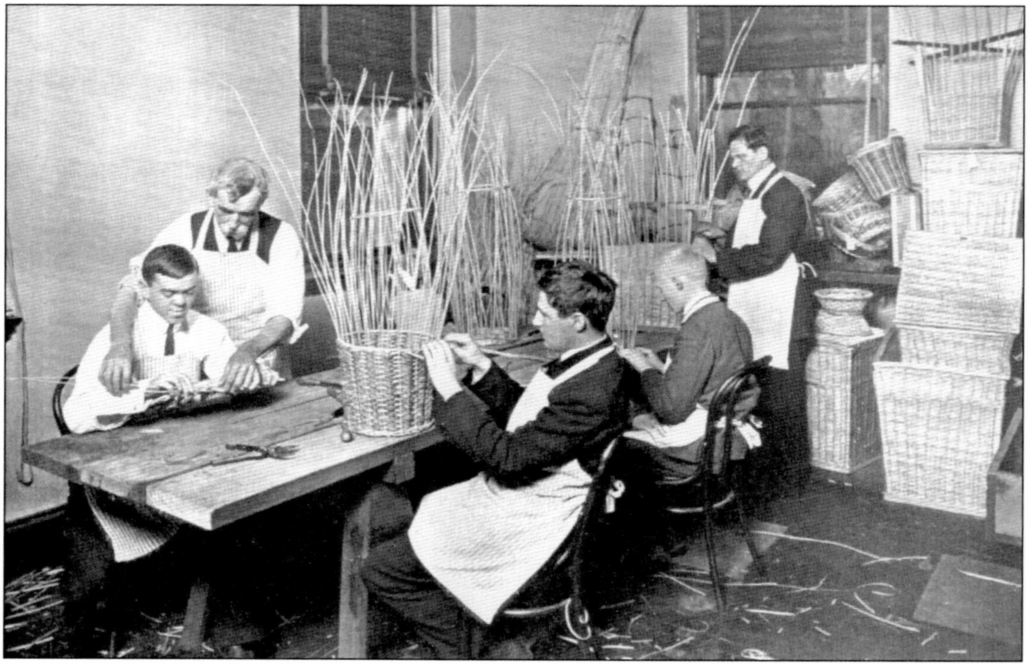

Making Baskets. Basketry, taught as part of the manual arts department, provided the students with the opportunity to learn a lifelong skill. The baskets were often sold at a store on Walnut Street. Here older boys sit at a table and use reed and cane to make their baskets.

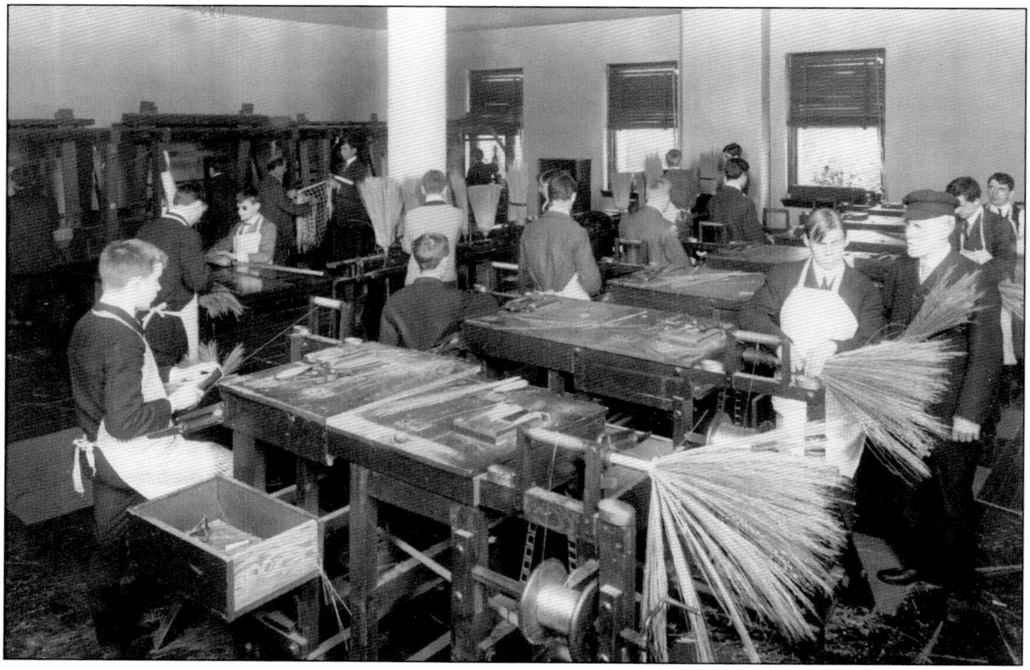

Broom-making Class, 1908. Boys learned how to make brooms, which were very popular because they were rugged and durable. Broom making was a skill that was very useful for students' future employment. In the rear of this photograph are looms used for creating hammocks.

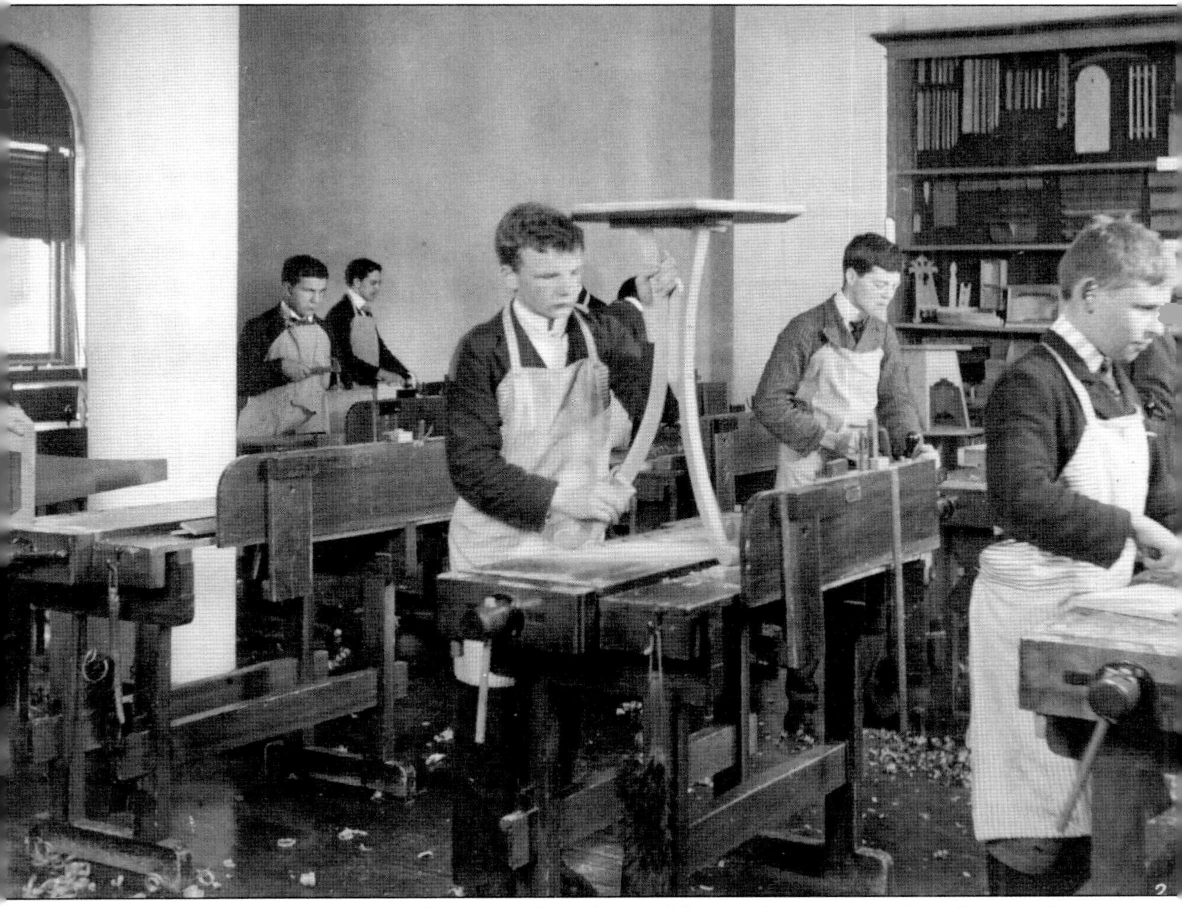

MANUAL TRAINING, 1889. Around 1889, a few of the older students were given lessons in woodworking, and by 1894, the subject had become part of the required instruction for all boys after kindergarten. The Sloyd course was then introduced. Founded by Uno Cygenaeus in Sweden, the Sloyd movement developed the use of practical handicrafts into manual training using principally wood. The work of the first year in elementary involved thin wood only and basic tools such as the knife, hammer, and nails. The work of the following years was more technical and made use of more tools, such as a level, mallet, and spoke shave. At this time, each grade of boys was given two hours of Sloyd.

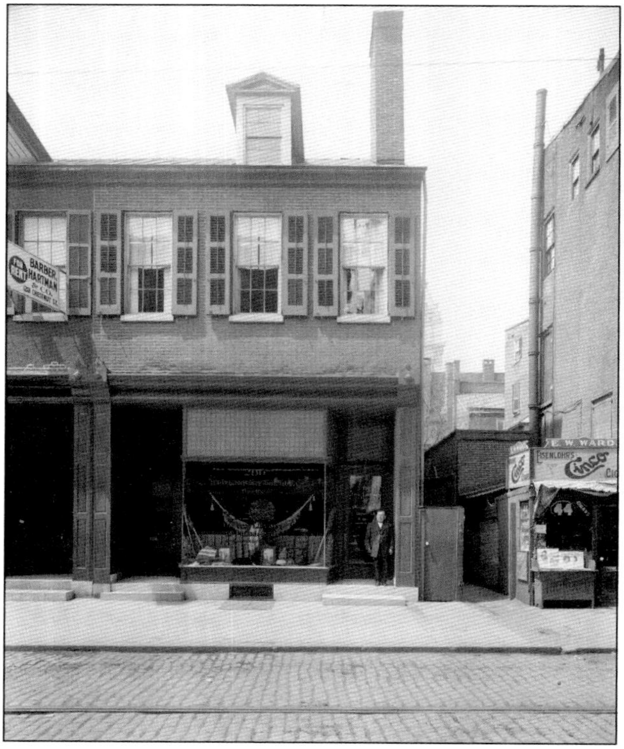

CENTER CITY STORE. Opening in 1911, the Overbrook Salesroom and Exchange Store sold goods made by students and blind adults. The building was located on South Thirteenth Street.

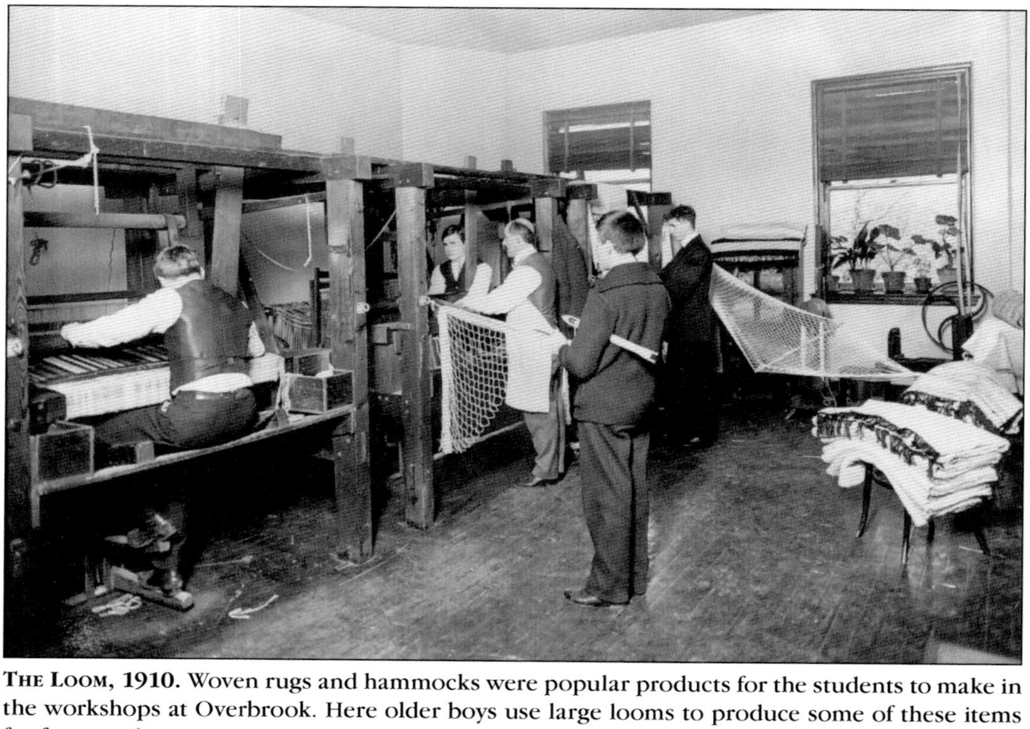

THE LOOM, 1910. Woven rugs and hammocks were popular products for the students to make in the workshops at Overbrook. Here older boys use large looms to produce some of these items for future sale.

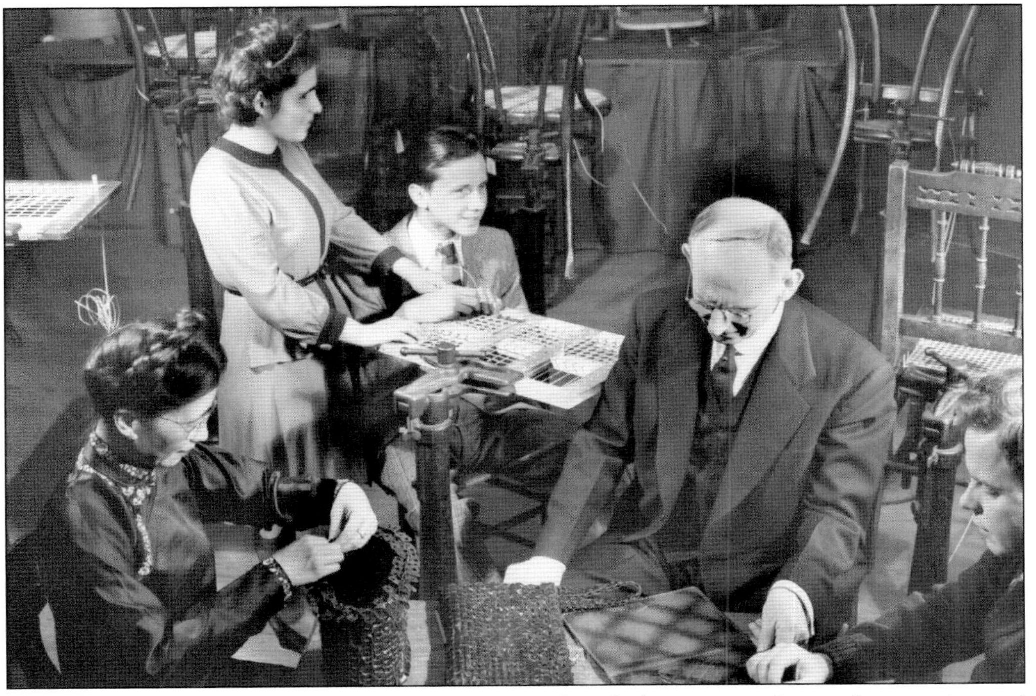

Caning and Leatherwork. Herbert Hartung, an Overbrook alumnus, teaches students caning and leatherwork. Some students make handbags while another works on a handwoven seat.

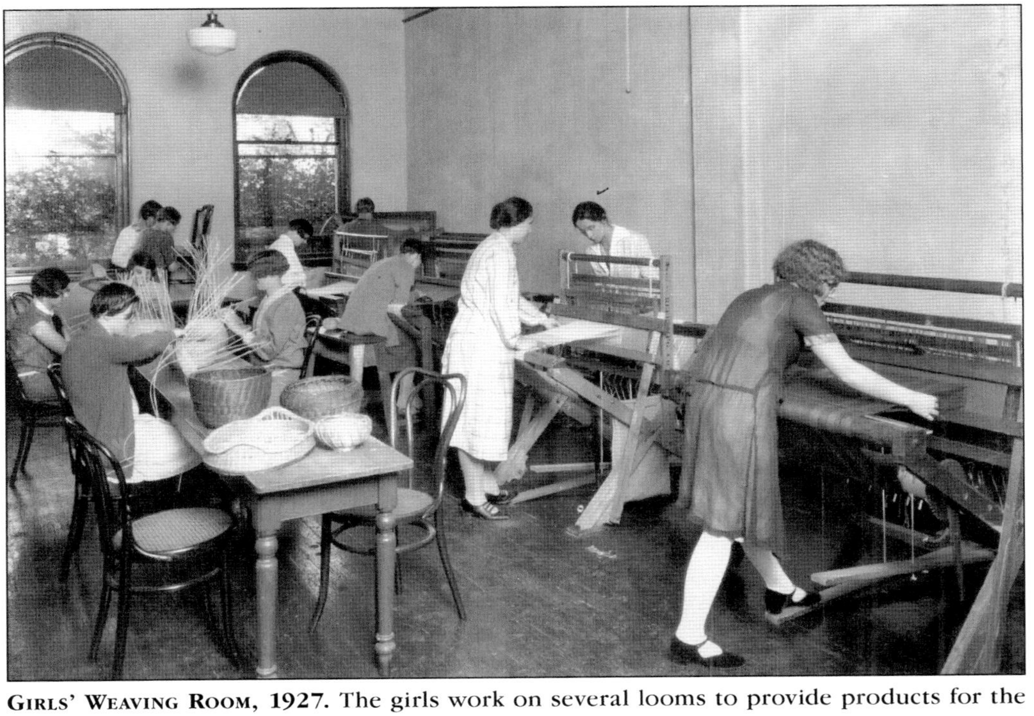

Girls' Weaving Room, 1927. The girls work on several looms to provide products for the Overbrook Salesroom and Exchange Store.

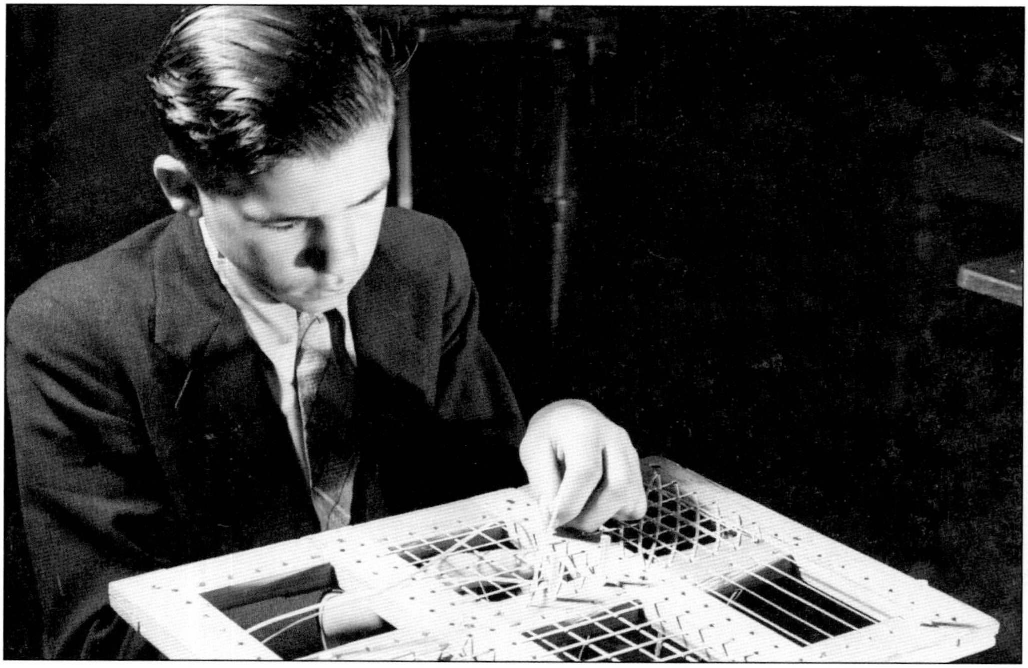

Caning, 1949. Career training was an important part of each student's educational program. Caning gave students an opportunity to earn money while in school and to learn a skill for future employment. In this photograph, a student practices his caning on a board held in place by a metal vice.

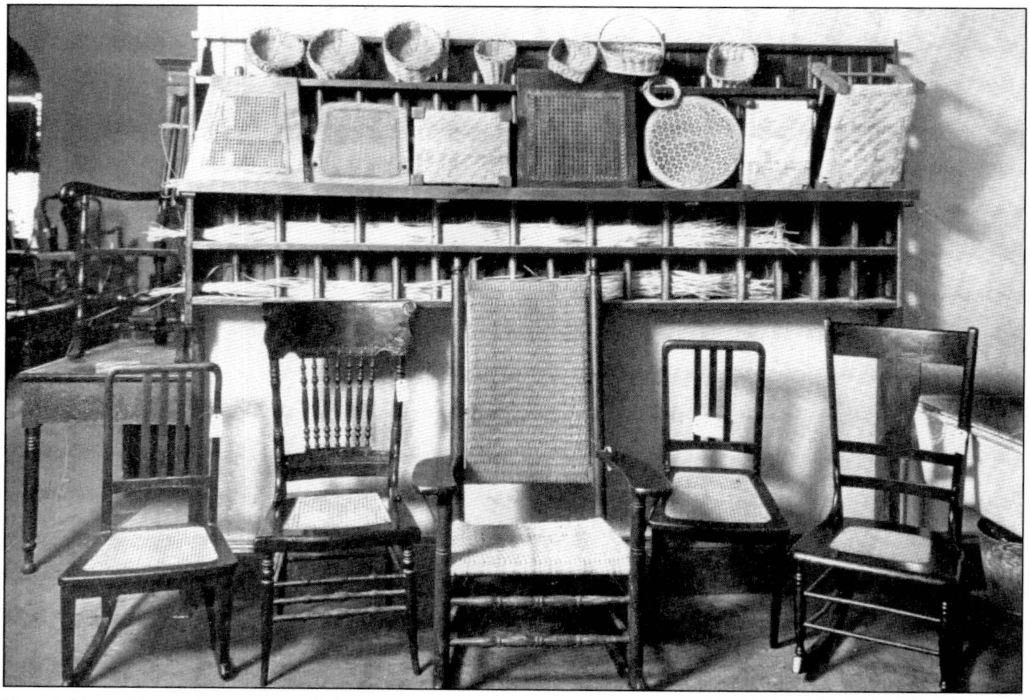

Boys' Cane Shop. A variety of chairs and baskets are made in the boys' cane shop.

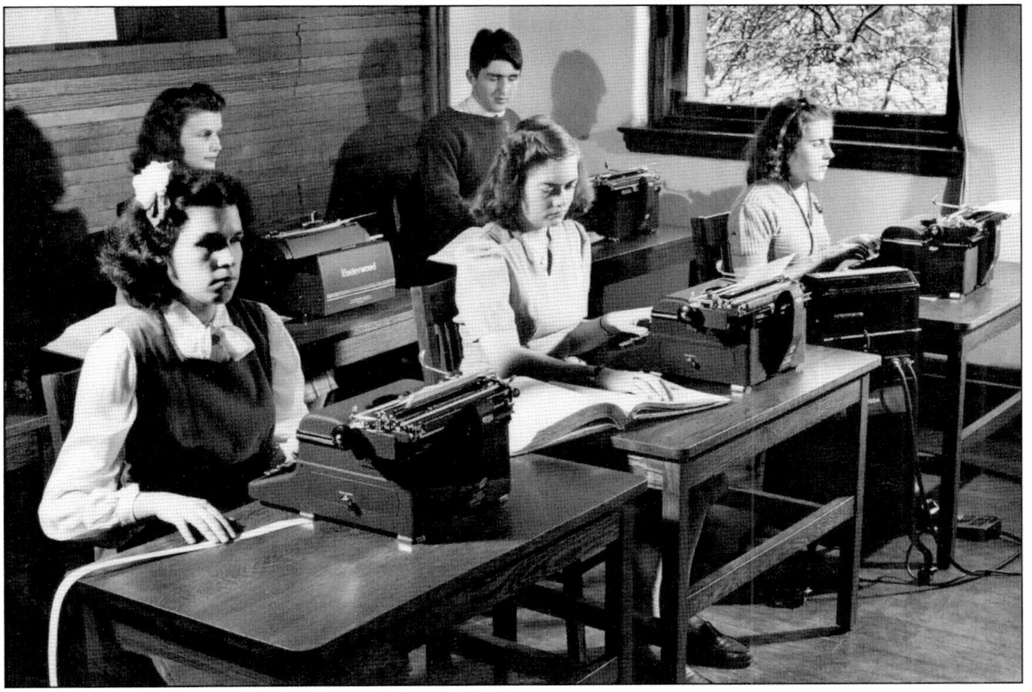

Typing and Ediphone Transcription. Overbrook involved students in the technology of the time so they could have jobs in competitive settings. In this class, four girls and one boy sit at wooden desks with typewriters. Some are transcribing using an ediphone while others just practice typing.

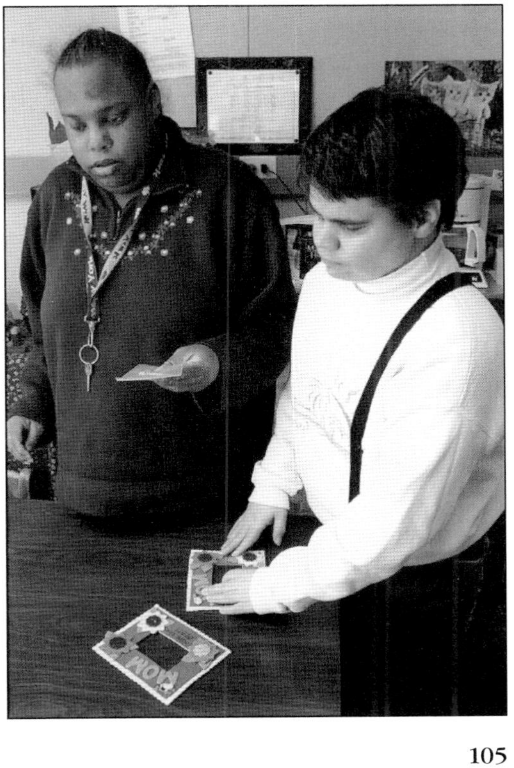

On Our Own. Learning does not end after graduation. To support adults and provide them with work opportunities, the school established the Overbrook Friedlander Programs in 1986. Graduates of Overbrook, as well as individuals from the community, live in apartments on campus and in the neighborhood. The men and women in the program work during the day or enjoy participating in community activities. These two women, for instance, make cards to sell during the holidays.

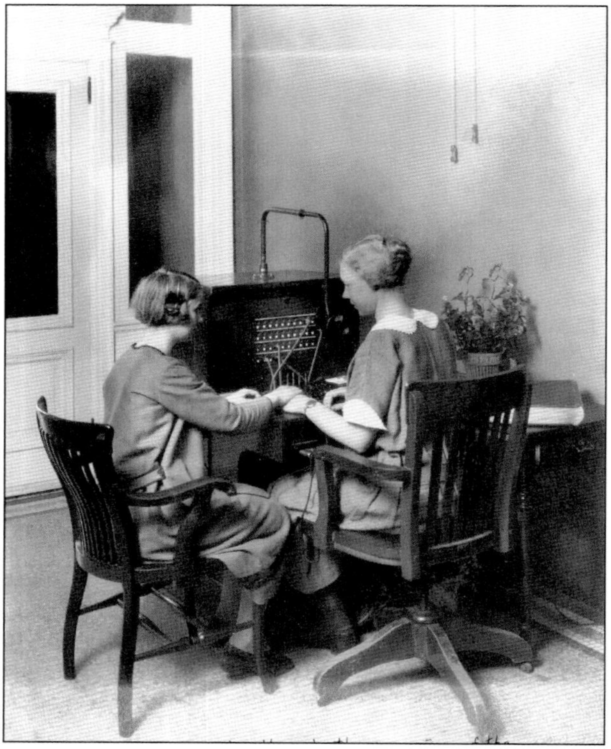

Early Communication, 1926. As soon as the technology was available, students were taught to run the telephone switchboard. In 1926, Agnes Locuson instructs Louise Hess in the switchboard's operation. Students looked forward to being the voice of Overbrook. Over the years, many students have had successful jobs as telephone operators in companies throughout the country.

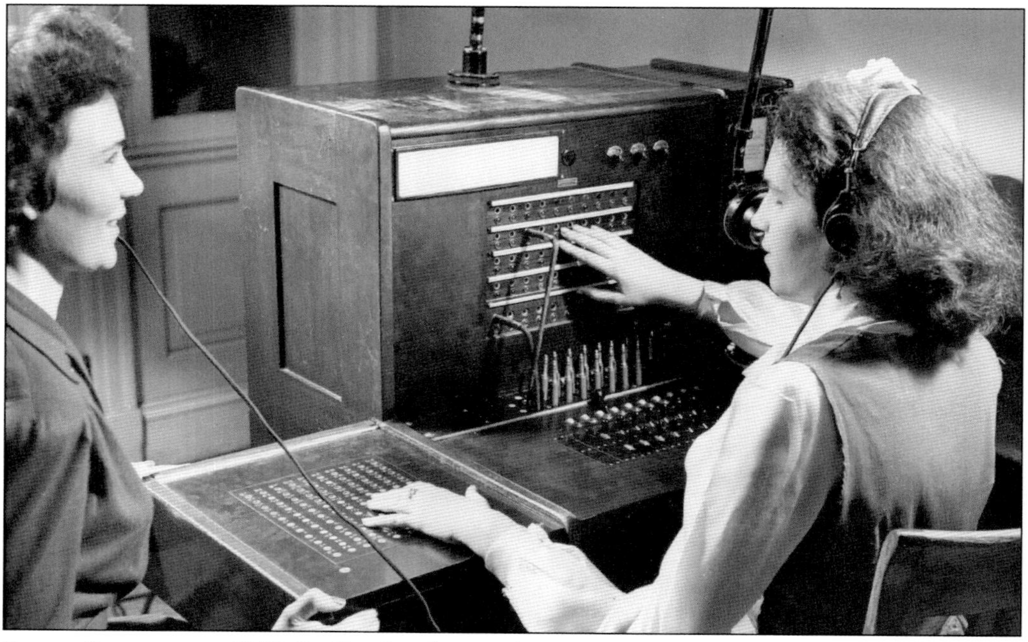

Braille Switchboard, 1948. Dr. Mae Davidow teaches a student to operate a braille PBX switchboard, a system with manual cords. Instead of lights flashing to indicate an incoming call, small pins pop up. The student feels along the board in front of her for the protruding pin, then finds the relevant extension and plugs in the cord to connect the call.

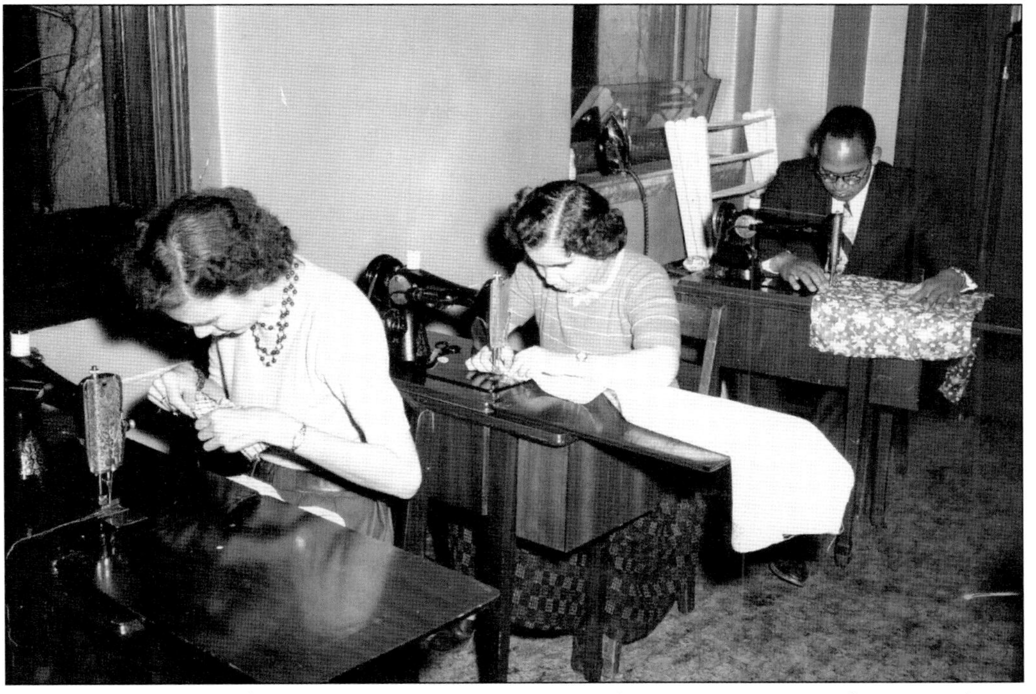

Pins and Needles, 1949. One male and two female students use sewing machines in a home economics class.

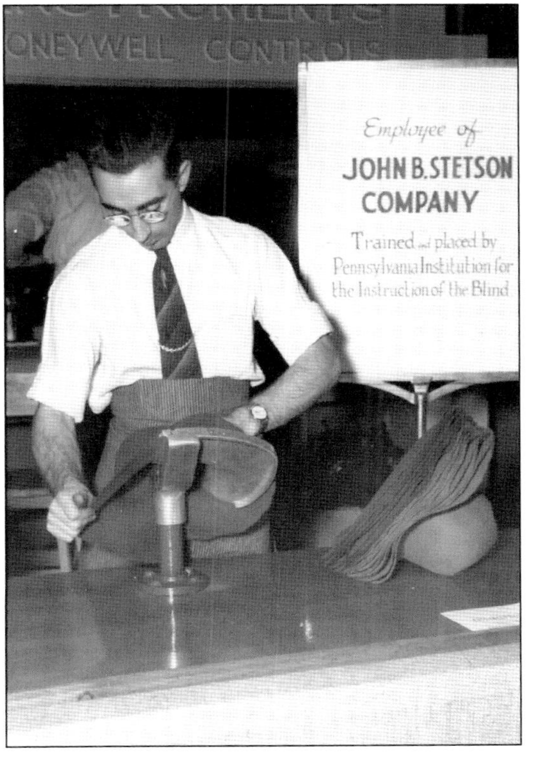

John B. Stetson Company, 1940. Using skills and confidence learned at school, an Overbrook graduate works as a hat shaper at the John B. Stetson Company.

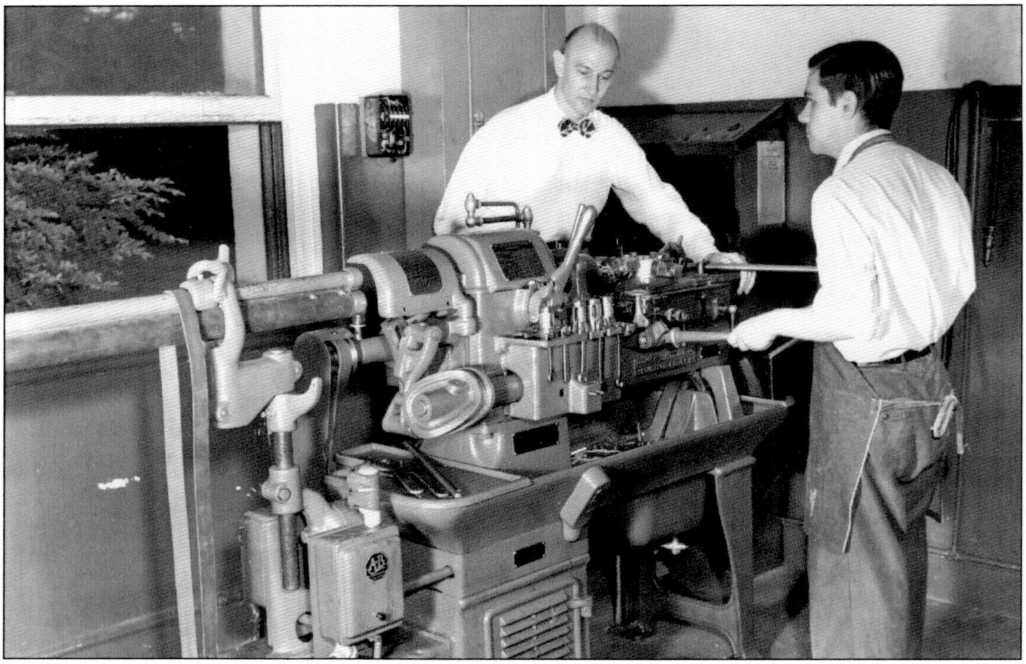

Industrial Arts, 1942. Typical machinery was used to learn mechanical trades. In this photograph, a student receives instruction on the Brown and Sharpe screw machine.

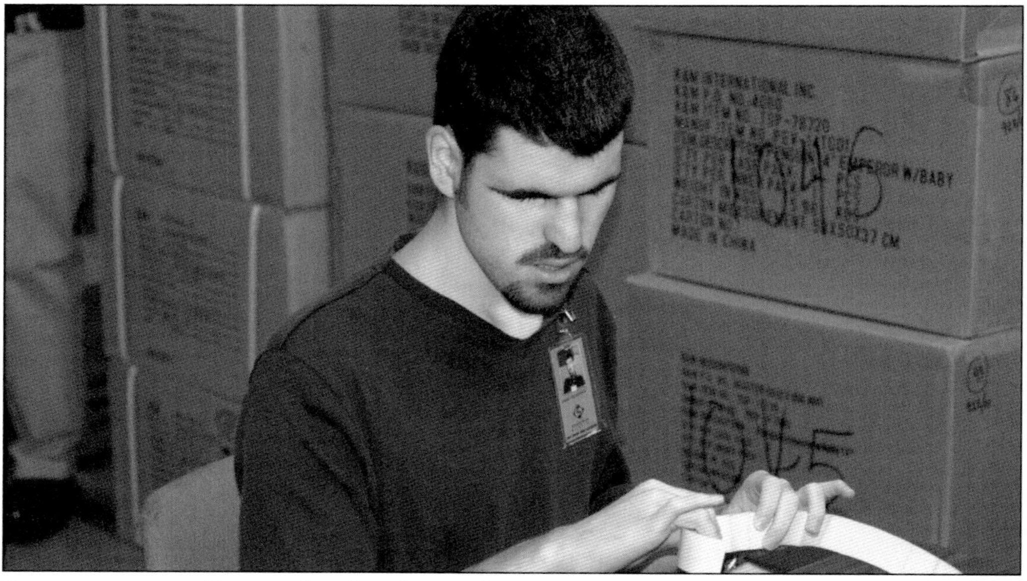

Preparing for the Future. Overbrook's production workshop is a facility where students fulfill work contracts the school secures from local manufacturers. In the workshop, students further develop their skills to complete tasks such as packaging parts, monitoring quality control, and operating equipment such as a heat sealer, a taping machine, a blister pack machine, and an automatic bagger. At the supported job site students can put into practice the interpersonal skills they have learned in the classroom, skills they will carry with them to all future jobs. Here a teenage boy seals a package.

Ham Radio Club, 1970. High in the tower of Overbrook, students gather to create their own radio program. The Ham Radio Club was made up of students interested in communications and electronics. In this photograph, three club members hold different communication devices.

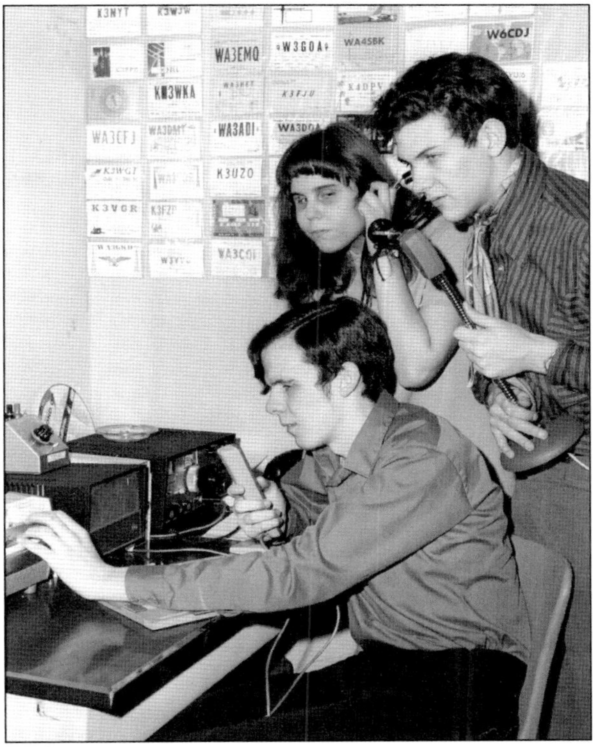

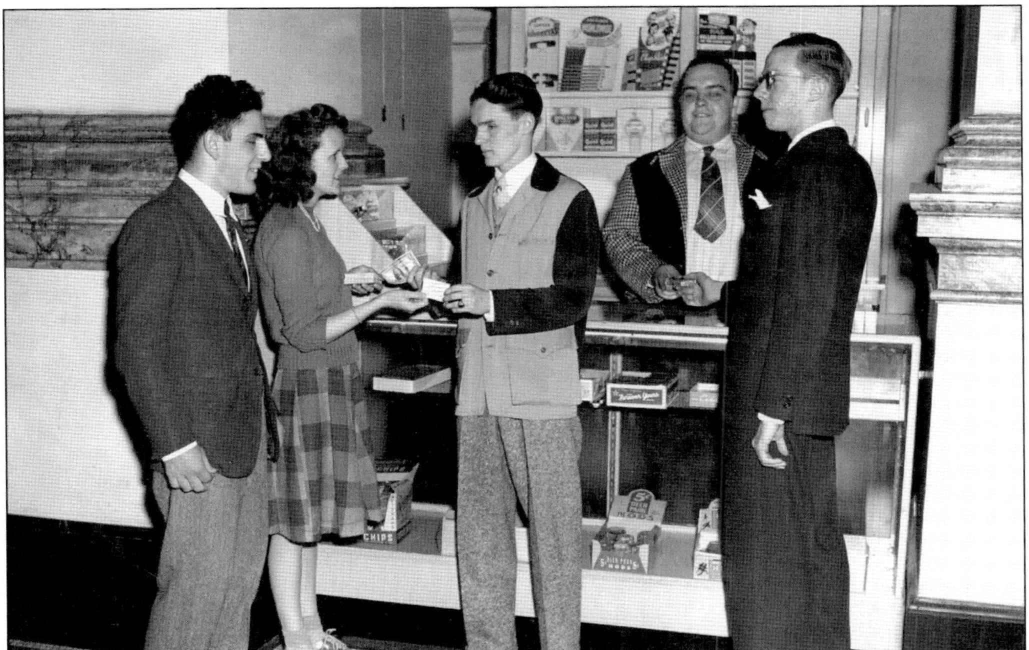

Vending Stand, 1947. Students line up to buy candy, ice cream, and toiletries from a vending stand operated by men and women who are blind. After World War II, Overbrook instituted a training course on how to run vending stands.

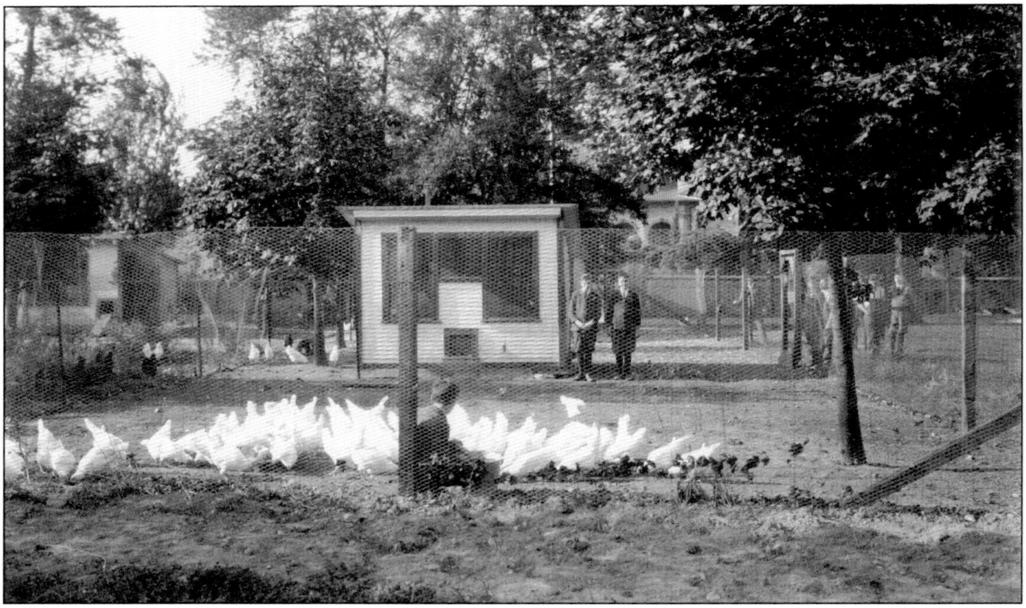

Poultry Raising. In 1921, the school decided to initiate an experiment in poultry husbandry. As part of the program, male students and their instructor constructed three houses, each with a capacity of four flocks of 30 birds each. There were also feeding and watering devices and a brooder stove. Very few of the pupils were expected to choose poultry raising as a vocation. The chief value of the program was a way to develop responsibility and provide a center of interest. In this photograph, students tend their flock.

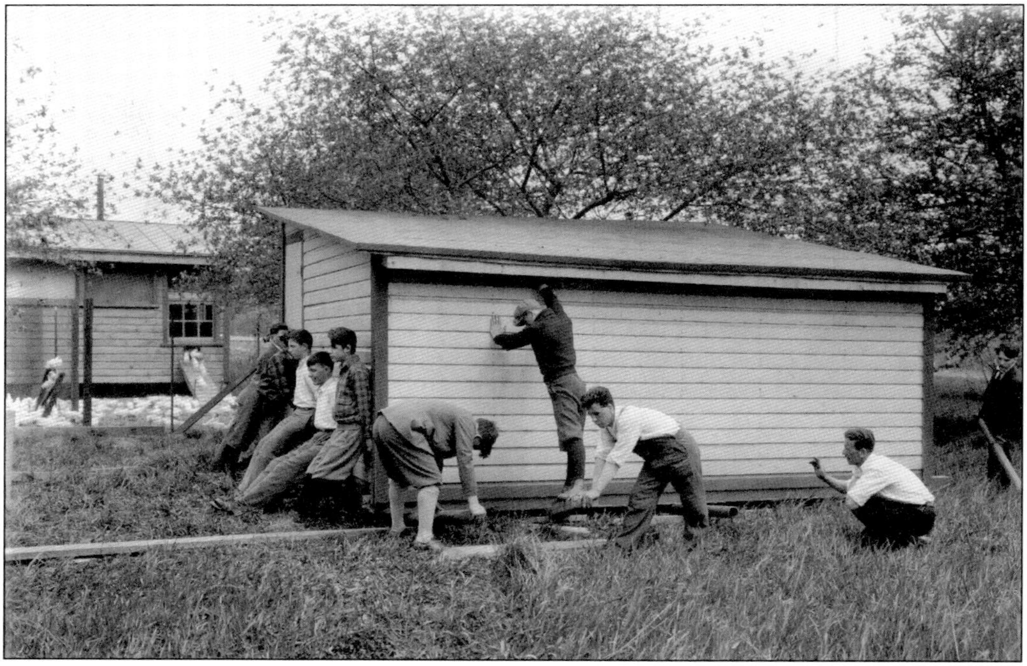

Poultry Keepers, 1925. A teacher instructs teenage boys on fundamental mechanical principles as they move a poultry house on skids.

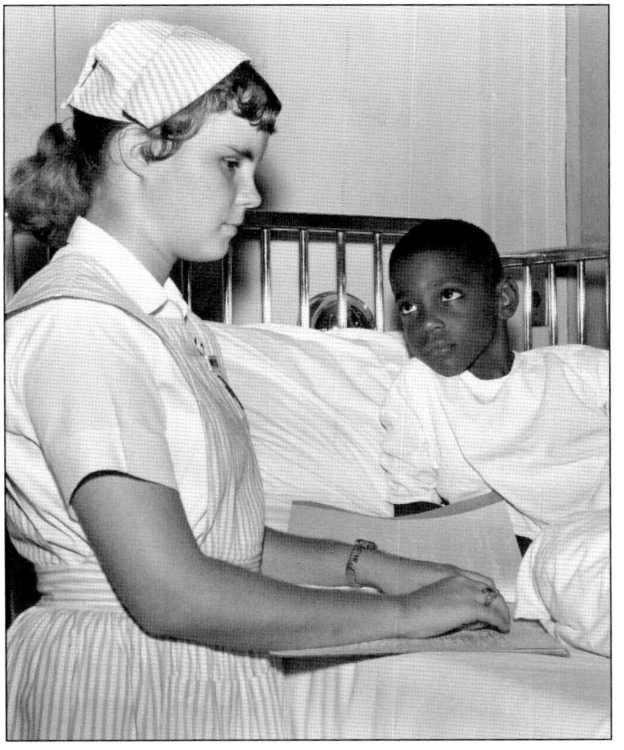

Red Cross Volunteer, 1968. This Overbrook senior was the only junior aide who was blind and worked in the American Red Cross volunteer program. She is pictured reading to a young patient in the Pediatrics Pavilion at the Delaware County Memorial Hospital.

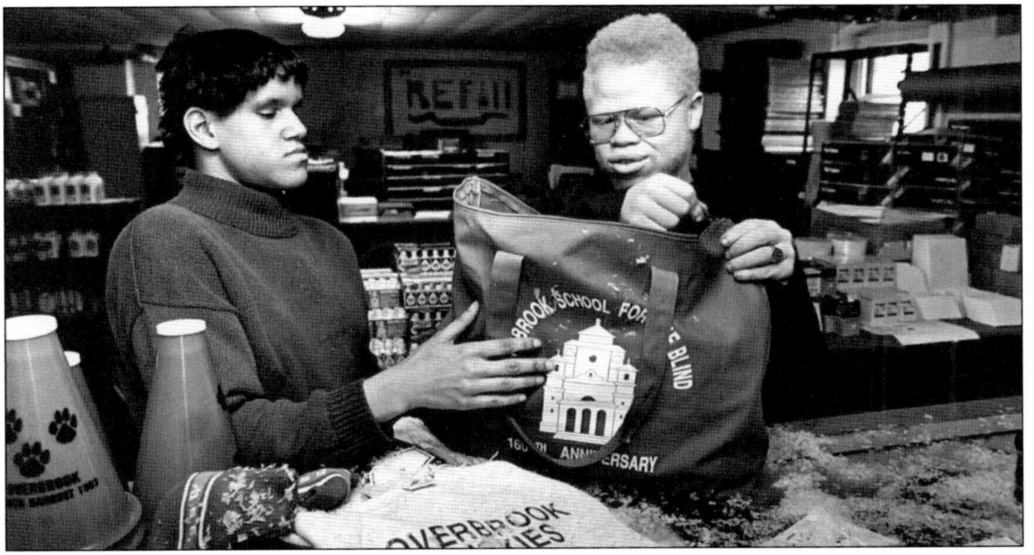

Paw Print Shop, 1995. Prevocational classes help students age 7 through 16 develop skills that are the foundation for getting and holding jobs. Staff members provide guidance on work-related behavior such as attendance, punctuality, and cooperation with coworkers. They also help students to develop the basic skills and attitudes, such as work-related vocabulary, manual dexterity, and gross and fine motor skills, they will need for success in life. The Paw Print Shop, which sells Overbrook insignia items and other school supplies, gives students the opportunity to work in a store setting. Here one student purchases an Overbrook bag from another.

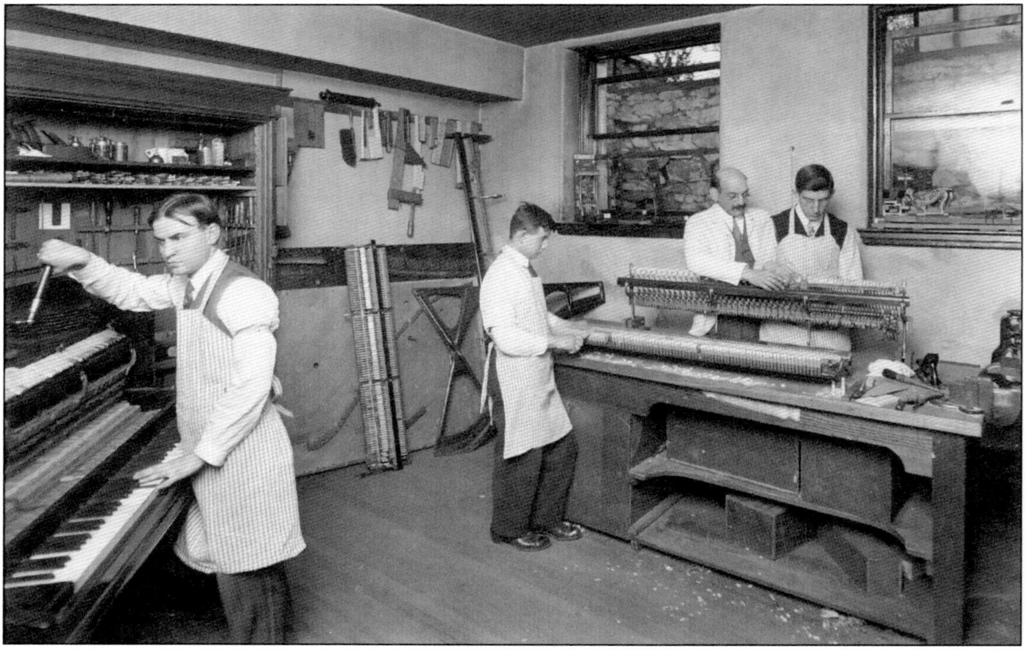

Piano Tuning. Piano tuning came to be a special branch in the music department. In this photograph, the boys are given a practical knowledge of the delicate machinery of the piano by participating in the instrument's construction.

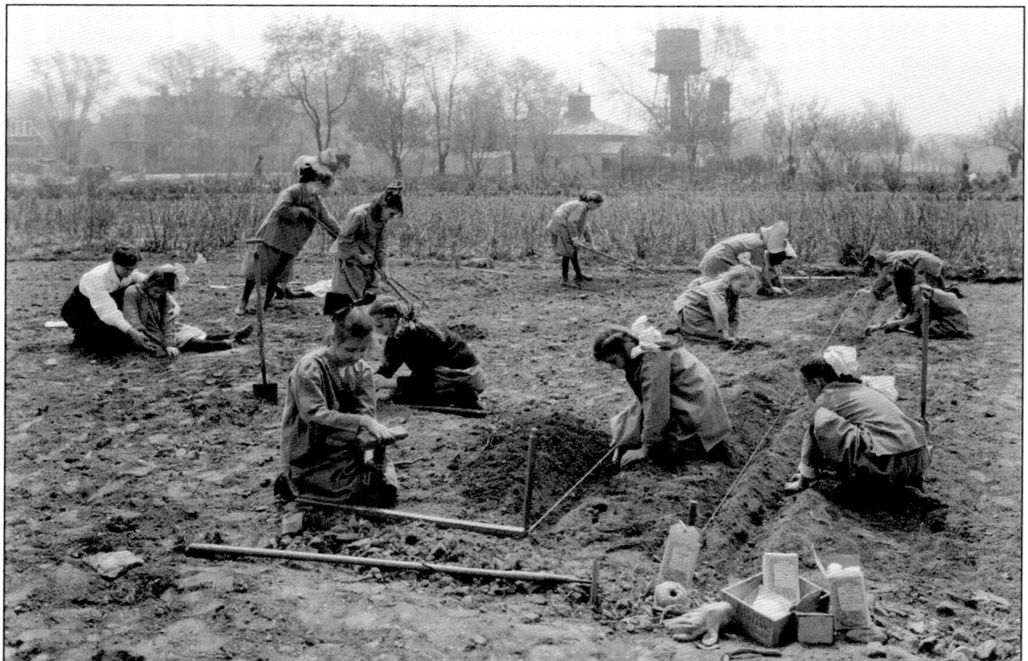

Tilling the Garden, 1912. Young girls till this garden to get it ready for planting. Seen in the background are the tanks for water from the artesian wells that supplied the school in the early years.

Eight

OUTREACH

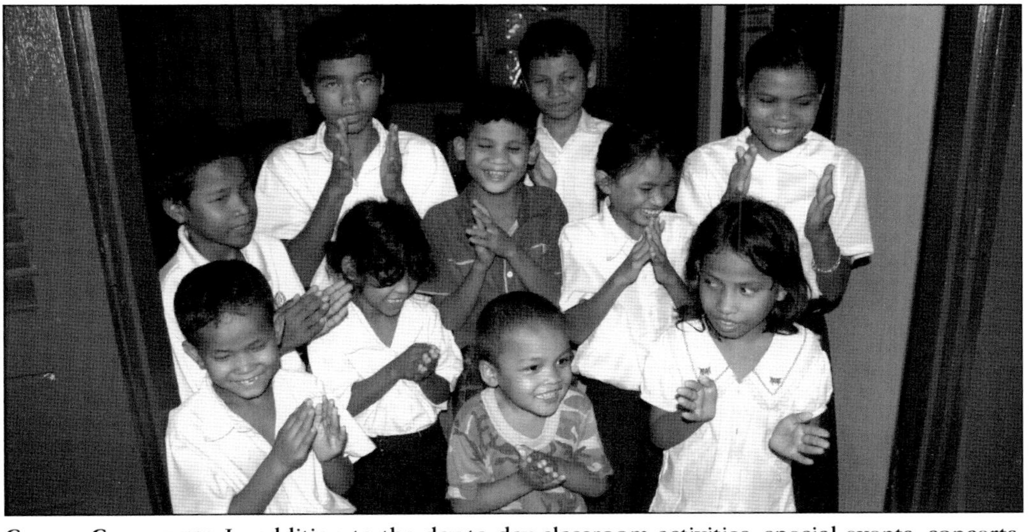

GLOBAL COMMUNITY. In addition to the day-to-day classroom activities, special events, concerts, competitions, and staff training sessions on Overbrook's campus, staff also work with local, state, national, and international communities to learn from others and to share their expertise. In the early years, students came from various countries around the world to complete their high school education. In some cases, Overbrook graduates developed services for the blind in the United States and abroad. Today local school districts, universities, and businesses receive assistance from Overbrook on how to make appropriate accommodations for people who are blind. During the 1980s, international students came to Overbrook to learn about assistive technology, to become independent travelers, to study English as a second language, and to develop leadership skills. These talented young people returned to their countries to demonstrate that individuals who are blind or visually impaired can compete alongside their sighted peers. During the years of the campus program, Overbrook developed a relationship with the Soros and the Nippon Foundations. These partnerships resulted in the development of international regional programs in eastern and central Europe and in Southeast Asia. Through these programs, Overbrook has assisted thousands of people throughout the world. Students have learned skills in assistive technology, entered school, and joined the workforce. Sharing information with others is key to the vision and the mission of Overbrook.

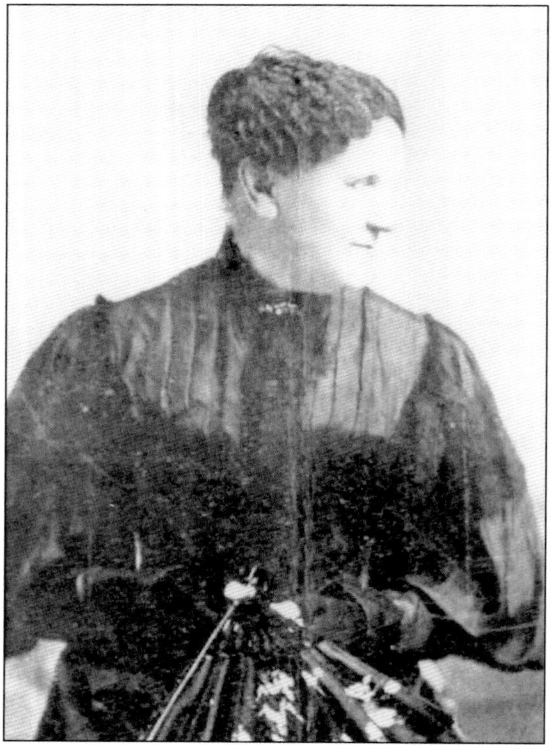

Hannah Guillian (1820–1898). Born in England and blind since age two, Hannah Guillian of Franklin County came to the Pennsylvania Institution for the Instruction of the Blind in 1834 as the 16th student under Julius Friedlander. She eventually became an instructor at the school, teaching reading and grammar, until 1852 when she transferred to the Georgia Academy for the Blind, where she remained principal until her death.

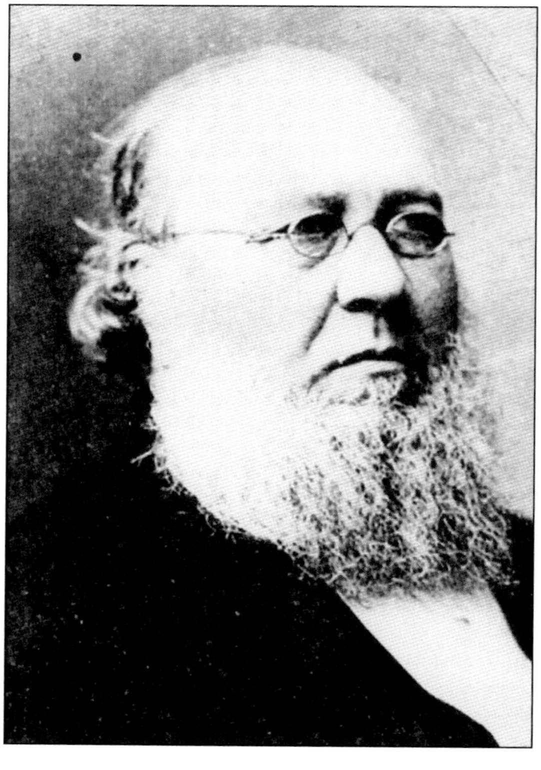

William Henry Churchman. Born in Baltimore of Quaker parents and blinded at age 15, William Henry Churchman entered the Pennsylvania Institution for the Instruction of the Blind and was a student under the direction of Julius Friedlander. After graduation, he started out as a private music teacher and later held teaching positions and principalships at the Tennessee School for the Blind, Indiana Institute for the Blind, and the Wisconsin School for the Blind. He was a founding member of the American Association of the Blind. This portrait of Churchman hangs in the Indiana School for the Blind.

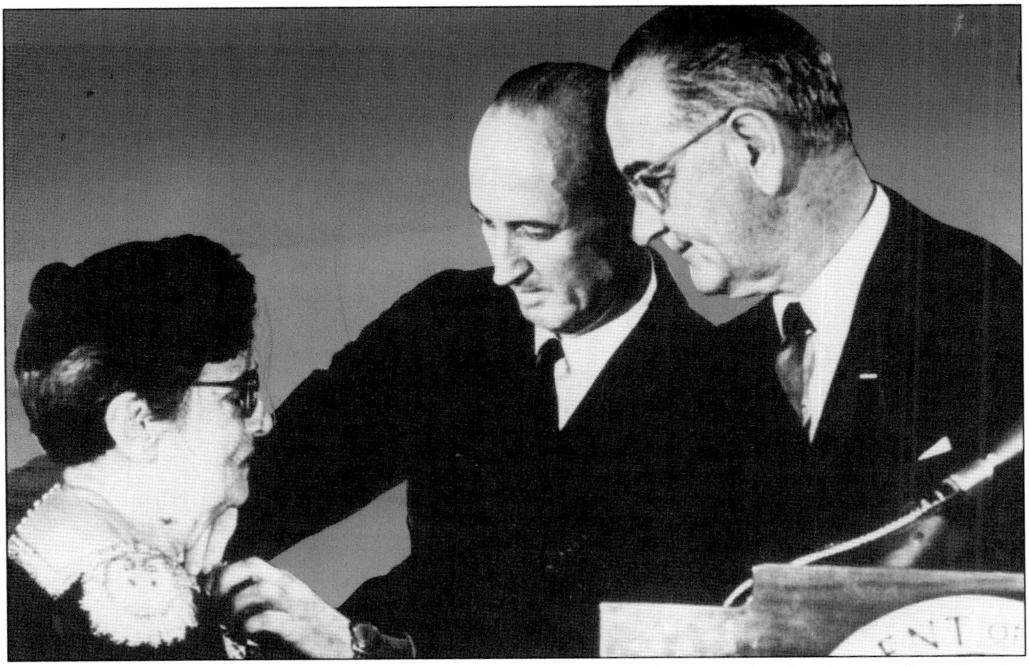

GENEVIEVE CAULFIELD (1888–1972). Genevieve Caulfield, blinded shortly after birth, transferred to the Pennsylvania Institution for the Instruction of the Blind in 1905. She received her teacher's certificate and bachelor of science degree from Columbia University in New York City. She went to Japan in 1923 and taught English to sighted people. In 1928, she traveled to Thailand, where she founded the first schools for the blind. In 1963, Caulfield was one of the first women to receive the National Honors Award, the Freedom Medal. In this photograph, Pres. Lyndon Johnson presents her with the medal.

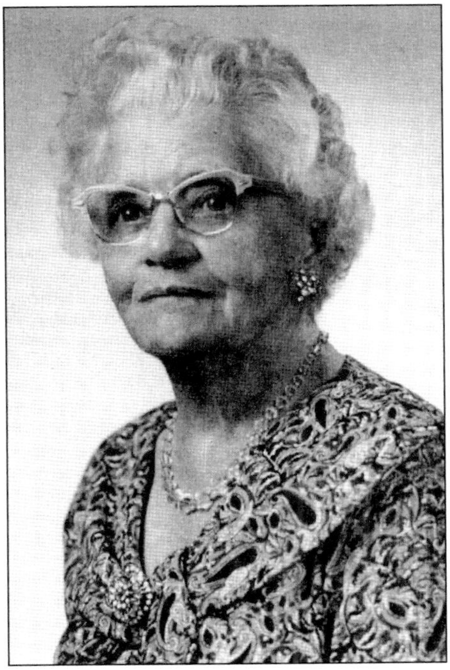

DR. JESSIE ROYER-GREAVES. In 1902, Dr. Edward Allen, principal of the Pennsylvania Institution for the Instruction of the Blind, hired Jessie Royer to become a teacher of physical expression on a part-time basis. The purpose of the class was to assist blind children in developing poise, balance, a muscular sense, and a sense of direction. Dr. Jessie Royer-Greaves went on to found the first school for children who were blind and mentally retarded in Strafford. Called Royer-Greaves School for the Blind, it was named for her husband and father.

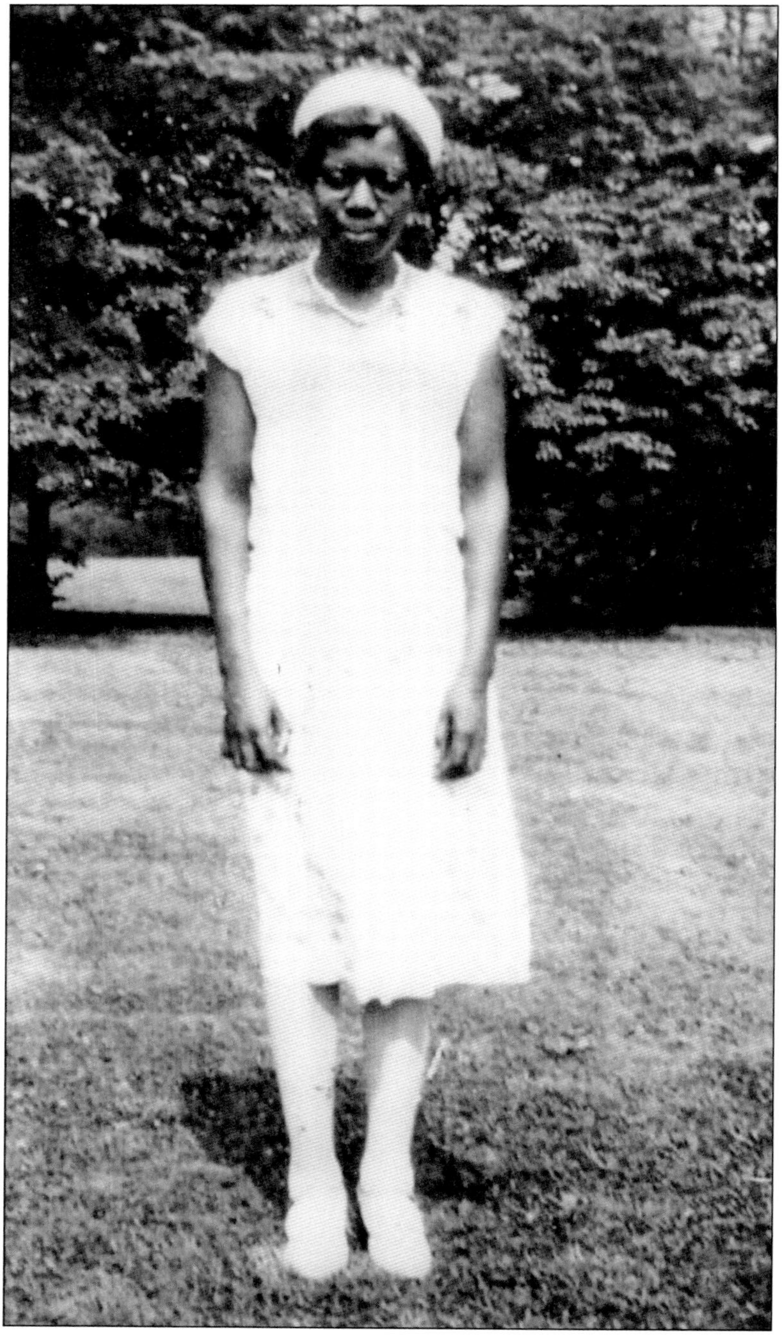

MARTHA MORROW FOX. Born in North Carolina in 1902, Martha Morrow Fox's family moved to Philadelphia in 1919, and she was admitted to the Pennsylvania Institution for the Instruction of the Blind. She graduated in 1928 and enrolled in the home teaching course. The course taught workers to go into homes of the blind to train the residents in living skills and handicrafts. Given the opportunity to teach a group of black children, however, Fox moved on to Mississippi and the Piney Woods Country Life School.

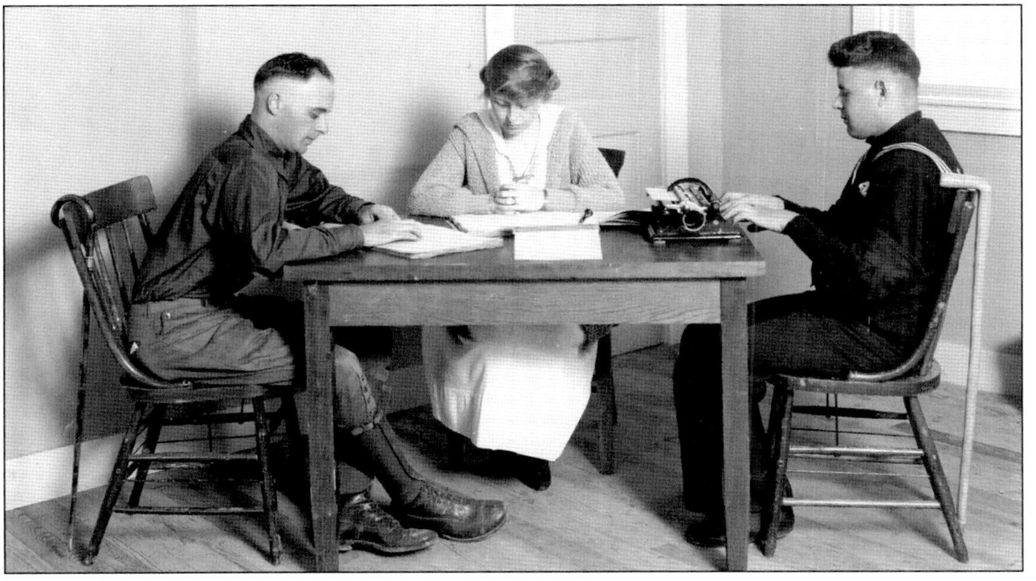

Assisting Veterans, 1918. In an announcement in the official bulletin of his office on April 2, 1918, the surgeon general of the United States defined a sweeping policy of thorough government care of every wounded or disabled man. Also announced at that time were the hospitals to begin the work of physical reconstruction of wounded American soldiers and sailors. General Hospital No. 7, or Evergreen, had been provided on the estate of Mrs. T. Garrison Garrett in Roland Park, Baltimore. Clara Croff Stilwell, shown here with a soldier and a sailor, had been a teacher at the Pennsylvania Institution for the Instruction of the Blind and was hired at Evergreen as a teacher of braille and writing.

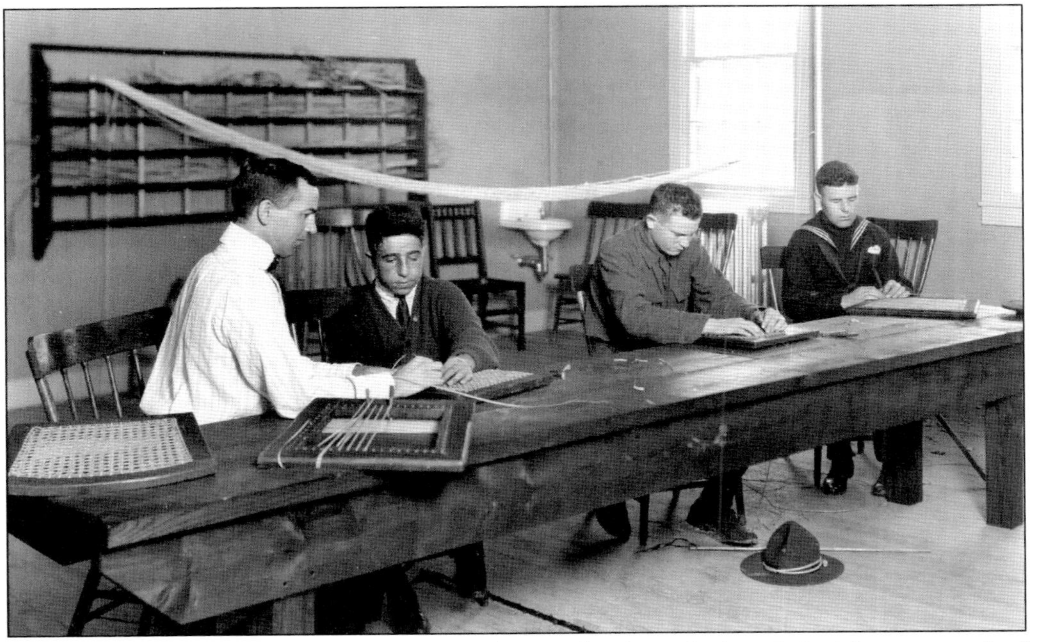

Learning New Skills. Wounded American soldiers and sailors who lost their vision as a result of the war receive training in how to cane chairs, at Evergreen.

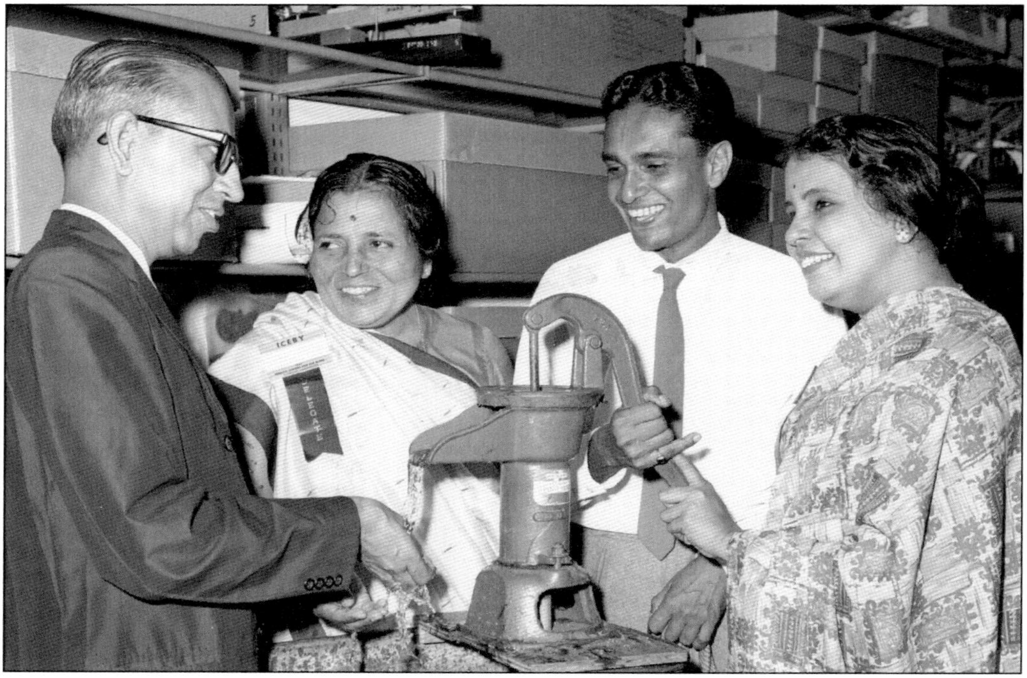

International Visitors, 1967. Delegates from India, en route to the International Conference of Education of Blind Youth, visit the Touch and Learn Center and examine the water pump.

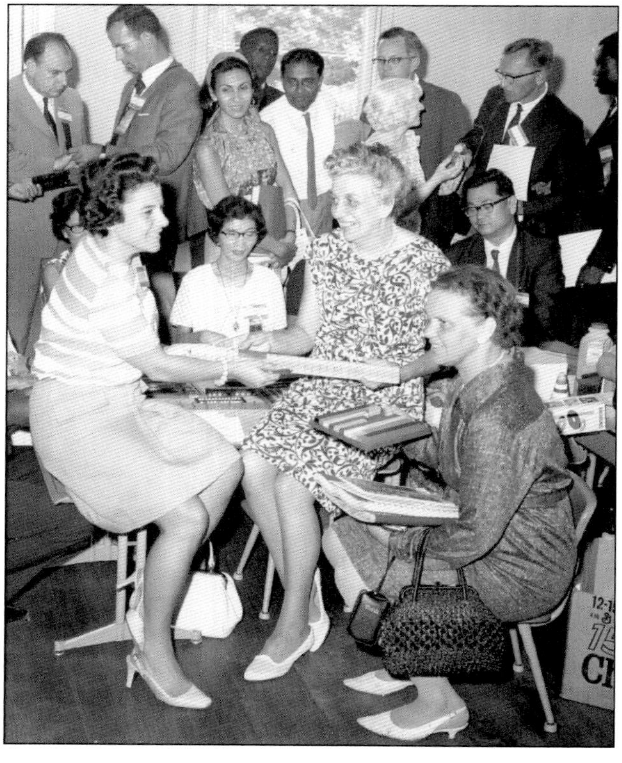

Learning from Each Other. Visitors from Finland and Portugal also visited Overbrook on their way to the International Conference of Education of Blind Youth. Elizabeth Sigafoos (center), supervisor of the primary school, goes over teaching aides for young pupils with this group of foreign educators.

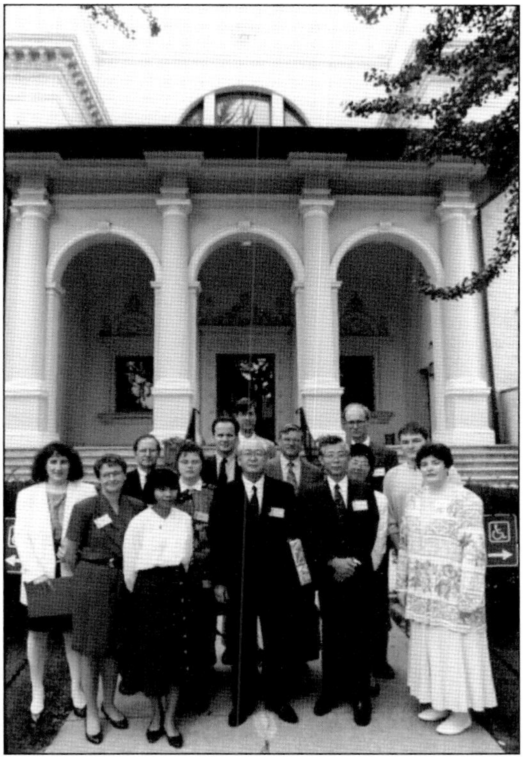

Welcoming Friends. Staff, board members, and students gather to welcome guests from the Nippon Foundation. In the late 1980s, the school was fortunate to receive an endowment for the International Student Program. From this partnership, Overbrook and Nippon strengthened their relationship, and once again the foundation gave a very generous endowment to develop regional programs in Southeast Asia.

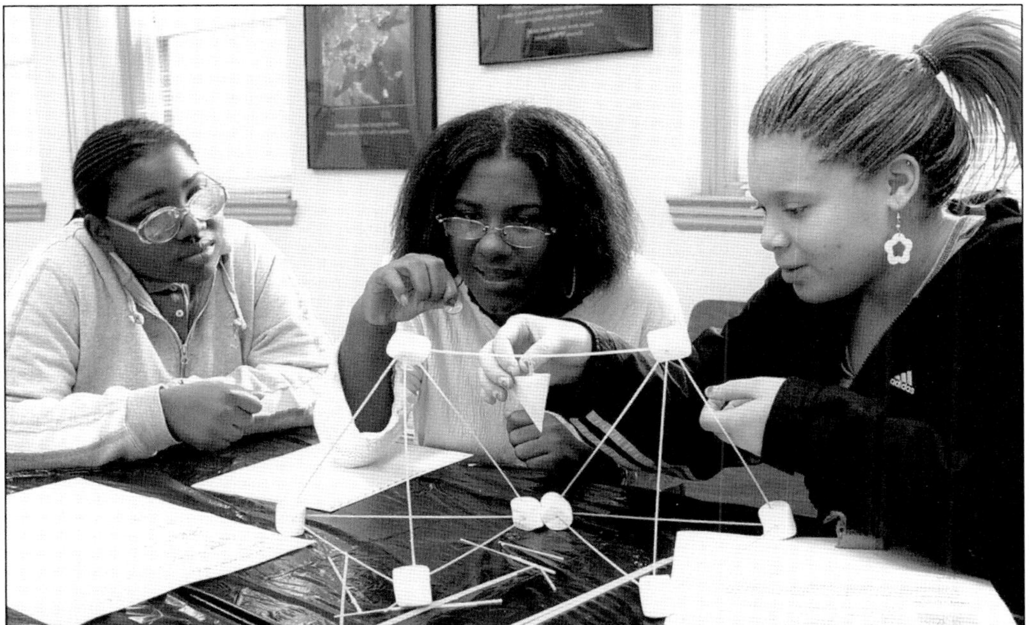

Exploring Technical Careers. Students at Overbrook have an opportunity to learn about careers in science, technology, engineering, and math through a partnership with IBM. The students work with IBM staff members to broaden their knowledge of careers they might pursue after graduation.

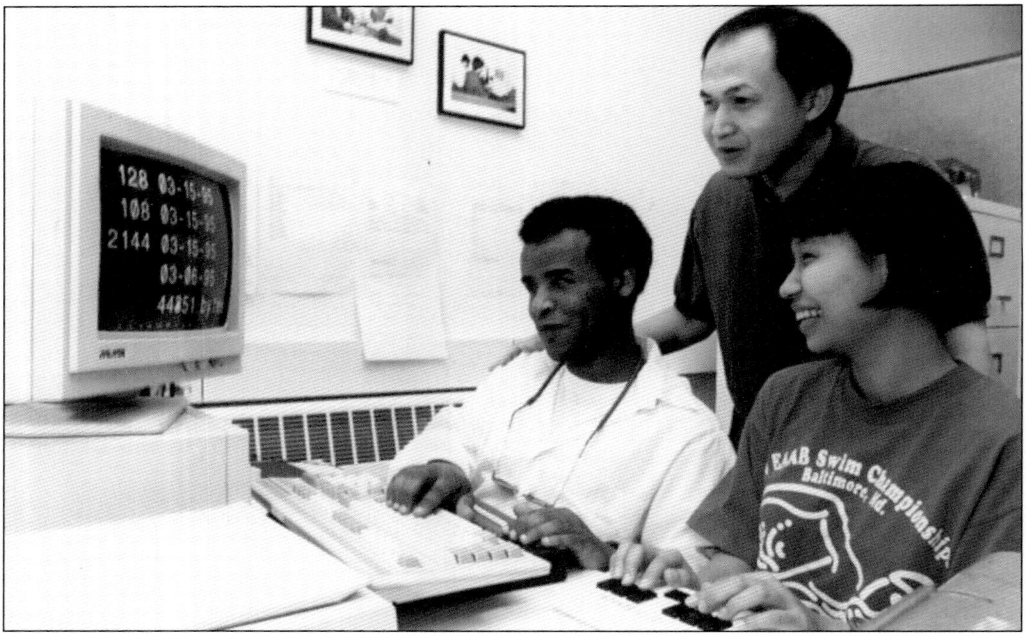

Opening the World. Learning on computers with appropriate access software and hardware expanded the educational and vocational opportunities for students in the International Program. When the students returned to their countries, they were able to enroll in universities and seek employment in more varied careers. During the yearlong program, students used computers in all their classes and spent many hours in the laboratory refining their skills. These students are working on a project with Wiraman Niyomphol, the computer technology teacher and a former student.

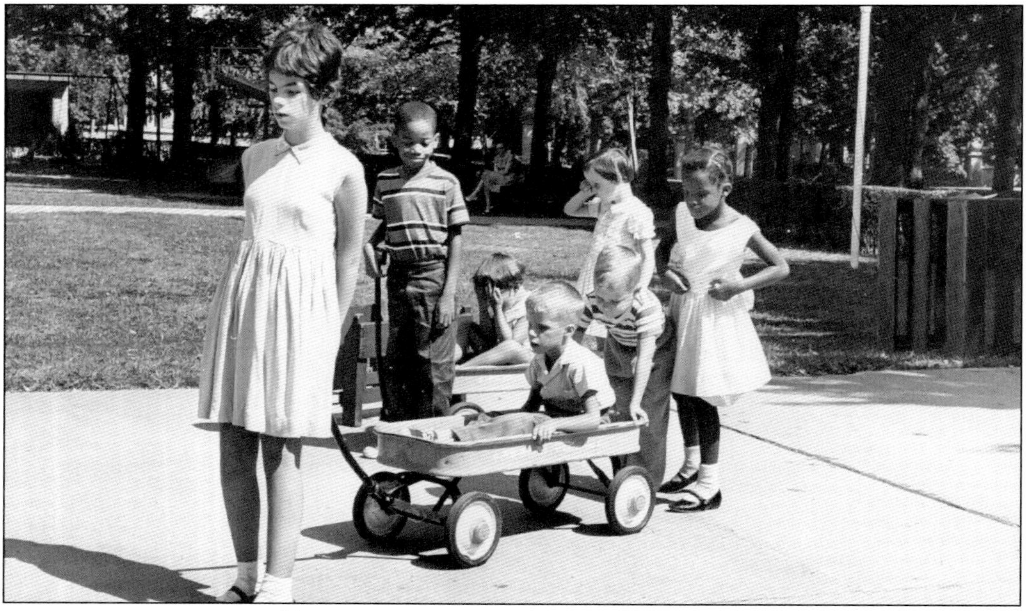

First Day of School, 1964. International student Milagros Ochoa, from Mexico, pulls a new American friend in a wagon on her first day of school at Overbrook. Throughout the years, students from different countries attended Overbrook.

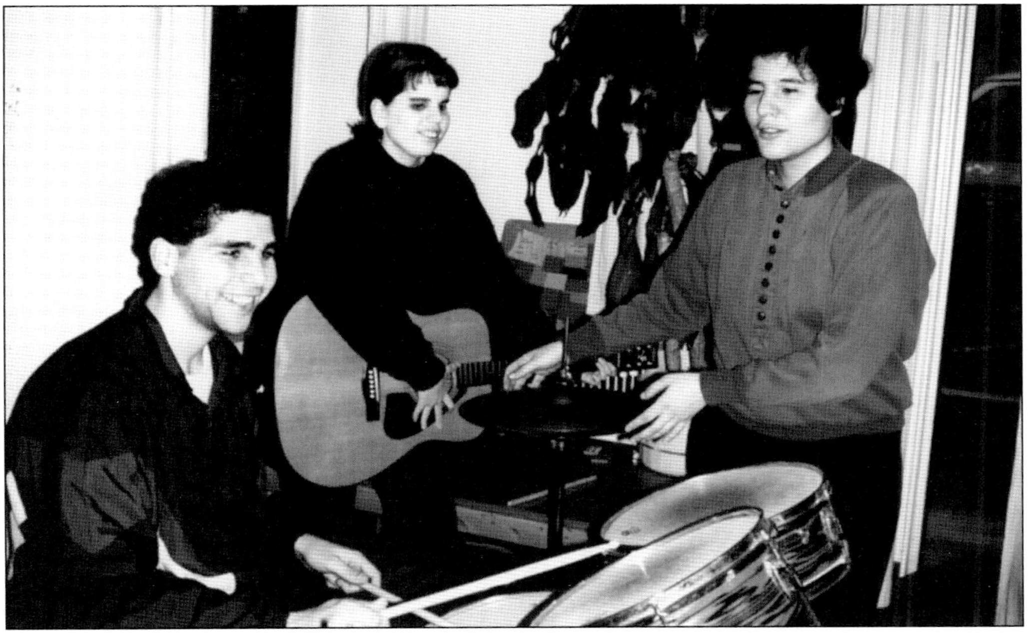

No Boundaries. Students from different countries enjoy making music together. The International Program included a strong academic regimen, and students learned much from sharing cultural music and working together to create shows for other students and staff. Those in this photograph are jamming in the living room in Friedlander Hall.

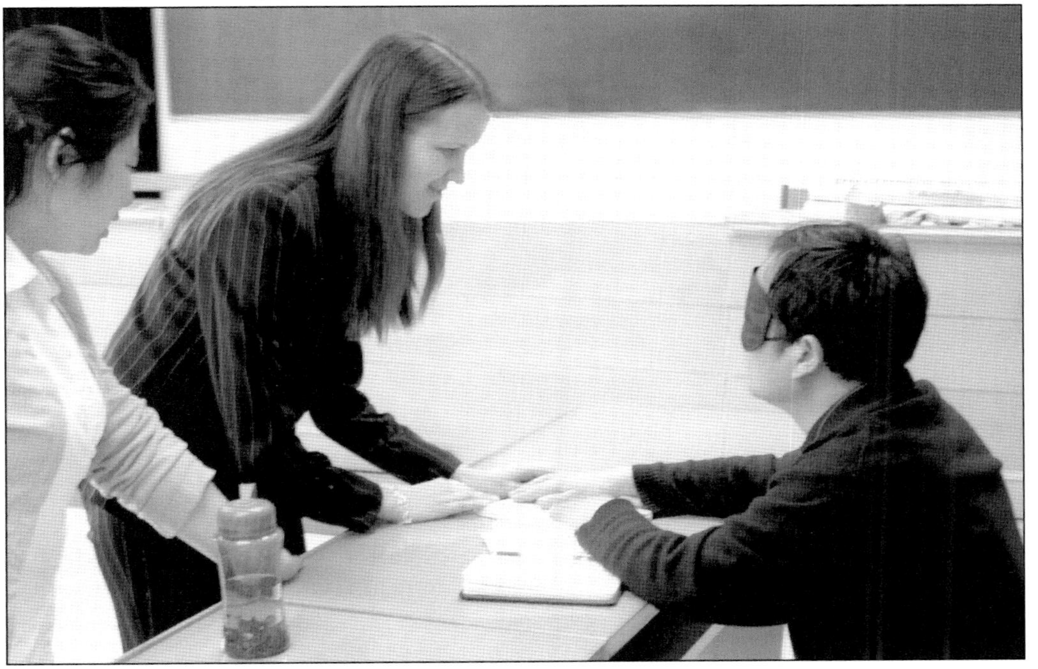

A Former International Student. Daniela Dimitrova, International Program alumnae, assists in training professionals from schools for the blind in China. During the training, she focused on creating high expectations for the students in the various schools.

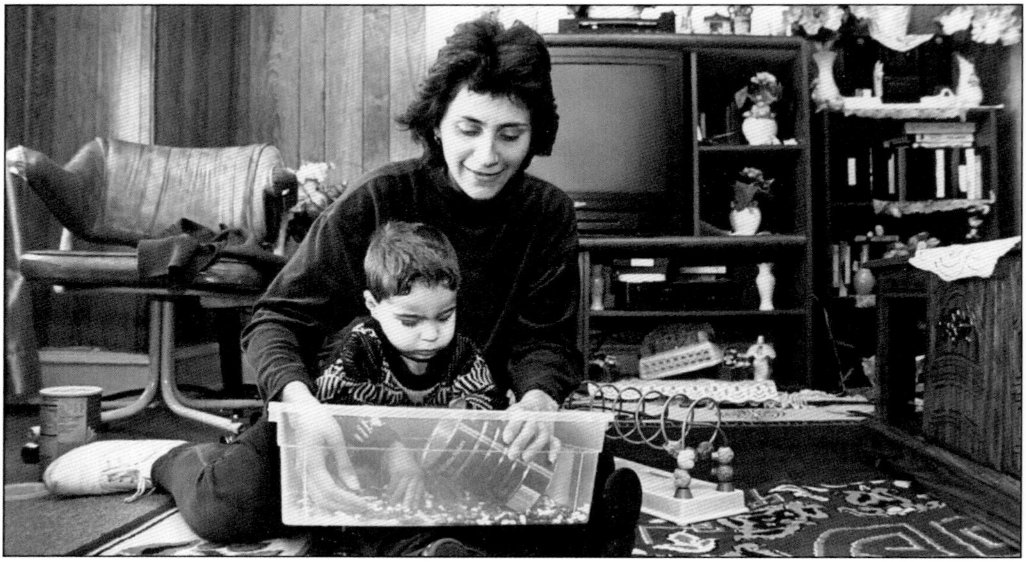

Playing at Home. Early intervention teachers visit the families of children ages newborn to three in their homes. During the visits, the teacher assists the parents in learning strategies they can incorporate into their daily routines. Here the teacher encourages the toddler to reach into a bin and find items to place in a can. Sensory experiences, especially touch, are important in the child's development.

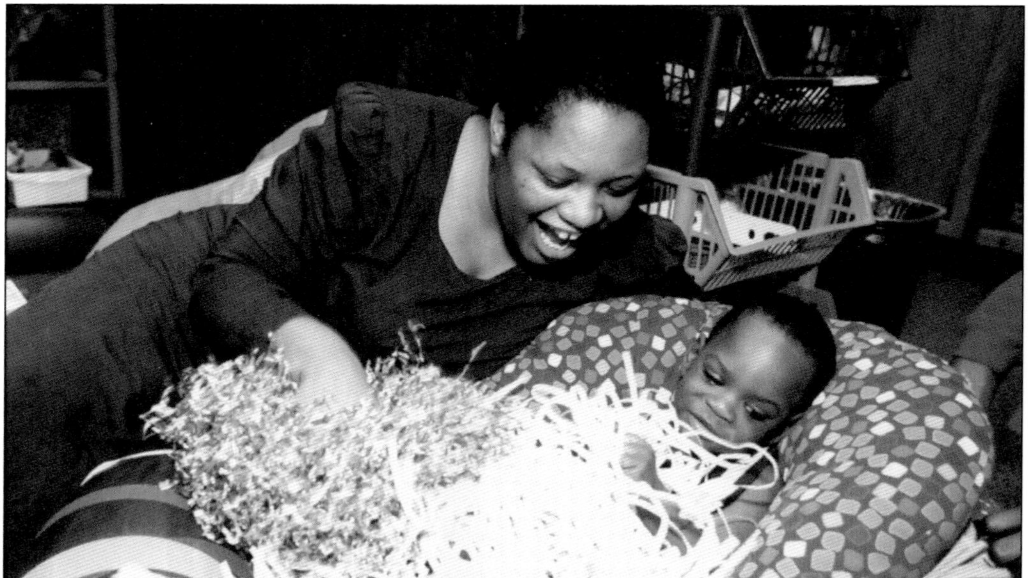

Learning with Their Children. In 1948, Overbrook established the Summer Nursery Program. Mothers came to Overbrook for two weeks to learn skills to help their babies attain typical developmental milestones. Over the years, the program has changed to meet the needs of the families. Today's program is a three-day workshop, and the baby comes with his or her mother, father, and sometimes even grandparents. The goals continue to be providing support for the family and an opportunity for families to meet and share their experiences. In this photograph, a parent and child play with metallic pom-poms.

INTERNATIONAL SUCCESS. Pecharat Techavachara was one of the early international students at Overbrook School for the Blind, and it was made possible by Genevieve Caulfield. After leaving Overbrook, he received a scholarship to Wharton School of the University of Pennsylvania and graduated with a bachelor's degree in economics. He was the first blind person from Thailand to earn a degree from a foreign university. He established the Foundation for the Employment Promotion of the Blind, a nonprofit organization established in July 1993, with the purpose of training blind people for various jobs. Blind men and women from throughout Thailand go to the foundation for the following courses: traditional Thai massage, braille, mobility and orientation skills, computer, telephone operator training, music, and astrology.

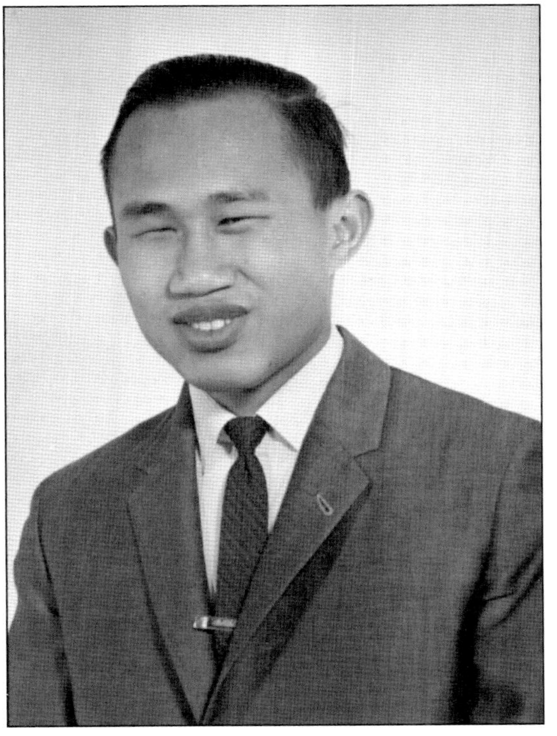

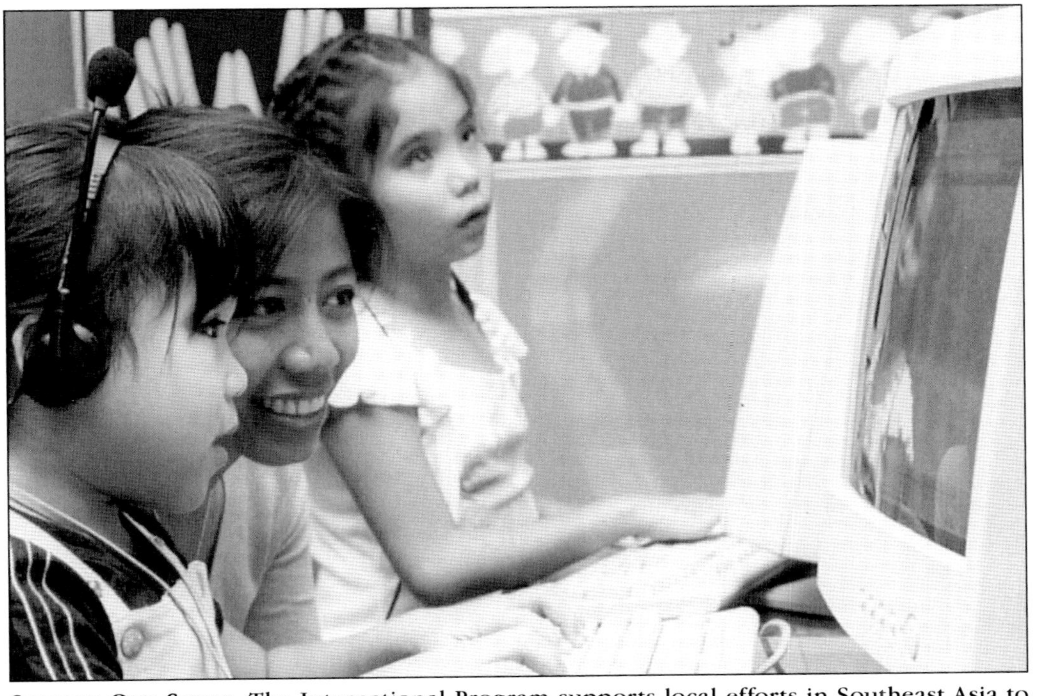

SHARING OUR SKILLS. The International Program supports local efforts in Southeast Asia to provide technology training for people who are blind. In this photograph, young students in the Philippines learn about access technology.

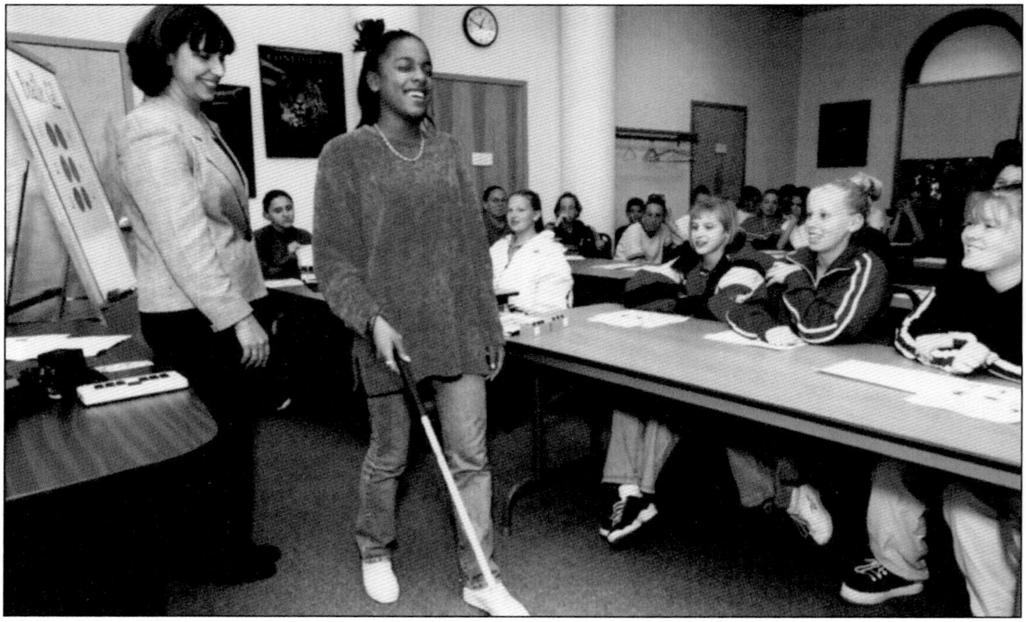

TRAINING SEMINAR. The Outreach Program runs workshops and training seminars for local school students and universities. Individuals may also come to the campus to learn more about visual impairment and blindness. In this photograph, Overbrook's outreach coordinator instructs a sighted high school student on how to hold a white cane.

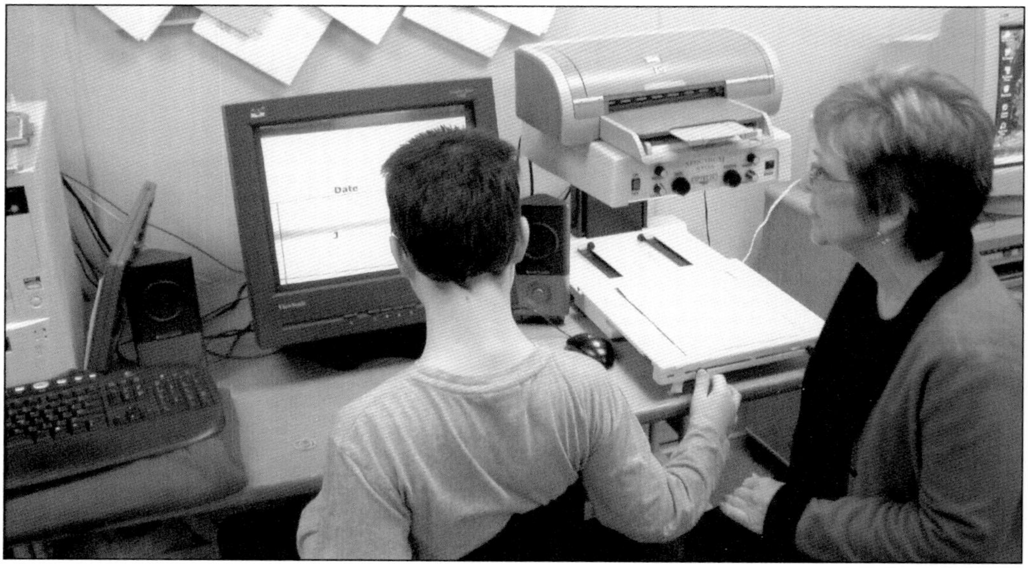

LOW VISION CLINIC. The Overbrook Low Vision Clinic is a collaborative effort between Overbrook School for the Blind and the Pennsylvania College of Optometry and serves the unique needs of Overbrook's students. At the Overbrook Low Vision Clinic, students receive thorough specialized eye examinations for the purpose of determining needed optical corrections and low-vision aids. Together eye care specialists and educators determine the essential training strategies that will promote optimal visual performance and learning potential. In this photograph, a student works with an Overbrook therapist on a specially equipped computer.

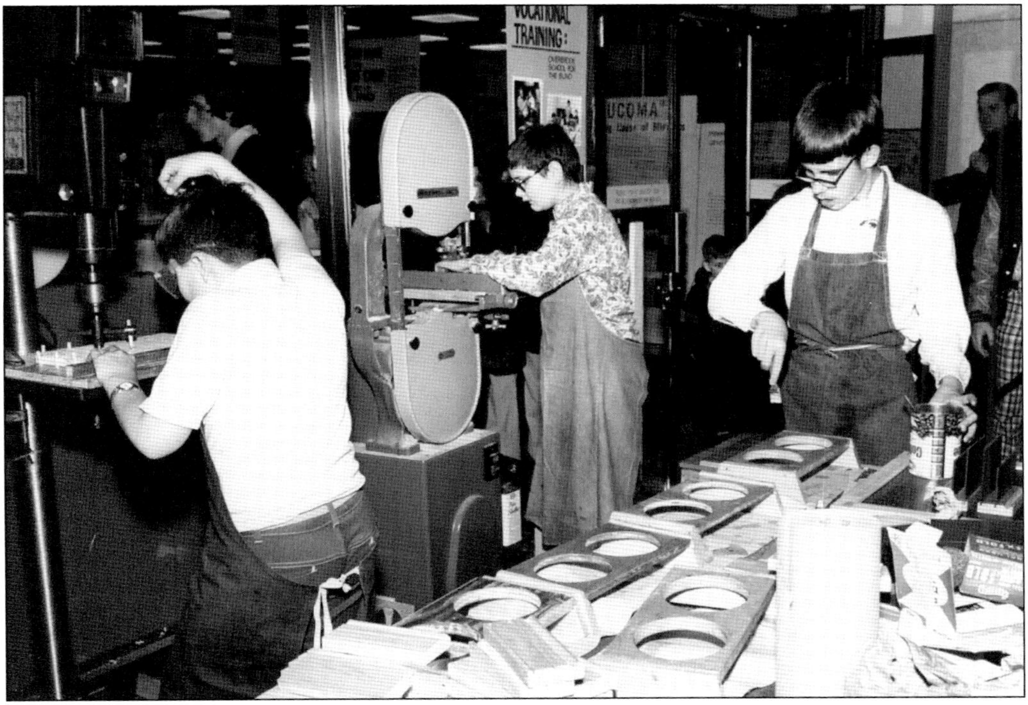

Broaden Your Vision, 1972. Overbrook students and faculty participated in Broaden Your Vision Day at a Boscov's department store. Students demonstrated their different skills by producing various items that were sold to the public. In the photograph above, students demonstrate their woodworking skills. In the photograph below, students make various baked goods.

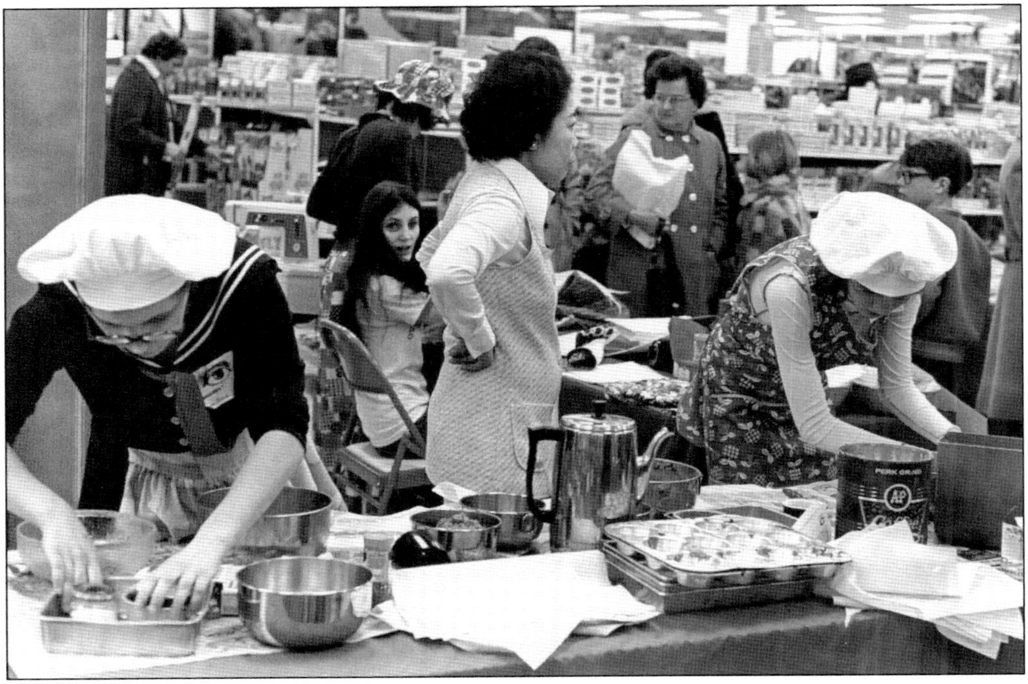

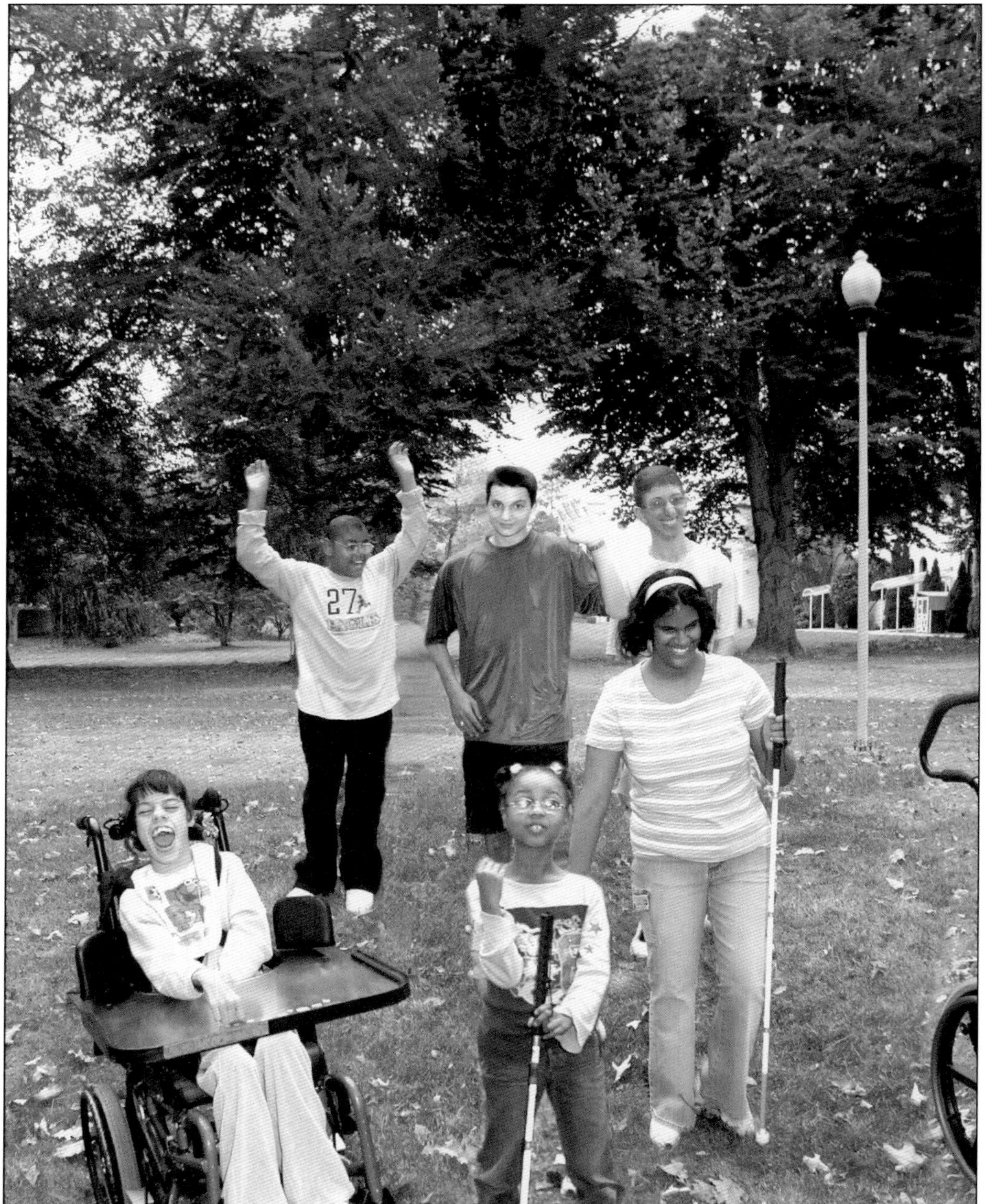

Learning and Friendships. Overbrook offers programs to students of all ages and ability levels. They have access to a well-rounded educational program and also develop lifelong friendships. The students are a part of the community on a regular basis through work experiences, participation in college classes, field trips, service learning projects, and just having fun on recreational outings.

BIBLIOGRAPHY

Most of the information in this book was obtained from the archives of Overbrook School for the Blind. For more information, please contact the development office at (215) 877-0313 or e-mail info@obs.org. Visit the Overbrook School for the Blind Web site at www.obs.org.

Harrison, Eliza Cope. *Best Companions*. Columbia, SC: University of South Carolina Press, 2001.
Weigley, Russell. *Philadelphia: A 300 Year History*. New York: W. W. Norton and Company, 1982.